Anonymous

Richard Frotscher's almanac

And garden manual for the southern states

Anonymous

Richard Frotscher's almanac
And garden manual for the southern states

ISBN/EAN: 9783337732691

Printed in Europe, USA, Canada, Australia, Japan

Cover: Foto ©ninafisch / pixelio.de

More available books at **www.hansebooks.com**

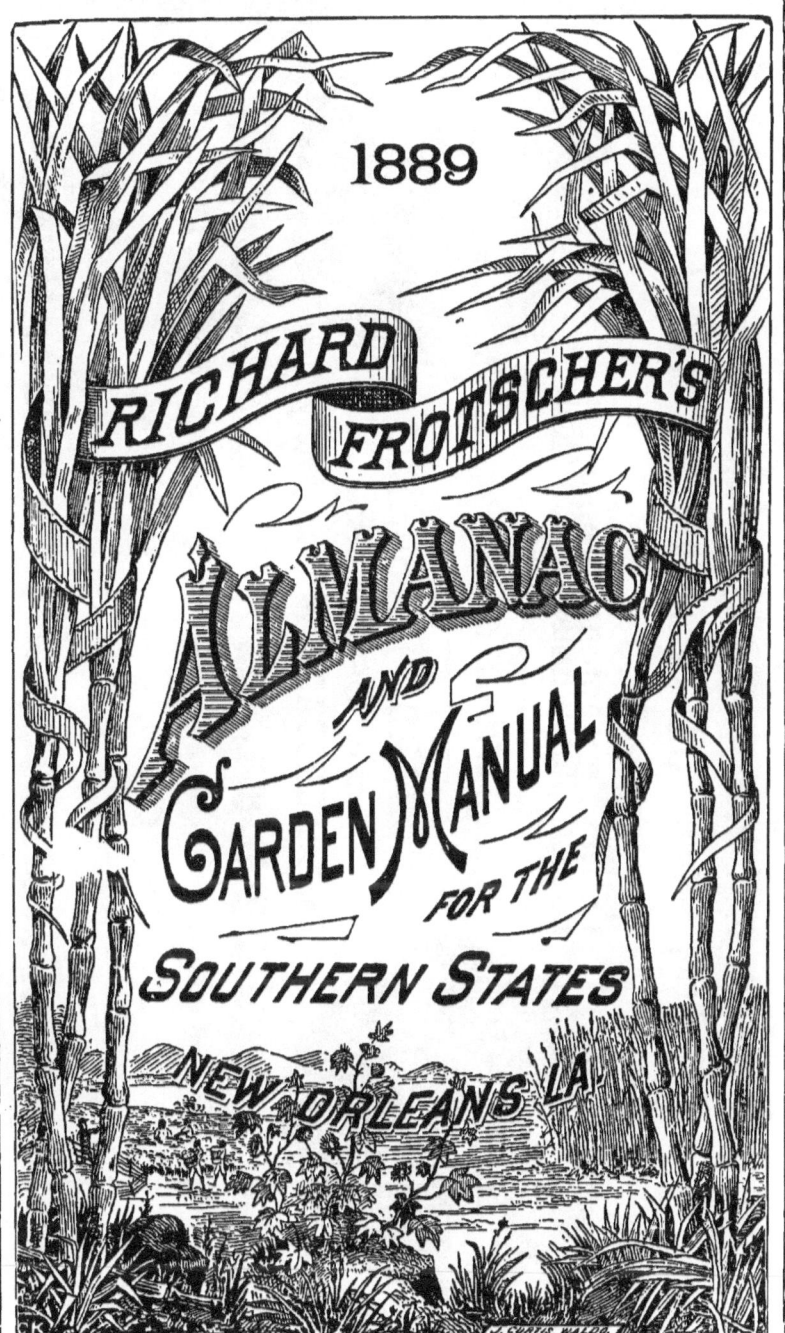

THE WORLD'S INDUSTRIAL AND Cotton Centennial Exposition.

CERTIFICATE OF AWARD.

RICHARD FROTSCHER,

NEW ORLEANS,

For Best CABBAGE, Winter Variety,

FIRST DEGREE OF MERIT,

In accordance with Act of Congress, approved February 10th, 1883.

New Orleans, May 30th, 1885.

S. H. Buck,
Director General.

E. Richardson,
President.

Gus. A. Breaux,
Chairman Committee of Awards.

RICHARD FROTSCHER'S

ALMANAC

—AND—

—FOR THE—

SOUTHERN STATES.

DESIGNED

To give Directions for the Cultivation of Vegetables, as practiced in the South.

Entered according to Act of Congress by RICHARD FROTSCHER, in the Office of the Librarian at Washington, in the year 1877.

WAREHOUSE:

15 & 17 DU MAINE STREET,

NEAR THE FRENCH MARKET,

NEW ORLEANS, LA.

GEO. MÜLLER, PRINTER, 50 BIENVILLE STREET.
1889.

INTRODUCTION.

In presenting to my friends and patrons the

Twelfth Annual Edition of my Almanac and Garden Manual,

I have sincere pleasure in congratulating them upon the great advance made in that special branch of commerce, Vegetables for the Markets, in which we are mutually interested.

Although I have exercised great care in the distribution of this work, desiring to place it only in the hands of those who practically benefit by its instructions, the inquiry for it has increased year by year, so that the supply has not equalled the demand; therefore, I shall publish of the present issue a still larger edition.

The information contained in these pages is based upon the actual experience of many years, and its correctness and value are well attested by the success attained by those who have followed the instructions given.

The many friendly and flattering encomiums bestowed upon my ALMANAC AND GARDEN MANUAL, and the steady increase in my business are gratifying evidences that my efforts towards the development and improvement of this important branch of Southern industry have been appreciated.

With assurances of my continued devotion to their interests, I tender to my patrons many thanks for their liberal favors in the past.

Yours Very Truly,

RICHARD FROTSCHER.

SEEDS BY MAIL.

Seeds can be sent by mail to any part of the United States in packages not exceeding four pounds, at eight cts. per pound, or one cent for two ounces, or fraction thereof. On seeds ordered in papers or by the ounce I prepay the postage, except on peas, beans and corn. This refers to large sized papers which are sold at one dollar per dozen. When ordered by the pound eight cents per pound postage has to be added to the price of the seeds; to peas, beans and corn, fifteen cts. per quart.

All packages are put up in the most careful manner, and every precaution taken to insure their reaching their destination in safety. Purchasers living at any place where my seeds are not sold, are requested to write to me to obtain their supplies. This will be more profitable than to buy from country stores where seeds left on commission, are often kept till all power of germination is destroyed. As seed merchants, who give their goods out on commission, rarely collect what is not sold, oftener than once every twelve or eighteen months, and as Lettuce, Spinach, Parsnip, Carrots, and many other seeds will either not sprout at all or grow imperfectly if kept over a summer in the South—to buy and plant such, is but money, time and labor wasted.

Here in our climate, where we plant garden vegetables as freely in autumn as in spring, and where often the seeds have to be put in the ground when the weather is very warm, it is an indispensable necessity to have perfectly fresh seeds.

My arrangements with my growers are made so that I receive the new crop, expressly cleaned for me, as soon as it is matured. The varieties which are not raised in the North, I order from Europe, and have them shipped so as to reach me about the beginning of August, just the time they are needed for fall planting. By following this plan I have always a full supply of fresh seeds of undoubted germinating qualities, while dealers, who sell on commission, have only those left from the winter previous.

On the receipt of one dollar I will mail thirteen large size papers of seeds, put up the same as seeds sold by the pound. These papers can be selected from this Catalogue, and include four papers of either Beans or Peas, if so wanted. Or, for the same amount, I will mail twenty smaller papers, including four papers of either Peas or Beans. This is done to enable consumers to get reliable seeds in good size papers in places where my seeds are not sold. The papers put up by Northern seedsmen are so small that of some varieties they hardly contain enough to do any good. The low prices charged to merchants are made at the expense of consumers. My papers are large and worth the full value of the money paid for them.

It cannot be too well impressed on the minds of all cultivators of vegetables, that seeds kept through a summer in this climate *will not grow*, and that all who use such seeds will be losers.

All seeds that leave my establishment are thoroughly tested.

Having received a great many complaints that letters which were addressed to me and contained money, were not answered, I must state that these letters never reached me, and, therefore, would caution my customers not to send any money in letters without registering same. By sending one dollar, or upwards, the cost, ten cents, can be charged to me. The cheapest and surest way is money order or draft, but where they cannot be had, letters have to be registered, which can be done at any Post Office.

A Few Remarks on Raising Vegetables for Shipping.

Within the past few years the raising of early vegetables for shipping West has become quite an item in the neighborhood of New Orleans. We have advantages here, which are not found elsewhere, for that branch of industry. Freights have been reduced to all points from here, and special cars, built expressly for carrying green vegetables and fruit, have been put on the Railroads. We are earlier here than at any other point, and with the rich ground we have, and the large supply of manure to be had for the hauling only, early vegetables can be raised very successfully.

Almost every kind of vegetables are shipped from here, but Beans, Cucumbers, Beets, Tomatoes, Cabbage and Peas form the bulk of shipment. For Beans, the Dwarf Wax, Improved Valentine and "Best of All" are principally planted for shipping purposes; the latter carry well and find ready sale. The Wax varieties do well in a dry season, but in a wet one they are apt to spot, which makes them unfit for shipping. If they have had a good season to grow, so they arrive in good order at destination, they will sell higher than any other variety. The Crease Back—a Pole Bean introduced here by me—is well adapted for shipping. It is very early and will follow the Dwarf Beans closely in maturing. Thousands of bushels of green pods are shipped from here to the Western markets. They are generally stenciled "Mobile Beans," which name is wrongly applied. Very few of this variety are planted at that place.

In the way of Cucumbers, the Improved White Spine and New Orleans Market are the best varieties, as they bear abundantly, keep their color better, and are superior for shipping to any other. I have been supplying the largest growers in that line with seed, the stock of which cannot be surpassed in quality. Of Beets only the dark red Blood Turnip or the Egyptian should be planted for shipping purposes. The Egyptian is a very quick growing variety, and should not be sown quite so early as the Blood Turnip, which ought to be sown in September and October; for the former variety, January is time enough.

For Tomatoes, the Extra Early Dwarf comes in bearing first, but should be planted only for the first crop, as when large varieties come in the market, the former do not sell as well. Great improvements have been made of late years in Tomatoes; the varieties raised and introduced by Livingston's Sons are perfect, and hardly any improvement can be made on such varieties as the Paragon, Favorite, Acme and Beauty. New Orleans is not a good point to ship Tomatoes from as they hardly ever arrive at destination in good condition. Along the Jackson R. R., where the land is more sandy, a better article is raised for shipping. Lettuce is shipped quite extensively; the Improved Passion is used principally for that purpose.

Potatoes and Onions are shipped in large quantities, but the former are very uncertain in regard to prices. Late shipped Onions generally pay better than those shipped too early. Owing to the unfavorable weather last winter and spring, the season has not been good for raisers and shippers of vegetables. The Winter Cabbage which is mostly sold in this market brought good prices; the crop was large, one of the best and finest that has ever been raised in this section. The Spring crop for shipping did not pay so well, except the shipments made early, mostly Brunswick. The Early Summer and Excelsior were later; the whole crop came in so late, that shipments had to be stopped, and the remainder of the crop sold here. We had rains almost every day during February and March, with cold weather, which retarded the growing crops of all kinds.

The surest plan is to sow the seed in cold frames in November, say from the middle to the twentieth, to have them for transplanting in January.

Beets and Cucumbers paid well, that is, the latter raised in frames; the open ground crop was almost a failure. Peas did very poorly owing to the very heavy rains during March. Beans came in too late, and very few of them paid; there came too many from along the line of the Jackson Rail Road to Chicago at the same time. Wax Beans did not arrive in good order, shipped from here, but have done finely from the line of the L. & N. R. R., between here and Mobile. The Wax Beans, when in good order, always bring higher prices than green podded varieties.

The potatoes brought to the market early realized fancy prices; most of them were shipped to different points from here; but owing to their poor quality, having been mostly dug before properly matured, the returns were bad, and prices fell so rapidly, that our main crop sold at very low prices. The principal reason of it was, that our crop shipped North and West came in competition with the foreign potatoes,—New York alone received over one million sacks from England. The yield of potatoes was very different, one from the other; some hardly returned the seeds, while others got from 15 to 20 barrels for one planted, from the same lot of seed potatoes.—Tomatoes paid well.

Along the line of the Jackson Rail Road too many Peas were planted, and owing to the late season, they all matured almost at the same time; the quantities shipped were too large to bring good prices. Owing to the rains and late frosts the quality was poor, and as they wilt quickly they were sold very low; in some instances not bringing the freight.

Gardeners and others who contemplate raising vegetables for shipping, are invited to give me a call. From the fact that all staple articles are raised for me by contract, in such sections best suited to mature the varieties we need for our climate, and the interest I take in the seed business, coupled with a thorough knowledge of same, enables me to assist in making selections of seeds for the purpose. The interest of my customers and mine are identical. My stock is the best selected and largest in the South.

☞ I receive a good many letters which are plainly enough written, except the signature. To insure prompt filling of orders, I ask all customers and others writing to me, to write their names plainly; at the same time, never fail to give the name of the nearest Post Office. Also, write out the order in columns, not in the body of the letter. Some letters came in without any signature; when the Post Office was properly given, I returned the letter to the Post Master of that place, and in some instances have traced up the writer in that way.

FOR THE SOUTHERN STATES. 7

1st Month.   JANUARY.   31 Days.

Calculated for the Latitude of the Southern States.

MOON'S PHASES.
New Moon.. 1d.   3h.   48m. Evening.
First Quarter .... 8d.   7h.   20m. Evening.
Full Moon ....17d. 12h. 16m. Morning.
Last Quarter ....24d. 10h. 37m. Forenoon.
New Moon ....31d.   3h.   49m. Morning.

DAY OF Month and Week.	Sun rises. h. m	Sun sets. h. m.	Moon r. & s. h. m.	CHRONOLOGY —OF— IMPORTANT EVENTS.
1 Tuesday	7 9	4 51	sets	Union of Ireland with Great Britain, 1801.
2 Wednesday	7 8	4 52	6 8	Gen. Wolf born, Westerham. Kent, 1727.
3 Thursday	7 8	4 52	7 9	Eliot Warburton, Hist. Novelist, died 1852.
4 Friday	7 8	4 52	8 20	Introduction of Silk manuf'es into Europe,
5 Saturday	7 7	4 53	9 27	Vigil of Epiphany. [1536.

1) Sunday after New Year.   Matth. 2.   Day's length, 9h. 46m.

6 **Sunday**	7 7	4 53	10 42	Epiphany, or 12th day, old Christmas Day.
7 Monday	7 7	4 53	11 47	Robert Nicoll, poet, born, 1814.
8 Tuesday	7 6	4 54	morn	Battle of N. O,, 1815 & Inaug. Gov. Nicholls,'77
9 Wednesday	7 6	4 54	12 16	Car. Lucr. Herschel, Astronomer, died, 1848.
10 Thursday	7 6	4 54	1 12	1st Steamboat, New Orleans from Pittsburg,
11 Friday	7 5	4 55	1 42	First Lottery drawn in England, 1569. [1812.
12 Saturday	7 4	4 56	2 30	St. Arcadius. Martyr.

2) 1st Sunday after Epiphany.   Luke 2.   Day's length, 9h. 54m.

13 **Sunday**	7 3	4 57	3 24	G. Fox, Founder Sect of Quakers, died, 1690
14 Monday	7 3	4 57	4 28	"Great Frost" in England, began 1205.
15 Tuesday	7 2	4 58	5 27	Thomas Crofton Croker, born, 1798.
16 Wednesday	7 1	4 59	6 27	Edmond Spencer, Poet, died, 1599.
17 Thursday	7 0	5 0	rises	Mozart, Musician, born, 1756.
18 Friday	7 0	5 0	6 45	Festival of St. Peter's Chair at Rome.
19 Saturday	6 59	5 1	7 42	James Watt, born, 1736.

3) 2nd Sunday after Epiphany.   John 2.   Day's length, 10h. 4m.

20 **Sunday**	6 58	5 2	8 52	Coldest day in the century, 1838.
21 Monday	6 58	5 2	9 56	St. Agnes, Virgin Martyr, 304.
22 Tuesday	6 57	5 3	10 59	Francis Bacon, born 1561.
23 Wednesday	6 56	5 4	11 59	Thanksgiving for victory of 8th, 1815.
24 Thursday	6 56	5 4	morn	Frederick the Great, born, 1712.
25 Friday	6 55	5 5	12 30	St. Paul's Day.
26 Saturday	6 54	5 6	1 24	Louisiana seceded, 1861.

4) 3rd Sunday after Epiphany.   Matth. 8.   Day's length, 10h. 14m.

27 **Sunday**	6 53	5 7	2 18	Admiral Lord Hood, died, 1816.
28 Monday	6 52	5 8	3 14	Henry VIII, died, 1547.
29 Tuesday	6 51	5 9	4 10	Emanuel de Swedenborg, born, 1688-89.
30 Wednesday	6 50	5 10	5 8	King Charles I, beheaded, 1649.
31 Thursday	6 50	5 10	sets	Ben. Johnston, born, 1574.

Jewish Festivals and Fasts.—5649.—January 3, Rosh Chodesh Shebat.

2d Month.   **FEBRUARY.**   28 Days.

Calculated for the Latitude of the Southern States.

MOON'S PHASES.

First Quarter .... 7d.   3h. 38m. Evening.
Full Moon .... 15d.   4h. 57m. Evening.
Last Quarter .... 22d.   6h. 5m. Evening.

DAY OF Month and Week.	Sun rises. h. m.	Sun sets. h. m.	Moon r. & s. h. m.	CHRONOLOGY —OF— IMPORTANT EVENTS.
1 Friday	6 49	5 11	5 42	Washington elected Pres't, 1789. [mas Day
2 Saturday	6 49	5 11	7 48	Purification of the Blessed Virgin, Candle-

5) 4th Sunday after Epiphany.   Matth. 8.   Day's length, 10h. 24m.

3 **Sunday**	6 48	5 12	8 49	Henry Cromwell, born, 1627. [gomery, 1861.
4 Monday	6 47	5 13	9 54	Delegates from Conf. States meet at Mont-
5 Tuesday	6 46	5 14	10 49	Ole Bull, born, 1810.
6 Wednesday	6 45	5 15	11 48	Charles II, King of England, died, 1865.
7 Thursday	6 44	5 16	morn	Charles Dickens, born, 1812.
8 Friday	6 43	5 17	12 18	Mary, Queen of Scots, beheaded, 1587.
9 Saturday	6 42	5 18	1 12	David Rezzio, murdered, 1565-66.

6) 5th Sunday after Epiphany.   Matth. 13.   Day's length, 10h. 38m.

10 **Sunday**	6 41	5 19	2 6	Riot at Oxford, 1354.
11 Monday	6 40	5 20	3 1	Mary, Queen of England, born, 1516.
12 Tuesday	6 39	5 21	3 57	Abraham Lincoln, born, 1809.
13 Wednesday	6 38	5 22	4 46	St. Gregory II, Pope, 631.
14 Thursday	6 37	5 23	5 42	St. Valentine's Day.
15 Friday	6 36	5 24	rises	Galilei Galileo, Astronomer, born, 1564.
16 Saturday	6 35	5 25	6 42	Dr. Kane, Am. Arctic Explorer, died, 1857.

7) Septuagesima Sunday.   Matth. 20.   Day's length, 10h. 52m.

17 **Sunday**	6 34	5 26	7 50	Columbia, S. C., burned, 1865.
18 Monday	6 33	5 27	8 50	Pope Gregory V, died, 999.
19 Tuesday	6 32	5 28	9 46	Eliz. Carter, classical scholar, died, 1806.
20 Wednesday	6 31	5 29	10 53	U. Gaghan & T. Connor, felon poets, hanged
21 Thursday	6 30	5 30	11 59	Pierre du Bose, born, 1623. [1749.
22 Friday	6 29	5 31	morn	George Washington, born, 1732.
23 Saturday	6 28	5 32	12 35	Battle of Buena Vista, 1847.

8) Sexagesima Sunday.   Luke 8.   Day's length, 10h. 6m.

24 **Sunday**	6 27	5 33	1 30	St. Matthias, Apostle.
25 Monday	6 26	5 34	2 25	Dr. Bucan, born, 1729.
26 Tuesday	6 25	5 35	3 20	Thomas Moore, poet, died, 1852.
27 Wednesday	6 24	5 36	4 19	Longfellow, born, 1807. [1447.
28 Thursday	6 23	5 37	5 17	Humphrey, Duke of Gloucester, murdered,

Jewish Festivals and Fasts.—5649.—February 1, Rosh Chodesh Adar Rischon.

3d Month. MARCH. 31 Days.

Calculated for the Latitude of the Southern States.

MOON'S PHASES.

New Moon	1d.	4h. 40m.	Evening.
First Quarter	9d.	12h. 39m.	Afternoon.
Full Moon	17d.	6h. 27m.	Morning.
Last Quarter	24d.	1h. 34m.	Morning.
New Moon	31d.	6h. 17m.	Morning.

DAY OF Month and Week.	Sun rises. h. m.	Sun sets. h. m.	Moon r. & s. h. m.	CHRONOLOGY —OF— IMPORTANT EVENTS.
1 Friday	6 22	5 38	sets	First No. of the Spectator published, 1711.
2 Saturday	6 21	5 39	6 47	Territory of Dakota organized, 1861.

9) Quinquagesima Sunday.   Luke 18.   Day's length, 11h. 22m.

3 **Sunday**	6 19	5 41	7 46	Edmond Waller, Poet, born, 1605.
4 Monday	6 17	5 43	8 53	Abraham Lincoln inaugurated, 1861.
5 Tuesday	6 16	5 44	9 56	Mardi Gras in New Orleans.
6 Wednesday	6 15	5 45	10 53	Great financial excitement, 1863.
7 Thursday	6 14	5 46	11 52	Blanchard, Aeronaut, died, 1809.
8 Friday	6 13	5 47	morn	King William III, of England, died, 1702.
9 Saturday	6 11	5 49	12 36	William Cobbett born, 1762.

10) 1st Sunday in Lent.   Matth. 4.   Day's length, 11h. 40m.

10 **Sunday**	6 10	5 50	1 26	The Forty Martyrs of St. Sebaste, 320.
11 Monday	6 9	5 51	2 15	First daily paper, "Daily Courant." Br. 1702.
12 Tuesday	6 8	5 52	2 48	St. Gregory the Great, Pope, 604.
13 Wednesday	6 7	5 53	3 50	Disc'ry of planet Uranus, by Herschel, 1781.
14 Thursday	6 6	5 54	4 26	Andrew Jackson, born, 1767.
15 Friday	6 5	5 55	5 12	Julius Cæsar, assassinated, B. C , 44,
16 Saturday	6 3	5 57	5 53	Prince Hohenlohe's miraculous cures, 1823.

11) 2nd Sunday in Lent.   Matth. 15.   Day's length, 11h. 56m.

17 **Sunday**	6 2	5 58	rises	St. Patrick, Apostle of Ireland.
18 Monday	6 1	5 59	7 32	Edward, King and Martyr, 978.
19 Tuesday	6 0	6 0	8 43	St. Joseph's day.
20 Wednesday	5 59	6 1	9 56	Vesta discovered, 1807.
21 Thursday	5 58	6 2	10 58	Louisiana ceded to France, 1800.
22 Friday	5 57	6 3	11 59	J. W. von Goethe. Germ. Poet, died, 1832.
23 Saturday	5 56	6 4	morn	Peter the Cruel, King of Castile, died, 1369.

12) 3rd Sunday in Lent.   Luke 11.   Day's length, 12h. 10m.

24 **Sunday**	5 55	6 5	12 31	Mahomet II, born, 1430.
25 Monday	5 54	6 6	1 28	Annunciation of the Blessed Virgin Mary.
26 Tuesday	5 53	6 7	2 20	Gov. Winthrop, died, 1640.
27 Wednesday	5 52	6 8	3 20	Vera Cruz captured, 1847.
28 Thursday	5 51	6 9	4 11	Planet Pallas, discoverd, 1802.
29 Friday	5 50	6 10	5 7	Mrs. Fitzherbert, died, 1837.
30 Saturday	5 49	6 11	5 42	Dr. William Hunter, died, 1783.

13) 4th Sunday in Lent.   John 6.   Day's length, 12h. 24m.

| 31 **Sunday** | 5 48 | 6 12 | sets | Beethoven, died, 1827. |

Jewish Festivals and Fasts.—5649.—March 2. Schekolim.   4. Rosh Chodesh Adar Scheni.   14. Zom Esther.   16. Parschoth Sochor.   17. Purim.   23. Parschoth Poroh.   30. Parschoth Hachodesh.

4th Month.   **APRIL.**   30 Days.

Calculated for the Latitude of the Southern States.

MOON'S PHASES.

First Quarter...	8d.	8h.	27m. Morning.
Full Moon	15d.	4h.	58m. Evening.
Last Quarter...	22d.	7h.	58m. Morning.
New Moon..	29d.	8h.	44m. Evening.

DAY OF Month and Week.	Sun rises. h. m.	Sun sets. h. m.	Moon r. & s. h. m.	CHRONOLOGY —OF— IMPORTANT EVENTS.
1 Monday	5 47	6 13	7 8	Earthquake at Melbourne, 1871.
2 Tuesday	5 46	6 14	7 58	Jefferson, born, 1743.
3 Wednesday	5 45	6 15	8 54	Washington Irving, born, 1783.
4 Thursday	5 44	6 16	9 48	Oliver Goldsmith, died, 1774.
5 Friday	5 43	6 17	10 44	St. Irgernach, of Ireland, 550.
6 Saturday	5 42	6 18	11 40	Battle of Shiloh, 1862.

14) 5th Sunday in Lent.   John 8.   Day's length, 12h. 38m.

7 **Sunday**	5 41	6 19	morn	St. Francis Xavier, Missionary, born, 1506.
8 Monday	5 40	6 20	12 30	Louisiana admitted to the Union, 1812.
9 Tuesday	5 39	6 21	1 33	Gen. R. E. Lee surrendered 1865.
10 Wednesday	5 38	6 22	2 21	St. Bademus, Abbot Martyr, 376.
11 Thursday	5 37	6 23	3 6	Geo. Canning, born, 1770.]Sumter.
12 Friday	5 36	6 24	3 47	First gun of Civil War fired, 1861, at Fort
13 Saturday	5 35	6 25	4 26	Sydney Lady Morgan, died, 1859.

15) Palm Sunday.   Matth. 21.   Day's length, 12h. 52m.

14 **Sunday**	5 34	6 26	4 59	Lincoln assassinated, 1865.
15 Monday	5 33	6 27	rises	Geo. Calvert. Lord Baltimore, died, 1632.
16 Tuesday	5 32	6 28	7 37	Battle of Culloden, 1746.
17 Wednesday	5 31	6 29	8 50	Dr. Benjamin Franklin, died, 1790.
18 Thursday	5 30	6 30	10 2	Shakespeare born, 1564.
19 Friday	5 29	6 31	11 6	Good Friday.
20 Saturday	5 28	6 32	morn	E. Barton, "Maid of Kent," executed, 1534.

16) Easter Sunday.   Mark. 16.   Day's length, 13h. 6m.

21 **Sunday**	5 27	6 33	12 19	Easter Sunday.
22 Monday	5 26	6 34	1 9	Madam De Stael, born 1766.
23 Tuesday	5 25	6 35	1 58	Shakespeare died, 1616.
24 Wednesday	5 24	6 36	2 36	Oliver Cromwell, born, 1599.
25 Thursday	5 23	6 37	3 7	St. Mark's Day.
26 Friday	5 22	6 38	3 59	David Hume, born, 1711.
27 Saturday	5 21	6 39	4 20	Sir Wm. Jones, Poet and Scholar, died, 1794.

17 1st Sunday after Easter.   John 20.   Day's length, 13h. 20m.

28 **Sunday**	5 20	6 40	5 2	Monroe, born, 1758.
29 Monday	5 18	6 42	sets	King Edward IV, of England, born, 1441.
30 Tuesday	5 17	6 43	7 25	Louisiana purchased from France by U. S.

Jewish Festivals and Fasts.—5649.— 2. April, Rosh Chodesh Nisan.   13., Schaboth Hagodol. 15., Erev Pessach. 16.—23., Pessach.

5th Month. MAY. 31 Days.

Calculated for the Latitude of the Southern States.

MOON'S PHASES.

First Quarter......	8d.	12h.	22m. Morning.
Full Moon	15d.	1h.	22m. Morning.
Last Quarter	21d.	4h.	33m. Evening.
New Moon	29d.	11h.	59m. Forenoon.

DAY OF Month and Week.	Sun rises. h. m.	Sun sets. h. m.	Moon r. & s. h. m.	CHRONOLOGY —OF— IMPORTANT EVENTS.
1 Wednesday	5 16	6 44	8 22	St. Philip and St. James, Apostles.
2 Thursday	5 15	6 45	9 19	William Camden, born, 1551.
3 Friday	5 14	6 46	10 14	Discovery of the Holy Cross, by St. Helena.
4 Saturday	5 14	6 46	11 16	Dr. Isaac Barrow, Eng. divine, died, 1677.

18) 2d Sunday after Easter. John 10. Day's length, 13h. 34m.

5 Sunday	5 13	6 47	morn	Emperor Justinian, born, 482.
6 Monday	5 12	6 48	12 30	Humboldt, died, 1859.
7 Tuesday	5 11	6 49	1 10	St. Benedict II, Pope, Confessor, 686.
8 Wednesday	5 10	6 50	1 50	Stonewall Jackson, died, 1863.
9 Thursday	5 10	6 50	2 32	Battle of Spottsylvania, 1864.
10 Friday	5 9	6 51	2 57	Pacific Railroad finished, 1869.
11 Saturday	5 8	6 52	3 31	Madame Ricamire, died, 1849.

19) 3d Sunday after Easter. John 16. Day's length, 13h. 46m.

12 Sunday	5 7	6 53	4 3	St. Pancras, Martyr, 304.
13 Monday	5 6	6 54	4 49	Jamestown, Va., settled, 1607.
14 Tuesday	5 5	6 55	5 4	Battle of Crown Point, 1575.
15 Wednesday	5 5	6 55	rises	St. Isidore, died, 1170.
16 Thursday	5 4	6 56	8 52	Sir William Petty, born, 1623.
17 Friday	5 3	6 57	9 50	J. Jay, died, 1829.
18 Saturday	5 2	6 58	10 49	Napoleon I, elected Emperor, 1804.

20) 4th Sunday after Easter. John. 16. Day's length, 13h. 56m.

19 Sunday	5 2	6 58	11 42	St. Dunstan, Archbishop of Canterbury, 988.
20 Monday	5 1	6 59	morn	Hawthorn, died, 1864.
21 Tuesday	5 1	6 59	12 35	Columbus, died, 1506.
22 Wednesday	5 0	7 0	1 11	Title of Baronet first conferred, 1611.
23 Thursday	4 59	7 1	1 43	Napoleon I, crowned King of Italy, 1805.
24 Friday	4 58	7 2	2 9	Bishop Jewell, born, 1522.
25 Saturday	4 58	7 2	2 39	Battle of Winchester, 1864.

21) 5th Sunday after Easter. John 16. Day's length, 14h. 6m.

26 Sunday	4 57	7 3	3 14	Fort Erie captured, 1813.
27 Monday	4 57	7 3	3 44	Dante, poet, born, 1265.
28 Tuesday	4 56	7 4	4 39	Noah Webster, died, 1843.
29 Wednesday	4 56	7 4	sets.	Paris burned, 1871.
30 Thursday	4 55	7 5	8 10	Ascension Day.
31 Friday	4 55	7 5	9 4	Joan of Arc burned, 1431.

Jewish Festivals and Fasts.—5649—May 1. and 2., Rosh Chodesh Iyar. 19., Lag Beomer. 31., Rosh Chodesh Siwan.

6th Month.   JUNE.   30 Days.

Calculated for the Latitude of the Southern States.

MOON'S PHASES.

First Quarter	6d.	2h.	41m.	Afternoon.
Full Moon	13d.	8h.	38m.	Forenoon.
Last Quarter	20d.	2h.	15m.	Morning.
New Moon	28d.	3h.	33m.	Morning.

DAY OF Month and Week	Sun rises. h. m.	Sun sets. h. m.	Moon r. & s. h. m.	CHRONOLOGY —OF— IMPORTANT EVENTS.
1 Saturday	4 54	7 6	10 11	Battle of Seven Pines, 1862.

22) 6th Sunday after Easter.   John 15.   Day's length, 14h. 12m.

2	**Sunday**	4 54	7 6	10 40	Battle of Cold Harbor, 1864.
3	Monday	4 53	7 7	11 14	S. A. Douglas died, 1861.
4	Tuesday	4 53	7 7	11 47	Lord R. Dudley marr'd A. Robsart, 1550.
5	Wednesday	4 52	7 8	morn	J. Pradier, Sculptor, died, 1852.
6	Thursday	4 52	7 8	12 32	Surrender of Memphis, Tenn., 1862.
7	Friday	4 51	7 9	1 6	First American Congress at New York, 1765.
8	Saturday	4 51	7 9	1 40	Emperor Nero, died, 68, Rome.

23) Whit Sunday.   John 14.   Day's length, 14h. 18m.

9	**Sunday**	4 51	7 9	2 9	Charles Dickens, died, 1870.
10	Monday	4 51	7 9	2 40	Battle of Big Bethel, 1861.
11	Tuesday	4 50	7 10	3 11	Sir John Franklin, died, 1847.
12	Wednesday	4 50	7 10	3 52	Harriet Martineau, Novelist, born, 1802.
13	Thursday	4 50	7 10	rises	General Scott, born, 1786.
14	Friday	4 50	7 10	8 46	St. Basil the Great, 379.
15	Saturday	4 50	7 10	9 44	Magna Charter, 1215.

24) Trinity Sunday.   John 3.   Day's length, 14h. 20m.

16	**Sunday**	4 50	7 10	10 33	Edward I, of England, born, 1239.
17	Monday	4 50	7 10	11 12	Battle of Bunker Hill, 1775.
18	Tuesday	4 49	7 11	11 45	War declared against Great Britain, 1812.
19	Wednesday	4 49	7 11	morn	Kearsage sunk the Alabama, 1864.
20	Thursday	4 49	7 11	12 20	Corpus Christi.
21	Friday	4 48	7 12	12 58	Anthony Collins, born, 1676.
22	Saturday	4 49	7 11	1 30	Napoleon I, abdicated, 1815.

25) 1st Sunday after Trinity.   Luke 16.   Day's length, 14h. 22m.

23	**Sunday**	4 49	7 11	1 59	Battle of Solferino, 1859.
24	Monday	4 49	7 11	2 31	Nativity of St. John the Baptist.
25	Tuesday	4 50	7 10	2 59	Battle of Bannockburn.
26	Wednesday	4 50	7 10	3 20	Dr. Philip Doddridge, born, 1702.
27	Thursday	4 50	7 10	3 47	John Murray, Publisher, died, 1843.
28	Friday	4 50	7 10	sets	Queen Victoria, crowned, 1838.
29	Saturday	4 50	7 10	8 31	St. Peter the Apostle, 68.

26) 2d Sunday after Trinity.   Luke 14.   Day's length, 14h. 20m.

30	**Sunday**	4 50	7 10	9 12	Bishop Gavin Dunbar, died, 1547.

Jewish Festivals and Fasts.—5649.—June 5. and 6., Schebuoth.   29. and 30., Rosh Chodesh Tamus.

FOR THE SOUTHERN STATES.

7th Month. JULY. 31 Days.

Calculated for the Latitude of the Southern States.

MOON'S PHASES.

First Quarter	6d.	12h.	38m. Afternoon.
Full Moon	12d.	3h.	41m. Evening.
Last Quarter	19d.	2h.	24m. Evening.
New Moon	27d.	6h.	52m. Evening.

DAY of Month and Week.	Sun rises. h. m.	Sun sets. h. m.	Moon r. & s. h. m.	CHRONOLOGY —OF— IMPORTANT EVENTS.
1 Monday	4 50	7 10	9 48	Battle of Malvern Hill, 1862.
2 Tuesday	4 51	7 9	10 22	Visitation of the Blessed Virgin Mary.
3 Wednesday	4 51	7 9	10 54	Quebec founded, 1608.
4 Thursday	4 51	7 9	11 24	Independence of the United States, 1776.
5 Friday	4 51	7 9	morn	Queen Magdalen of Scotland, died, 1537.
6 Saturday	4 52	7 8	2 10	Th. More, Chancel. of Eng. beheaded, 1535.

27) 3d Sunday after Trinity. Luke 15. Day's length, 14h. 16m.

7 **Sunday**	4 52	7 8	12 47	Dog days begin.
8 Monday	4 52	7 8	1 14	John de la Fontaine, born, 1621.
9 Tuesday	4 53	7 7	1 47	Zachary Taylor, died, 1850.
10 Wednesday	4 53	7 7	2 40	John Calvin, theologian, born, 1509,
11 Thursday	4 54	7 6	3 30	J. Q. Adams, born, 1767.
12 Friday	4 54	7 6	rises	Robt. Stevenson, engineer, etc., died, 1850.
13 Saturday	4 55	7 5	8 22	Pope, John III, died, 573.

28) 4th Sunday after Trinity. Luke 6. Day's length, 14h. 8m.

14 **Sunday**	4 56	7 4	9 7	John Hunter, eminent surgeon, born, 1728.
15 Monday	4 56	7 4	9 43	St. Swithin's Day.
16 Tuesday	4 57	7 3	10 19	Great riot in New York city, 1863.
17 Wednesday	4 57	7 3	10 42	Dr. Isaac Watts, born, 1647.
18 Thursday	4 58	7 2	11 14	St. Symphorosia and 7 sons, Martyrs, 120.
19 Friday	4 59	7 1	11 45	St. Vincent de Paul, confessor, 1660.
20 Saturday	4 59	7 1	morn	Confed. Congress at Richmond, 1861.

29) 5th Sunday after Trinity. Luke 15. Day's length, 14h. 00m.

21 **Sunday**	5 0	7 0	12 27	Battle of Bull Run, 1861.
22 Monday	5 1	6 59	12 56	Urania discovered, 1824.
23 Tuesday	5 1	6 59	1 37	First Olympiad, 776, B. C.
24 Wednesday	5 2	6 58	2 30	Curran, born, 1750.
25 Thursday	5 2	6 58	2 59	St. James the Great.
26 Friday	5 3	6 57	3 58	Flood at Pittsburg, 1874.
27 Saturday	5 4	6 56	sets	Atlantic cable laid, 1866.

30) 6th Sunday after Trinity. Matth. 5. Day's length, 13h. 52m.

28 **Sunday**	5 4	6 56	7 56	Battle before Atlanta, Ga., 1864.
29 Monday	5 5	6 55	8 36	Albert I, Emp. of Germany, born, 1289.
30 Tuesday	5 6	6 54	9 0	Westfield Explosion, N. Y. Harbor, 1871.
31 Wednesday	5 7	6 53	9 30	St. Ignatius Loyola, died, 1556.

Jewish Festivals and Fasts.—5649.—July 16., Zom Tamus. 29., Rosh Chodesh Ab.

8th Month. **AUGUST.** 31 Days.

Calculated for the Latitude of the Southern States.

MOON'S PHASES.

First Quarter	4d.	8h.	6m. Forenoon.
Full Moon	10d.	11h.	22m. Evening.
Last Quarter	18d.	5h.	31m. Morning.
New Moon	26d.	8h.	40m. Morning.

DAY OF Month and Week.	Sun rises. h. m.	Sun sets. h. m.	Moon r. & s. h. m.	CHRONOLOGY —OF— IMPORTANT EVENTS.
1 Thursday	5 7	6 53	9 58	Harriet Lee, Novelist, died, 1851.
2 Friday	5 8	6 52	10 34	Mehemed Ali, Pasha of Egypt, died, 1849.
3 Saturday	5 9	6 51	10 58	Crown Point taken, 1759.

31) 7th Sunday after Trinity.   Mark. 8.   Day's length, 13h. 40m.

4	**Sunday**	5 10	6 50	11 30	John Banim, Irish Novelist, died, 1842.
5	Monday	5 11	6 49	morn	First Atlantic Cable landed, 1858.
6	Tuesday	5 12	6 48	12 32	Transfiguration of our Lord.
7	Wednesday	5 13	6 47	1 47	Leonidas, Spartan Hero, slain 480, B. C.
8	Thursday	5 14	6 46	2 51	Fr. Hutcheson, Moral Phil., born, 1694.
9	Friday	5 15	6 45	3 59	Isaac Walton, born, 1593.
10	Saturday	5 16	6 44	rises	Battle of Weisenburg, 1870.

32) 8th Sunday after Trinity.   Matth. 7.   Day's length, 13h. 26m.

11	**Sunday**	5 17	6 43	7 40	Viscount Rowland Hill, born, 1772.
12	Monday	5 18	6 42	8 12	Pope Gregory IX, died, 1241.
13	Tuesday	5 19	6 41	8 40	Earthquake in Scotland, 1816.
14	Wednesday	5 19	6 41	9 10	G. Coleman, the elder, Dramatist, died, 1794.
15	Thursday	5 20	6 40	9 30	Ascension of the Blessed Virgin Mary.
16	Friday	5 21	6 39	10 10	Battle of Bennington, 1777.
17	Saturday	5 22	6 38	10 40	Frederick the Great, died, 1786.

33) 9th Sunday after Trinity.   Luke 16.   Day's length, 13h. 14m.

18	**Sunday**	5 23	6 37	11 18	John Earl Russell, born, 1792.
19	Monday	5 24	6 36	11 48	Dog days end.
20	Tuesday	5 25	6 35	morn	Robert Herrick, English Poet, born, 1591.
21	Wednesday	5 26	6 34	12 29	Lady Mary Wortley Montague, died, 1762.
22	Thursday	5 27	6 33	1 19	Dr. F. J. Gall, founder of phrenology, died,
23	Friday	5 28	6 32	1 46	Wallace, beheaded, 1305. [1828.
24	Saturday	5 29	6 31	2 36	St. Bartholomew, Apostle.

34) 10th Sunday after Trinity.   Luke 19.   Day's length, 13h. 00m.

25	**Sunday**	5 30	6 30	3 54	25th or 27th, Landing of Cæsar in England,
26	Monday	5 31	6 29	sets	Sir Rob. Walpole born, 1676. [55 B. C.
27	Tuesday	5 32	6 28	7 48	Battle of Long Island, 1776.
28	Wednesday	5 33	6 27	8 18	Leigh Hunt, died, 1859.
29	Thursday	5 34	6 26	8 48	John Locke, Philosopher, born, 1632.
30	Friday	5 35	6 25	9 4	Union defeat at Richmond, Ky.
31	Saturday	5 36	6 24	9 35	John Bunyan, died, 1683.

Jewish Festivals and Fasts.—5649.—August 6., Tischo beab. 10., Schaboth Nachmu. 12., Chamischo Osor. 27. and 28., Rosh Chodesh Elul.

FOR THE SOUTHERN STATES. 15

9th Month.　　　　SEPTEMBER.　　　　30 Days.

Calculated for the Latitude of the Southern States.

MOON'S PHASES.
First Quarter	2d.	2h.	14m. Afternoon.
Full Moon	9d.	8h.	32m. Forenoon.
Last Quarter	16d.	11h.	28m. Evening.
New Moon	24d.	9h.	21m. Evening.

DAY OF Month and Week	Sun rises. h. m.	Sun sets. h. m.	Moon r. & s. h. m.	CHRONOLOGY —OF— IMPORTANT EVENTS.
35) 11th Sunday after Trinity.			**Luke 18.**	**Day's length, 12h. 46m.**
1 Sunday	5 37	6 23	10 8	Napoleon III, captured at Sedan, 1870.
2 Monday	5 38	6 22	10 53	Great fire in London, 1666.
3 Tuesday	5 40	6 20	11 47	Cromwell died, 1658.
4 Wednesday	5 42	6 18	morn	Pindar, Lyric poet, 518, B. C.
5 Thursday	5 43	6 17	12 55	Confederates entered Maryland, 1862.
6 Friday	5 44	6 16	2 3	Geo. Alex. Stevens, writer, died, 1784.
7 Saturday	5 45	6 15	3 4	Independence of Brazil, 1822.
36) 12th Sunday after Trinity.			**Mark 7.**	**Day's length, 12h. 28m.**
8 Sunday	5 46	6 14	4 14	Nativity of the Blessed Virgin.
9 Monday	5 47	6 13	rises	James IV, of Scotland, killed, 1513.
10 Tuesday	5 48	6 12	7 21	Mungo Park, African Traveler, born, 1771.
11 Wednesday	5 50	6 10	7 45	James Thomson, poet, born, 1700.
12 Thursday	5 51	6 9	8 15	St. Guy, Confessor, 11th century.
13 Friday	5 52	6 8	8 41	Sir Wm. Cecil, Lord Burleigh, born, 1520.
14 Saturday	5 53	6 7	9 15	Uprising of the People of New Orleans against the usurping government.
37) 13th Sunday after Trinity.			**Luke 10.**	**Day's length, 12h. 12m.**
15 Sunday	5 54	6 6	9 51	Capture Harper's Ferry by St'll Jackson,'62.
16 Monday	5 55	6 5	10 33	Gabriel Daniel Fahrenheit, died, 1736.
17 Tuesday	5 56	6 4	11 25	Battle of Antietam, 1862.
18 Wednesday	5 57	6 3	morn	Gilbert Bishop Burnet, historian, born, 1643.
19 Thursday	5 58	6 2	12 24	First Battle of Paris, 1870.
20 Friday	5 58	6 2	1 24	Alexander the Great, born, 356, B. C.
21 Saturday	5 59	6 1	2 31	St. Matthew, Apostle and Evangelist.
38) 14th Sunday after Trinity.			**Luke 17.**	**Day's length, 12h. 00m.**
22 Sunday	6 0	6 0	3 39	Beginning of Autumn.
23 Monday	6 1	5 59	4 51	Wm. Upcott, Manusc. Collec., died, 1845.
24 Tuesday	6 2	5 58	sets	Pepin, King of France, 768.
25 Wednesday	6 3	5 57	6 48	Pacific Ocean discovered, 1513.
26 Thursday	6 4	5 56	7 26	Saints Cyprian and Justina, Martyrs, 304.
27 Friday	6 5	5 55	7 59	Strassburg fell, 1870.
28 Saturday	6 6	5 54	8 38	Sir Wm. Jones, Oriental Scholar, born, 1746.
39) 15th Sunday after Trinity.			**Matth. 6.**	**Day's length, 11h. 46m.**
29 Sunday	6 7	5 53	9 19	Michaelmas Day.
30 Monday	6 8	5 52	10 10	Yorktown invested, 1781.

Jewish Festivals and Fasts.—5649.—Sept. 22., Maschkimim Lislichos. 26. and 27., Rosh Haschonoh. 5650. 28., Schaboth Teschuvoh. 29., Zom Gedaljah.

10th Month.   OCTOBER.   31 Days.

Calculated for the Latitude of the Southern States.

MOON'S PHASES.

First Quarter	1d.	8h.	13m. Evening.
Full Moon	8d.	8h.	5m. Evening.
Last Quarter	16d.	7h.	17m. Evening.
New Moon	24d.	9h.	5m. Morning.
First Quarter	31d.	3h.	10m. Morning.

DAY of Month and Week.		Sun rises. h. m.	Sun sets. h. m.	Moon r. & s. h. m.	CHRONOLOGY —OF— IMPORTANT EVENTS.
1	Tuesday	6 9	5 51	11 6	Fulton's first Steamboat trip, 1807.
2	Wednesday	6 10	5 50	morn	André executed as a spy, 1780.
3	Thursday	6 11	5 49	12 7	Black Hawk, died, 1838.
4	Friday	6 12	5 48	1 14	Battle of Germantown, 1777.
5	Saturday	6 14	5 46	2 24	Horace Walpole, born, 1717.

40) 16th Sunday after Trinity.   Luke 7.   Day's length, 11h. 30m.

6	**Sunday**	6 15	5 45	3 30	Jenny Lind, born, 1820.
7	Monday	6 16	5 44	4 44	Margaret, Maid of Norway, died, 1290.
8	Tuesday	6 17	5 43	rises	Battle of Perryville, Ky., 1862.
9	Wednesday	6 18	5 42	6 45	Great fire in Chicago, 1871.
10	Thursday	6 19	5 41	7 16	Benjamin West, Painter, born, 1738.
11	Friday	6 20	5 40	7 46	America discovered, 1492.
12	Saturday	6 21	5 39	8 22	St. Wilfrid, Bishop of York, 709.

41) 17th Sunday after Trinity.   Luke 14.   Day's length, 11h. 14m.

13	**Sunday**	6 23	5 37	8 59	Battle of Queenstown, 1812.
14	Monday	6 24	5 36	9 40	Battle of Jena, 1806.
15	Tuesday	6 25	5 35	10 32	Virgil, Latin Poet, born, 70 B. C.
16	Wednesday	6 26	5 34	11 32	Marie Antoinette beheaded, 1793.
17	Thursday	6 27	5 33	morn	Burgoyne surrendered, 1777.
18	Friday	6 28	5 32	12 18	Last State Lottery drawn in England, 1826.
19	Saturday	6 29	5 31	1 23	Cornwallis surrendered, 1781.

42) 18th Sunday after Trinity.   Matth. 22.   Day's length, 11h. 00m.

20	**Sunday**	6 30	5 30	2 32	M. Dahl, Swed. Portrait Painter, died, 1743.
21	Monday	6 31	5 29	3 35	Battle of Trafalgar, 1805.
22	Tuesday	6 32	5 28	4 38	Charles Martel, died, 741.
23	Wednesday	6 33	5 27	5 48	Dr. John Jortin, Critic, born, 1698.
24	Thursday	6 34	5 26	sets.	Daniel Webster, died, 1852.
25	Friday	6 35	5 25	6 48	Dr. James Beattie, Poet, born, 1735.
26	Saturday	6 36	5 24	7 26	Hogarth, died, 1765.

43) 19th Sunday after Trinity.   Matth. 9.   Day's length, 10h. 46m.

27	**Sunday**	6 37	5 23	8 14	Cuba discovered, 1492.
28	Monday	6 38	5 22	9 10	Battle at White Plains, 1776.
29	Tuesday	6 39	5 21	10 15	Surrender of Metz, 1870.
30	Wednesday	6 40	5 20	11 14	Solomon's Temple dedicated, 1004 B. C.
31	Thursday	6 41	5 19	morn	All Hallow Eve.

Jewish Festivals and Fasts.—5650.—October 5., Yom Kippur. 10. and 11., The First days of Suckoth: 12., Chol Hamoeid. 16., Hoschano Rabo. 17., Schemini Azereth. 18., Simchoth Torah. 25. and 26., Rosh Chodesh Marcheschwan.

11th Month. NOVEMBER. 30 Days.

Calculated for the Latitude of the Southern States.

MOON'S PHASES.

Full Moon................................. 7d.	10h.	45m.	Morning.
Last Quarter ....15d.	3h.	15m.	Morning.
New Moon................................22d.	8h.	20m.	Evening.
First Quarter ....29d.	12h.	8m.	Afternoon.

DAY OF Month and Week.	Sun rises. h. m.	Sun sets. h. m.	Moon r. & s. h. m.	CHRONOLOGY —OF— IMPORTANT EVENTS.
1 Friday	6 42	5 18	12 40	All Saints Day.
2 Saturday	6 43	5 17	1 40	All Souls Day.

1) 20th Sunday after Trinity.   Matth. 22.   Day's length, 10h. 32m.

3 **Sunday**	6 44	5 16	2 18	Malachy, Archbishop of Armagh, 1148.
4 Monday	6 45	5 15	3 39	George Peabody, died, 1869.
5 Tuesday	6 45	5 15	4 40	The American 74 launched, 1782.
6 Wednesday	6 46	5 14	5 41	Battle of Port Royal, 1861.
7 Thursday	6 47	5 13	rises	John Kyrle, "The Man of Ross," died 1724.
8 Friday	6 48	5 12	5 59	Cortez entered Mexico, 1519.
9 Saturday	6 49	5 11	6 58	Great fire in Boston, 1872.

45) 21st Sunday after Trinity.   John 4.   Day's length, 10h. 20m.

10 **Sunday**	6 50	5 10	7 45	Mahomet, Arabian Prophet, born, 570.
11 Monday	6 51	5 9	8 20	Mortinmas.
12 Tuesday	6 52	5 8	9 18	Sherman left Atlanta, 1864.
13 Wednesday	6 53	5 7	10 12	French entered Vienna, 1805.
14 Thursday	6 54	5 6	11 10	Sir Chas. Lyell, Geologist, born, 1797.
15 Friday	6 54	5 6	morn	John Keppler, great Astronomer, died, 1630.
16 Saturday	6 55	5 5	12 25	Tiberius, Roman Emperor, born, 42 B. C.

46) 22nd Sunday after Trinity.   Matth. 18.   Day's length, 10h. 8m.

17 **Sunday**	6 56	5 4	1 26	Suez Canal opened 1869.
18 Monday	6 57	5 3	2 30	Fort Lee taken by the British, 1776.
19 Tuesday	6 57	5 3	3 31	St. Elizabeth of Hungary, Widow, 1231.
20 Wednesday	6 58	5 2	4 32	Thomas Chatterton, Poet, born, 1752.
21 Thursday	6 59	5 1	5 31	Presentation of the Blessed Virgin.
22 Friday	7 0	5 0	sets	Professor Dugald Stewart, born, 1753.
23 Saturday	7 1	4 49	6 10	Th. Henderson, Prof. of Astron., died, 1844.

47) 23rd Sunday after Trinity.   Matth. 22.   Day's length, 9h. 38m.

24 **Sunday**	7 1	4 49	6 54	Battle of Lookout Mountain, 1863.
25 Monday	7 2	4 48	7 51	Evacuation of New York, 1783.
26 Tuesday	7 2	4 48	8 49	John Elwes, noted Miser, died, 1789.
27 Wednesday	7 3	4 47	9 47	Steam Printing, 1814.
28 Thursday	7 3	4 47	10 47	Washington Irving, died, 1859.
29 Friday	7 3	4 47	11 44	Sir Philip Sidney, Poet, born, 1554.
30 Saturday	7 4	4 46	morn	U. S. took possession of Louisiana, 1803.

Jewish Festivals and Fasts.—5650.—24. November, Rosh Chodesh Kislev.

12th Month. DECEMBER. 31 Days.

Calculated for the Latitude of the Southern States.

MOON'S PHASES.

Full Moon	7d.	4h.	32m. Morning.
Last Quarter	15d.	9h.	38m. Morning.
New Moon	22d.	7h.	32m. Morning.
First Quarter	29d.	11h.	56m. Evening.

DAY of Month and Week.	Sun rises. h. m.	Sun sets. h. m.	Moon r. & s. h. m.	CHRONOLOGY —OF— IMPORTANT EVENTS.
48) 1st Sunday in Advent.				Matth. 21. Day's length, 9h. 50m.
1 **Sunday**	7 5	4 55	12 20	Princess A. Comnena, Historian, born, 1083.
2 Monday	7 6	4 54	1 21	Hernan Cortez, died, 1547.
3 Tuesday	7 6	4 54	2 22	Robert Bloomfield, Poet, born, 1776.
4 Wednesday	7 7	4 53	3 28	Pope John XXII, died, 1334.
5 Thursday	7 7	4 53	4 32	Carlyle, born, 1795.
6 Friday	7 7	4 53	5 36	St. Nicholas, Archbishop of Myra, 342.
7 Saturday	7 8	4 52	rises	Cicero, Roman orator, assassinated, 43 B. C.
49) 2d Sunday in Advent.				Luke 21. Day's length, 9h. 44m.
8 **Sunday**	7 8	4 52	5 59	Immaculate Conception of Blessed Virgin.
9 Monday	7 8	4 52	6 41	Milton, born, 1608.
10 Tuesday	7 9	4 51	7 38	Louis Napoleon, elected President, 1848.
11 Wednesday	7 9	4 51	8 34	Louis, Prince of Conde, died 1686.
12 Thursday	7 9	4 51	9 32	St. Columba, Abbot in Ireland, 584.
13 Friday	7 9	4 51	10 29	Battle of Fredericksburg, 1862.
14 Saturday	7 10	4 50	11 32	Washington, died, 1799.
50) 3d Sunday in Advent.				Matth. 11. Day's length, 9h. 40m.
15 **Sunday**	7 10	4 50	morn	David Don, Botanist, died, 1841.
16 Monday	7 10	4 50	12 2	Great Fire in New York, 1835.
17 Tuesday	7 10	4 50	1 24	Ludw. Beethoven, emin. comp., born, 1770.
18 Wednesday	7 11	4 49	2 30	St. Winebald, Abbot and Confessor, 760.
19 Thursday	7 11	4 49	3 40	Capt. W. Ed. Parry, Arct. Nav., born, 1790.
20 Friday	7 11	4 49	4 50	Secession ord. passed in S. Carolina, 1860.
21 Saturday	7 12	4 48	5 58	St. Thomas, Apostle.
51) 4th Sunday in Advent.				John 1. Day's length, 9h. 38m.
22 **Sunday**	7 11	4 49	sets.	Emp. Vitellius, beheaded at Rome, 69 A. D.
23 Monday	7 11	4 49	6 9	Newton, born. 1642.
24 Tuesday	7 11	4 49	7 20	Treaty of Ghent, 1814.
25 Wednesday	7 11	4 49	8 30	Nativity of our Lord. Christmas Day.
26 Thursday	7 10	4 50	9 40	Battle of Trenton, 1776.
27 Friday	7 10	4 50	10 45	St. John, Apostle and Evangelist.
28 Saturday	7 10	4 50	11 54	Macauley, died, 1859.
52) Sunday after Christmas.				Luke 2. Day's length, 9h. 42m.
29 **Sunday**	7 9	4 51	morn	Union repulsed at Vicksburg, Miss., 1862.
30 Monday	7 9	4 51	12 39	Titus, Roman Emperor, born, 41 A. D.
31 Tuesday	7 9	4 51	1 37	Battle of Murfreesboro, 1862.

Jewish Festivals and Fasts,—5650.—December 18., Chanukah.
23. and 24., Rosh Chodesh Thebet.

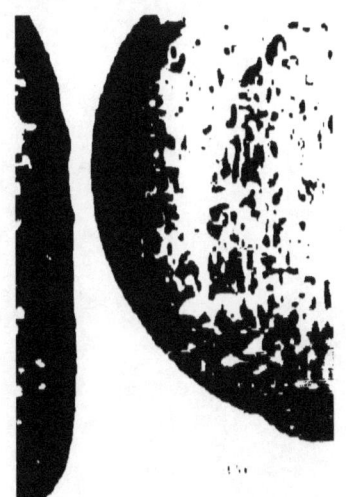

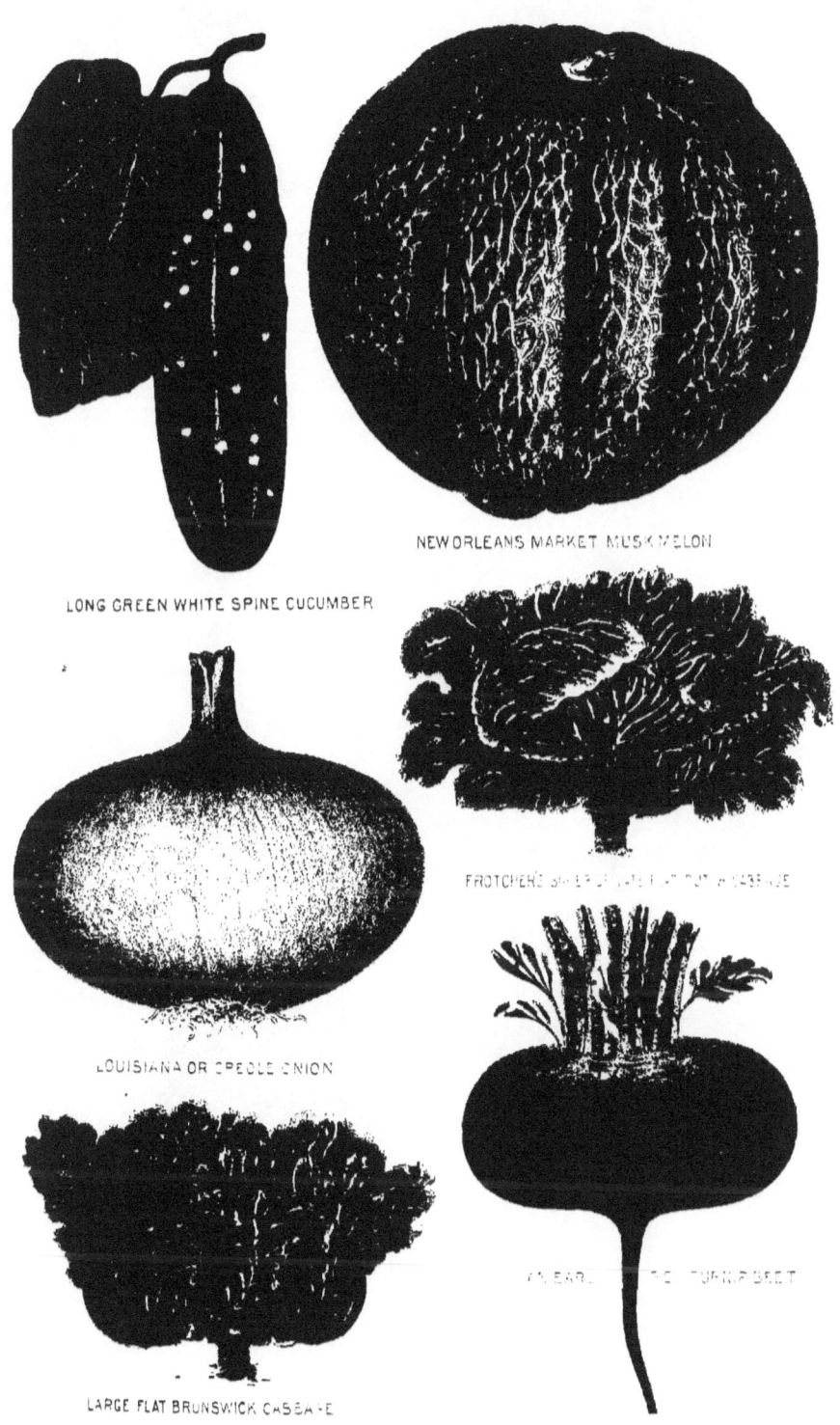

THE VEGETABLE GARDEN.

The size depends upon the purposes for which it is intended; whether the family is large or small, and the time which can be devoted to its cultivation. The most suitable soil for a garden is a light loam. When the soil is too heavy, it ought to be made light by applying stable manure, and working up the ground thoroughly. Trenching as done in Europe, or North, is not advisable. at least where there is any cocoa, as by trenching the roots of this pest will get so deeply incorporated with the soil that trouble will be met with afterwards to get rid of it. Exposure towards the east is desirable. If there are one or more large trees in the garden, or on the immediate outside, their shade can be used in which to sow Celery, Cabbage and other seeds during the hot summer months, which will be an advantage. The seed beds for this purpose should be so arranged as to receive only the morning or evening sun. It is of the greatest importance that the ground should be well drained, otherwise it will be impossible to raise good vegetables. The most reliable manure for general purposes is well decomposed stable or barnyard manure. Cow manure will suit best for light, sandy soil, and horse manure for heavy, stiff clay lands. For special purposes, Peruvian Guano, Blood Fertilizer, Raw Bone, Cotton Seed Meal and other commercial manures may be employed with advantage. Of late years most gardeners who work their land with a plow, use Cow peas as a fertilizer with excellent result. They are sown broad-cast at the rate of 1½ bushels to the acre, and when large enough they are turned under. Where the land is very sandy, cotton seed meal has the most lasting effect. For quick growing crops, such as Melons, Cucumbers, etc., the Blood Fertilizer and Guano applied in the hills are very good. Soap suds are good for Celery; it is astonishing to perceive the difference in the size of those stalks which are watered every few days with the suds, and others on the same ground which are not. Wood ashes are best for Peas, either used as a top dressing when the Peas just come out of the ground, or else sprinkled in the rows when planted. The New Orleans market gardeners raise as fine vegetables as can be produced anywhere; in fact, some varieties cannot be excelled, and very few gardeners use anything but stable manure.

Rotation of Crops is another important item. Beets, Carrots and other roots should not be grown in succession on the same ground, but should be changed to those which grow above ground, such as Lettuce, Beans, Peas, etc. Good seed, good ground and good cultivation are essential in order to raise good vegetables. When plants are up, the ground should be stirred frequently; weeds ought not to be suffered to go into seed, but should be destroyed as soon as they appear. Hoeing and working the young crops during dry weather is very beneficial, because the weeds are then easily killed, and hoeing the ground will make it retain moisture better than if it were left alone.

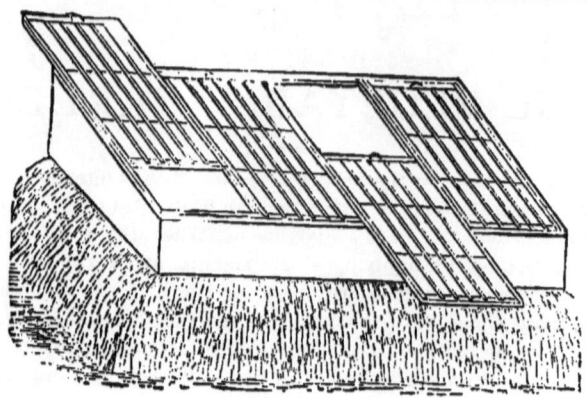

THE HOT BED.

Owing to the open winters in the South, hot beds are not so much used as in the North, except to raise such tender plants as Egg-Plants, Tomatoes and Peppers. There is little forcing of vegetables done here, except as regards Cucumbers and Lettuce; and, if we do not have any hard frosts, the latter does better in the open ground than under glass. To make a hot bed is a very simple thing. Any one who has the use of tools can make the wooden frame; the sashes may be obtained from any sash factory. I consider a wooden frame from five to six feet wide and ten feet six inches long a very good size. It should be at least six inches higher at the back than in the front, and covered by three sashes 3½x5 feet. The manure ought not to be over one month old; it should be thrown together in a heap, and when commencing to heat, be worked over with a fork, and all the long and short manure evenly mixed. In this State the ground is generally low, and to retain the heat of the manure for a longer time it is best to put the manure on top of the ground—that is, make a bank two feet longer and two feet wider than the frame. Keep the edges straight and the corners firm; when thrown up about eighteen inches trample the manure down to six or eight inches, then put on another layer of eighteen inches and trample down again; place thereon the frame and sash, and fill in six inches of good earth. After about five days stir the ground to kill the weeds which may have come up, then sow the seeds. In lower Louisiana the ground is too wet to dig out eighteen inches deep, throw in the manure and trample down as recommended in the North; by a few hard rains, such as we frequently have in winter, the manure would become so soaked beneath the ground that the heat would be gone. Another advantage, when the frame is put above the ground, is, that it will go down with the manure gradually, and there remains always the same space between the glass and the ground. If the ground is dug out and the manure put into the frame, the ground will sink down so low, after a short time, that the sun will have little effect upon it, and plants will become spindly.

SOWING SEEDS.

Some seeds are sown at once where they are to remain and mature. Others are sown in seed beds and transplanted afterwards. Seeds should be covered according to their sizes, a covering of earth twice the size of the seed is about the maximum. Some seeds, such as Beans, Corn and Peas, can be covered from one to two inches, and they will come up well. Here is a difference again: Wrinkled Peas and Sugar Corn have to be covered lighter and more carefully than marrowfat Peas or the common varieties of Corn. It depends upon the nature of the soil, season of the year, etc. For instance, in heavy wet soils seeds have to be covered lighter than in sandy light ground. Seeds which are sown during summer in the open ground, such as Beets and Carrots, should be soaked over night in water and rolled in ashes or plaster before sowing; they will come up quicker. When they are sown in a seed bed, the ground should be light enough not to bake after a rain. Some varieties of seeds require shade when sown during the summer, such as Cauliflower, Celery and Lettuce. Care should be taken to have the shade at least three feet from the ground, and shade only after the sun has been on the bed for two or three hours; and remove again early in the afternoon, so the plants may become sturdy. If too much shaded they will be drawn up, long-legged, and not fit to be set out in the open ground. The most successful cabbage planters in this neighborhood sow their seeds in the open ground, towards the end of July and during August, and give them no shade but water, and keep the ground moist from the day of sowing till the plants are transplanted. Seeds should be sown thinly in the seed bed. If plants come up too thickly they are apt to damp off.

Lettuce seed should be sprouted during the hot months before sowing, according to directions given for June.

To sow Turnips on a large scale during late summer and early fall months, the ground should be prepared in advance, and the seed sown just before or during a rain. Small pieces of ground, of course, can be sown at any time and watered afterwards. For covering all kinds of seeds, a fork is preferable to a rake; with either implement, care must be taken not to cover the seeds too deep. Beans, Peas and Corn are covered with the hoe. Some fine seeds, such as Thyme or Tobacco, are covered enough when pressed with the back of the spade to the ground. The seedsman is often blamed for selling seeds which have not come up, when the same are perfectly good, but, perhaps, through ignorance the party by whom they were sown, placed them too deep or too shallow in the ground, or the ground may have been just moist enough to swell the seeds, and they failed to come up. At other times washing rains after sowing beat the ground and form a crust that the seeds are not able to penetrate, or, if there is too much fresh manure in the ground, it will burn the seed, and destroy its vitality.

When seeds, such as Beans, Cucumbers, Melons and Squash, are planted before it is warm enough, they are very apt to rot if it rains.

Seeds requisite to produce a given number of Plants and sow a given amount of ground.

	Quantity per acre.		Quantity per acre.
Artichoke, 1 oz. to 500 plants.	½ lb.	Garlic, bulbs, 1 lb. to 10 feet of drill	
Asparagus, 1 oz. to 200 plants.	5 lbs.	Hemp	½ bu.
Barley	2½ bu.	Kale, 1 oz. to 3,000 plants.	2 oz.
Beans, dwarf, 1 quart to 150 feet of drill	1½ "	Kohl-Rabi, 1 oz. to 200 feet of drill	1½ lbs.
Beans, pole, 1 quart to 200 hills	½ "	Leek, 1 oz. to 250 feet of drill	4 "
Beet, garden, 1 oz. to 100 feet of drill	10 lbs.	Lettuce, 1 oz. to 250 feet of drill	3 "
Beet, Mangel, 1 oz. to 150 feet of drill	6 "	Melon, Musk, 1 oz. to 100 hills	1¾ "
Broccoli, 1 oz. to 3,000 plants	5 oz.	Melon, Water, 1 oz. to 25 hills	1½ "
Broom Corn	10 lbs.	Nasturtium, 1 oz. to 50 feet of drill	10 "
Brussels Sprouts, 1 oz. to 3,000 plants.	5 oz.	Oats	2½ bu.
Buckwheat	½ bu.	Okra, 1 oz. to 50 feet of drill	10 lbs.
*Cabbage, 1 oz. to 3,000 plants	5 oz.	Onion Seed, 1 oz to 200 feet of drill	4 "
Carrot, 1 oz. to 250 feet of drill	2½ lbs	" for Sets	30 "
*Cauliflower, 1 oz. to 3,000 plants.	5 oz.	Onion Sets, 1 quart to 20 feet of drill	8 bu.
*Celery, 1 oz. to 10,000 plants	4 "	Parsnip, 1 oz. to 250 feet of drill	5 lbs.
Clover, Alsike and White Dutch	6 lbs	Parsley, 1 oz. to 250 feet of drill	8 "
" Lucerne, Large Red & Crimson		Peas, garden, 1 quart to 150 feet of drill	1½ bu.
Trefoil	8 lbs.	" field	2½ "
" Medium	10 lbs.	Pepper, 1 oz. to 1,500 plants.	4 oz.
*Collards, 1 oz. to 2,500 plants	6 oz.	Potatoes.	10 bu.
Corn, sweet, 1 quart to 500 hills	8 qts.	Pumpkin, 1 quart to 300 hills	4 qts.
Cress, 1 oz. to 150 feet of drill	8 lbs.	Radish, 1 oz. to 150 feet of drill	8 lbs.
Cucumber, 1 oz. to 80 hills	1¼ "	Rye	1½ bu.
Egg Plant, 1 oz. to 2,000 plants.	3 oz	Salsify, 1 oz. to 60 feet of drill.	8 lbs.
Endive, 1 oz. to 300 feet of drill	3 lbs.	Spinach, 1 oz. to 150 feet of drill	10 "
Flax, broadcast	½ bu.	Summer Savory, 1 oz. to 500 feet of drill	2 "
Gourd, 1 oz. to 25 hills	2½ lbs	Squash, summer, 1 oz. to 40 hills	2 "
Grass, Blue Kentucky.	2 bu.	" winter, 1 oz. to 10 hills	3 "
" Blue English	1 "	Tomato, 1 oz. to 3,000 plants.	3 oz.
" Hungarian and Millet.	½ "	Tobacco, 1 oz. to 5,000 plants	2 "
" Mixed Lawn.	3 "	Turnip, 1 oz. to 250 feet of drill	1½ lbs.
" Orchard, Perennial Rye, Red Top, Fowl Meadow and Wood Meadow	2 "	Vetches	2 bu.
		Wheat	1 to 2 "

* The above calculations are made for sowing in the spring; during the summer it requires double the quantity to give the same amount of plants.

Number of Plants or Trees to the Acre at given distances.

Dis. apart.	No. Plants.	Dis. apart.	No. Plants.	Dis. apart.	No. Plants.	Dis. apart.	No. Plants.
½ foot	174,240	3 feet by 3 feet	4,840	6 feet	1,210	12 feet	302
1 "	43,560	4 " 1 foot	10,888	7 "	889	15 "	193
1½ feet	19,360	4 " 2 feet	5,444	8 "	680	18 "	134
2 "	10,890	4 " 3 "	3,629	9 "	573	20 "	108
2½ "	6,969	4 " 4 "	2,722	10 "	435	25 "	69
3 feet by 1 foot	14,520	5 " 5 "	1,742	11 "	360	30 "	49
3 " 2 feet	7,260						

Standard Weight of Various Articles.

Apples		per bush.	48 lbs.	Onions		per bush.	54 lbs.
" dried.		"	22 "	Peas		"	60 "
Barley		"	48 "	Plastering Hair.		"	8 "
Beans		"	60 "	Rape		"	50 "
Buckwheat		"	48 "	Rye		"	56 "
Broom Corn		"	46 "	Red Top Seed.		"	14 "
Blue Grass, Kentucky.		"	14 "	Salt, Coarse.		"	50 "
" " English		"	24 "	Salt, Michigan		"	56 "
Bran		"	20 "	Sweet Potatoes		"	56 "
Canary Seed		"	60 "	Timothy Seed		"	45 "
Castor Beans		"	46 "	Turnips		"	58 "
Clover Seed		"	60 "	Wheat		"	60 "
Corn, shelled		"	56 "	Beef and Pork, per bbl., net			200 "
" on ear		"	70 "	Flour, per bbl., net			196 "
Corn Meal		"	50 "	White Fish and Trout, per bbl., net.			200 "
Charcoal		"	22 "	Salt, per bbl.			280 "
Coal, Mineral		"	80 "	Lime			220 "
Cranberries		"	40 "	Hay, well settled, per cubic foot.			4½"
Dried Peaches		"	28 "	Corn, on cob, in bin		"	22 "
Flax Seed		"	56 "	" shelled		"	45 "
Hemp Seed		"	44 "	Wheat,	"	"	48 "
Hungarian Grass Seed		"	48 "	Oats,	"	"	25½"
Irish Potatoes, heaping measure.		"	60 "	Potatoes,	"	"	38½"
Millet		"	50 "	Sand, dry,	"	"	95 "
Malt		"	38 "	Clay, compact,	"	"	135 "
Oats		"	32 "	Marble,	"	"	169 "
Osage Orange		"	33 "	Seasoned Beech Wood, per cord			5,616 "
Orchard Grass		"	14 "	" Hickory,	"		6,960 "

DESCRIPTIVE CATALOGUE of VEGETABLE SEEDS.

ARTICHOKE.
ARTICHAUT (Fr.) ARTISCHOKE (G.) ALCACHOFA (Sp.)

Large Green Globe. This is a very popular vegetable in the South, and much esteemed by the native as well as the foreign population from the South of Europe. It is extensively cultivated for the New Orleans market. It is best propagated from suckers which come up around the large plants. Take them off during the fall and early winter months; plant them four feet apart each way. Every fall the ground should be manured and spaded or plowed between them; at the same time the suckers should be taken off. If planted by seed, sow them in drills during winter or early spring, three inches apart and one foot from row to row; cover with about one-half inch of earth. The following fall the plants can be transplanted and cultivated as recommended above. The seeds I offer are imported by me from Italy, and of superior quality; I can also furnish sprouts or plants in the fall of the year, at $1.50 per 100.

Green Globe Artichoke.

Early Campania. An early variety imported by me from Italy and which fruited for the first time three years ago. The cut represents as it grows, and has been taken from a branch brought to me; it is flatter at the base than the Globe; it is very early, but has not proven itself as hardy as the foregoing kind.

Early Campania.

ASPARAGUS.
ASPERGE (Fr.), SPARGEL (Ger.), ESPARAGOS (Sp.)

Purple Top. The Asparagus is not extensively cultivated in the South; not that it is not liked well enough, but from the fact that it does not succeed as well as in more Northern latitudes. It seems that it is short-lived, the roots giving out soon or throwing up very small shoots.

The ground should be well manured and prepared before either the roots or seeds are planted. For this climate the sowing of seed is preferable. Roots are generally imported from the North, and I have found that the roots raised here, one year old, are as strong as those received from the North three years old. Plant the seed in early spring. Soak over night in water; plant in rows, or rather hills, one foot apart and two feet between; put from four to five seeds in each hill; when well up thin out to two plants. The following winter, when the stalks are cut off, cover with a heavy coat of well rotted manure and a sprinkling of salt; fishbrine will answer the same purpose. In the spring fork in the manure between the rows, and keep clean of weeds. The same treatment should be repeated every year. The bed should not be cut before being three years established. Care must be taken not to cut the stalks too soon in the fall of the year—not until we have had a frost. If cut before, it will cause the roots to throw up young shoots, which will weaken them.

BUSH BEANS.
CULTURE.

Place in rows eighteen inches apart; drop a bean every two or three inches. Plant from end of February, and for succession, every two or three weeks to May. Bush Beans planted in this latitude during June and July, will not produce much. August and September are good months in which to plant again; they will produce abundantly till killed by the frost. Do not cover the seeds more than two inches.

POLE BEANS.

Lima Beans should not be planted before the ground has become warm in spring. Strong poles ought to be set in the ground from four to six feet apart, and the ground drawn around them before the seed is planted. It is always best to plant after a rain and with the eye of the bean down. The other varieties can be planted flat, and not more than three to four feet apart, and hilled after they are up. Do not cover the seeds more than two inches; one inch is enough for the Southern Prolific and Crease Back.

BEANS.
(DWARF, SNAP or BUSH).

HARICOT (Fr.), BOHNE (Ger.), FRIJOLENANO (Sp.)

Extra Early Six Weeks, or Newington Wonder.
Early Valentine Red Speckled,
Early Mohawk Six Weeks.
Early Yellow Six Weeks.
German Dwarf Wax.
White Kidney.

Red Speckled French.
Early China Red-Eye.
Red Kidney.
Dwarf Golden Wax,
Best of All.
Improved Valentine.
Wardwell's New Dwarf Kidney Wax.

Extra Early Six Weeks, or Newington Wonder. Is very early, but the pods are small and round. Good for family use.

Early Valentine, one of the best varieties; pods round, tender and quite productive; not much planted for the market. Excellent for shipping.

Early Mohawk Six weeks. This is a long podded variety, and very hardy.

It is used to a large extent for the market for the first planting; very productive.

Early Yellow Six Weeks. This is the most popular sort among market gardeners. Pods flat and long; a very good bearer, but not so good for shipping as the Mohawk or Valentine.

German Dwarf Wax. A good variety which is unsurpassed as a snap bean. Pods are of a wax color and have no strings; quite productive. Has come into general cultivation; cannot be too highly recommended.

White Kidney. A good strong growing variety, not much planted.

Red Speckled French is another strong growing variety, planted a good deal for the New Orleans market as a second crop, being about ten days later than the Mohawk and yellow Six Weeks. It is hardy and productive.

Early China Red-Eye. Early and of good quality, but not very popular.

Red Kidney. This variety is largely planted for the New Orleans market. It is a coarse growing variety, and much used for shelling when the pods turn yellow, so that the beans are well developed, but yet soft.

Dwarf Golden Wax. A dwarf variety with flat pods, longer than the Dwarf German Wax; entirely stringless and white, mottled with purplish red. This variety will come into general cultivation, and will in time take the place of the black seeded Wax, being earlier and more productive.

Best of All. A new variety from Germany of great merit, introduced here by me. It is green podded, long and succulent; it is prolific and well flavored. An excellent variety for shipping and family use. It is not quite so early as the Mohawk, but is of superior quality for shipping, and, therefore, is almost

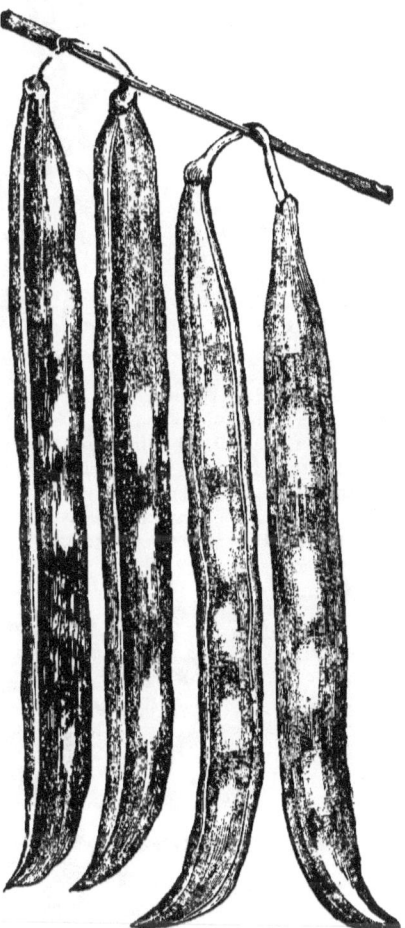

Dwarf Golden Wax Bean.　　Best of All Bean, ⅔ natural size

the only kind planted here for that purpose. The cut is a good representation as it grows; it shows only two-thirds of its natural size. Can not be too highly recommended. I expect to have a full supply this year.

Improved Valentine. This variety has all the good qualities of the old Valentine; only, it is ten days earlier, a great consideration when planted for the market; it will supersede the old variety of Valentine.

Wardwell's New Dwarf Kidney Wax. This kind was introduced two years ago. It is the best dwarf Wax Bean in cultivation; it is quite early; the pods are of similar shape as the Golden Wax, but longer; color of a beautiful golden yellow. They are very prolific and hardy, surpassing any other Dwarf Wax Bean that I know of. The color of the bean is somewhat like the Golden Wax, but more kidney-shaped and more spotted with dark purple. It has done best here among the Dwarf Wax Beans. Of all the many new kinds I have tried, I found none to excel it.

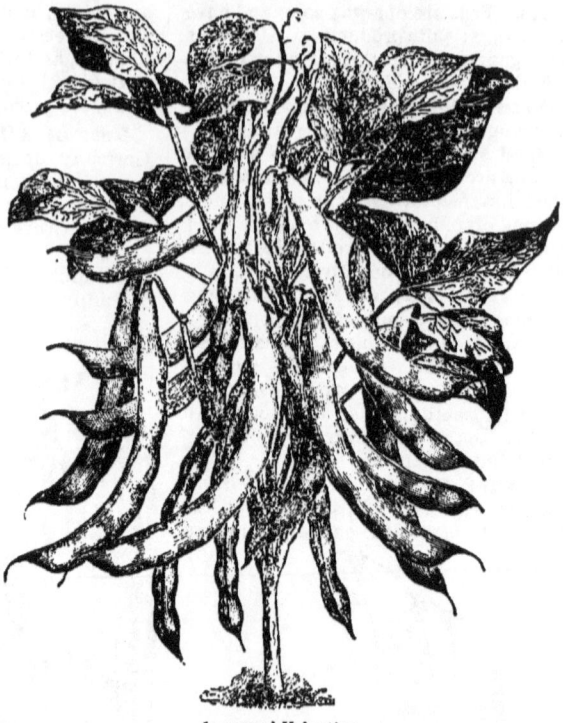

Improved Valentine.

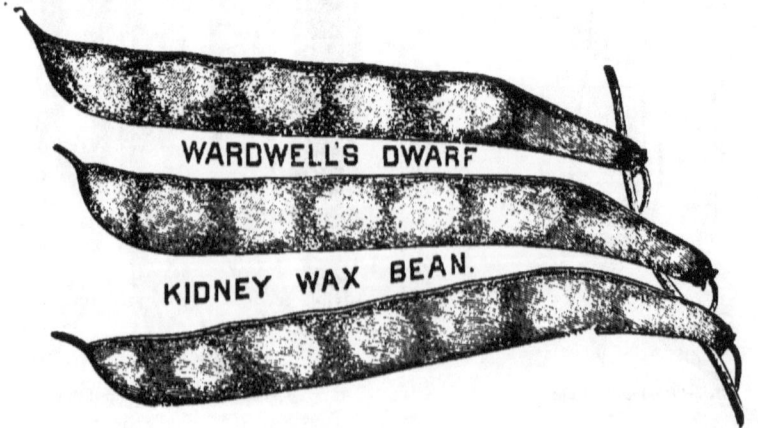

BEANS.
POLE OR RUNNING.
HARICOTS A RAMES (Fr.), STANGEN-BOHNEN (Ger.), FRIJOL VASTAGO (Sp.).

Large Lima.
Carolina or Sewee.
Horticultural or Wren's Egg.
Dutch Case Knife.
German Wax or Butter.

Southern Prolific.
Crease Back.
New Golden Wax Flageolet.
Lazy Wife's.
Southern Willow-leaved Sewee or Butter.

Large Lima. A well-known and excellent variety. It is the best shell bean known. Should have rich ground, and plenty room to grow.

Carolina or Sewee. A variety similar to the Lima; the only difference is, the seeds and pods are smaller. It is generally cultivated, being more productive than the Large Lima.

Horticultural or Wren's Egg, does not grow very strong; bears well, pods about six inches long, which are roundish and very tender.

Dutch Case Knife. A very good pole bean; it is early; pods broad and long, somewhat turned towards the end.

German Wax. This is a fine variety, and has the same good qualities as the German Dwarf Wax. Pods have a waxy appearance; very succulent and tender.

Southern Prolific. No variety will continue longer in bearing than this. It stands the heat of the summer better than any other, and is planted to succeed the other kinds. It is a very strong grower; pods about seven inches long and flat; seeds are dark yellow or rather light brown. It is the standard variety for the New Orleans market, for late spring and summer.

Crease Back. A variety of Pole Beans which has been cultivated in the South for a long time, but has never come into the trade till introduced by me. It is an excellent bean, earlier than the "Southern Prolific." Seeds white; pods round, with a crease in the back, from which the name. It is a good grower, bears abundantly, and, if shipped, will keep better than most other kinds. It sells better in the spring than any other for shipping purposes; and when in season, it can not be surpassed. For early summer, the Southern Prolific is preferable, standing the heat better. Several years ago I received half a bushel from near Mobile, Ala., and all the beans of this variety about here can be traced back to that half bushel. I supplied two growers in Georgia where it was not known at that time. I expect to have a full supply this season. There is a light brown bean, streaked and mottled with dark brown and

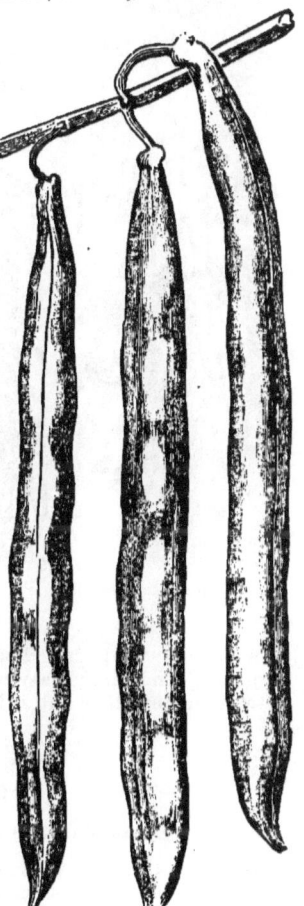

White Crease Back Beans.

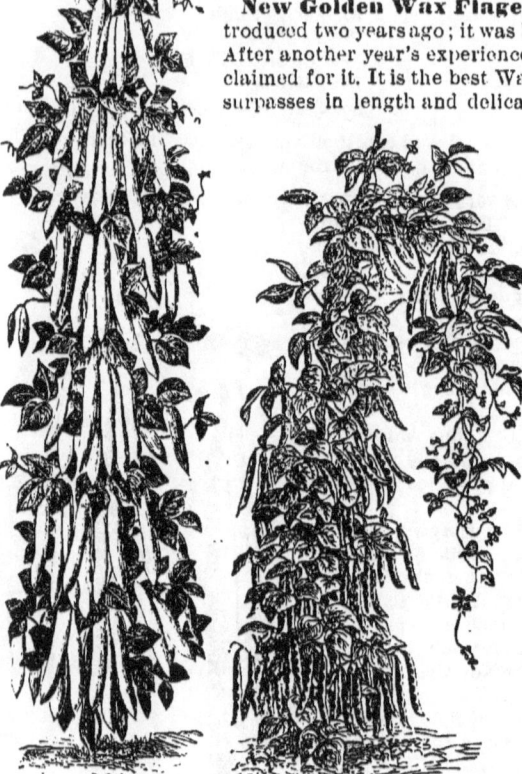

New Golden Wax Flageolet Pole Beans

Lazy Wife's Pole Beans.

black of the same name; but it is not equal to the white variety. In some localities this kind is called "Calico Crease Back." The white seeded variety is also known in some sections by the name of "Fat Horse."

New Golden Wax Flageolet. This variety was introduced two years ago; it was brought out from Germany. After another year's experience I can confirm all what is claimed for it. It is the best Wax Pole Bean in cultivation, surpasses in length and delicacy of flavor all other Wax varieties. It is a very strong grower, which is wanting by most of the Wax Pole kinds. It bears abundantly, is entirely stringless, and does not spot, even by too much rain or other untoward weather. Cannot be too highly recommended. The Golden Wax Pole Bean, brought out last year, I have dropped, as it can stand no comparison with the Golden Wax Flageolet.

Lazy Wife's. A new Pole Bean from Pennsylvania. The pods are entirely stringless, 4—5 inches long, and have a fine flavor when cooked. They retain their rich flavor until nearly ripe. The Beans are white, and as fine as a shell Bean.

Southern Willow-leaved Sewee or Butter. This is a variety which is grown by the market gardeners about New Orleans; the pods and beans are the same as the Sewee or Carolina Bean; it is quite distinct in the leaves, being narrow like the willow. It stands the heat better than any other Butter Bean, and is very productive. Try it.

ENGLISH BEANS.

FEVE DE MARAIS (Fr.), PUFF-BOHNE, (Ger.), HABA COMUN (Sp.).

Broad Windsor. Not so much cultivated here as in some parts of Europe. It is much liked by the people of the Southern part of Europe. Ought to be planted during November; as, if planted in the spring, they will not produce much.

BEETS.

BETRAVE (Fr.), RUNKELRUEBE (Ger.), REMOLACHA (Sp.).

Extra Early or Bassano.
Simon's Early Red Turnip.
Early Blood Turnip.
Long Blood.
Half Long Blood.
Egyptian Red Turnip.

Long Red Mangel Wurzel.
White French Sugar.
Silver or Swiss Chard.
Eclipse.
Lentz Beet.

CULTURE.

The ground for beets should be rich and well spaded or plowed. Sow in drills twelve to eighteen inches apart, cover the seed about one inch deep. When about a month old, thin them out to four or six inches apart. In this latitude beets are sown from January till the end of April, and from the middle of July till the middle of November; in fact, some market gardeners sow them every month in the year. In the summer and fall, it is well to soak the seeds over night and roll in plaster before sowing.

Extra Early, or Bassano, is the earliest variety, but not popular on account of its color, which is almost white when boiled. Earliness is not of so much value here, where there are beets sown and brought to the market the whole year around. In the North it is different, where the first crop of beets in the market in spring will bring a better price than the varieties which mature later.

Simon's Early Red Turnip. This is earlier than the Blood Turnip, smooth skin and of light red color; planted a good deal by the market gardeners about New Orleans.

Early Blood Turnip. The most popular variety for market purposes as well as family use. It is of a dark red color and very tender. This is the principal variety planted for shipping. My stock is raised for me from dark selected roots, and can not be excelled.

Long Blood. Is not quite so tender as the foregoing variety; it is not planted at all for the market, and very little for family use. In the North it is chiefly planted for winter use; here we have Turnip Beets the whole winter from the garden; therefore it has not the same value.

Half Long Blood. A very dark red variety of a half long shape; a good kind for family use.

Egyptian Red Turnip. This is a new variety, sent out by "Benary"

Simon's Early Red Turnip Beet.   Silver Beet or Swiss Chard.   Early Blood Turnip Beet.

some years ago. It is very early, tender, deep red and of Turnip shape. Leaves of this variety are smaller than of others. The seeds are also much smaller. I recommend it and consider it a good acquisition. The seed of this variety is obtained by me from the original source and is the finest stock offered.

Eclipse. A new Beet from Germany, very regular, of globular shape. It has a small top, is of dark red blood color, sweet and fine grained flesh. It comes as early as the Egyptian.

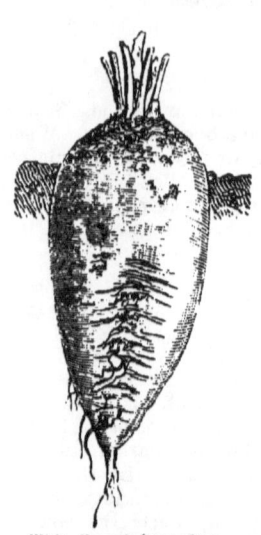

White French Sugar Beet.

Egyptian Red Turnip Beet.

Eclipse Beet.

Long Red Mangel Wurzel. This is raised for stock; it grows to a large size. Here in the South where stock is not stabled during the winter, the raising of root crops is much neglected. Being very profitable for its food it ought to be more cultivated.

White French Sugar, is used the same as the foregoing; not much planted.

Silver Beet, or Swiss Chard. This variety is cultivated for its large succulent leaves, which are used for the same purposes as Spinach. It is very popular in the New Orleans market.

Lentz Beet. This new strain of Blood Turnip Beet originated with one of the most prominent market gardeners around Philadelphia. This beet, as selected and grown by him, has had a great reputation, in the surroundings of the above place, but the seed has been carefully guarded and kept until recently, when it fell into the hands of a seed grower, from whom I have received my supply. It is fully as early as the Egyptian Beet, but larger and of better quality; it has a fine turnip form with smooth roots, dark blood red flesh, tender and sweet at all times, never becoming tough and stringy, even when old. The cut is an exact representation of its shape. Give it a trial.

BORECOLE, OR CURLED KALE.

Chou-vert (Fr.), Grüner Kohl (Ger.), Breton (Sp.).

Dwarf German Greens.

A vegetable highly esteemed in the Northern part of Europe, but very little cultivated in this country. It requires frost to make it good for the table. Treated the same as cabbage.

BROCCOLI.

Chou Brocoli (Fr.), Spargel-Kohl (Ger.), Broculi (Sp.).

Purple Cape.

Resembles the Cauliflower, but not forming such compact heads, and not quite so white, being of a greenish cast. We raise such fine Cauliflower here that very little Broccoli is planted.

The Purple Cape is the most desirable variety; cultivated the same as Half Early Cauliflower; further North than New Orleans, where Cauliflower does not succeed, the Broccoli may be substituted, being hardier.

BRUSSELS SPROUTS.

Chou de Bruxelles (Fr.), Rosen or Sprossen Kohl (Ger.), Breton de Bruselas (Sp.).

A vegetable cultivated the same as the Cabbage, but very little known here. The small heads which appear along the upper part of the stalk between the leaves, make a fine dish when well prepared. Should be sown during August and September.

Brussels Sprouts.

CABBAGE.

CHOU POMME (Fr.), KOPFKOHL (Ger.), REPOLLO (Sp.).

Early York.
Early Large York.
Early Sugar Loaf.
Early Large Oxheart.
Early Winningstadt.
Jersey Wakefield.
Early Flat Dutch.
Early Drumhead.
Large Flat Brunswick.

Improved Early Summer.
Improved Large Late Drumhead.
Frotscher's Superior Late Flat Dutch.
Red Dutch (for pickling).
Green Globe Savoy.
Early Dwarf Savoy.
Drumhead Savoy.
St. Denis or Chou Bonneuil.
Excelsior.

During the past "World's Exposition" I exhibited different vegetables as they were in season. Many visitors will recollect the fine specimens of Cabbage, Beets, Celery, Cauliflower, Lettuce, Cucumbers, etc., they saw there displayed. I received the Prize for **"Frotscher's Flat Dutch Cabbage"** and Early Blood Turnip Beets. Ten heads of Cabbage, devoid of all outside leaves, weighed one hundred and seventy-three pounds. They were raised on Captain Marcy's place, one mile below Algiers.—I did not exhibit them for competition, but merely to show to our Northern visitors what fine vegetables we have here during the winter, when at their homes everything is covered with snow and ice. The Committee of Awards on Vegetables gave me the Prize without any solicitation on my part,—they thinking it well merited. (See inside cover.)

CULTURE.

Cabbage requires a strong, good soil, and should be heavily manured. To raise large Cabbage without good soil and without working the plants well, is an impossibility. Cabbage is sown here almost in every month of the year, but the seed for a main crop should be sown from July to September. Some sow earlier, but July is time enough. For a succession, seed can be sown till November. The main crop for Spring should be sown from end of October to end of November, as stated before. The raising of Cabbage for spring has become quite an item of late years; Brunswick should be sown a little earlier than the Early Summer or the Excelsior, —the two latter kinds not till November, but in a frame, so the young plants can be protected against cold weather, which we generally have between December and January. After the middle of January, setting out can be commenced with. These early varieties of Cabbage require special fertilizing to have them large. Early varieties are sown during winter and early spring. Cabbage is a very important crop, and one of the best paying for the market gardener. It requires more work and attention than most people are willing to give, to raise cabbage plants during the months of July and August. I have found, by careful observation, that plants raised in August are the surest to head here. The most successful gardeners in raising cabbage plants sow the seeds thinly in seed beds, and water several times during the day; in fact, the seed-bed is never allowed to get dry from the sowing of the seed till large enough to transplant. There is no danger, in doing this, of scalding the plants, as many would suppose; but on the contrary, the plants thrive well, and so treated, will be less liable to be attacked by the cabbage-flies, as they are too often disturbed during the day. Tobacco stems chopped up and scattered between the plants and in the walks between the beds, are a preventative against the fly.

Early York. This is an early variety, but very little grown here except for family use. As we have cabbage heading up almost the whole year, it has not the same value as in Northern climates, where the first cabbage in spring brings a good price.

Large York. About two to three weeks later than the above, forming hard heads; not grown for the market. Recommended for family use.

Early Sugar Loaf. Another pointed variety, with spoon-shaped leaves; sown in early spring for an early summer cabbage.

Early Large Oxheart. An excellent variety, which is later than the Large York, and well adapted for sowing in fall or early spring.

Early Winningstadt. This is a very fine solid-heading variety; pointed and of good size, of the same season as the Oxheart. It is very good for family use. It does not suit the market, as no pointed cabbage can be sold to any advantage in the New Orleans market.

Jersey Wakefield. Very popular in the North; but little planted here. It is of medium size and heads up well.

Early Flat Dutch. An intermediate variety between the early pointed and late varieties. It is not, on an average, as heavy as the Oxheart or Winningstadt; but, if raised for the market, more salable on account of being flat. Very good variety for family use.

Early Drumhead. A similar variety to the above; a little earlier, and not making as many leaves, it can be planted close. A good early spring cabbage.

Large Flat Brunswick. This is a late German variety, introduced by me over twenty years ago. It is an excellent variety, and when well headed up the shape of it is a true type of a Premium Flat Dutch Cabbage. It requires very rich ground if sown for winter crop, and should be sown early, as it is a little more susceptible of frost than the Superior Flat Dutch. It is well adapted for shipping, being very hard, and does not wilt so quick as others. At Frenier, along the Jackson R. R. this is the kind principally planted, and is preferred over all other varieties. The people living there plant nothing else but cabbage, and have tried nearly all highly recommended varieties, and this is their choice. At that place the seeds are sown in October and November. The bulk of the cabbage raised there is shipped North in April and May, and is the finest which comes to the Chicago market.

Improved Early Summer. This cabbage is of recent introduction. It is not quite so large as the Brunswick; for fall it can be sown in August; for spring, in November and as late as January. It heads up very uniform and does not produce many outside leaves. It is hardier than the Brunswick, and stands the cold and heat better. The seed I offer is of the best strain cultivated, and can be planted closer together than the late varieties—say about 8000 to the acre. The finest crop of this variety (one hundred and fifty thousand heads of cabbage) I ever saw, was raised three years ago near the city. The grower could commence on one end of the row to cut, and continue to the end, all well headed. They averaged about 7 pounds.

Improved Large Late Drumhead. Fine large variety; should be sown early in the fall for winter, or during December and January for late spring use; it will stand more cold weather than the Brunswick.

Superior Late Flat Dutch. This is the most popular variety for winter cabbage, and cultivated by almost every gardener who plants for the New Orleans market. My stock is of superior quality, and I venture to say that seventy-five per cent. of all cabbage sold in the New Orleans market are of seeds which have been obtained from my store. During winter and spring, specimens which are brought as samples to my establishment, weighing from fifteen to twenty-five pounds, can frequently be seen. In regard to the time of planting, see remarks under

Early Winningstadt.

St. Denis, or Chou Bonneuil.

Drumhead Savoy.

Large York.

Green Globe Savoy.

Early Flat Dutch.

Frotscher's Superior Late Flat Dutch.

Early Large Oxheart

Early York.   Large Flat Brunswick.   Early Dwarf Savoy.

Early Drumhead Cabbage.

Improved Early Summer.

head of "Cabbage" in the directions for planting for July. I have tried seed of the Flat Dutch from different growers, but have found none yet to equal the stock I have been selling for years, and which is raised for me by contract.

Red Dutch. Mostly used for pickling or salads. Very little cultivated.

Green Globe Savoy. Medium sized heads, not very hard, but all the leaves can be used. This and the following varieties are of fine flavor, and preferred by many over the other kinds.

Early Dwarf Savoy. Heads rather small, but solid; leaves very curled and succulent; of a dark green color. Very fine for family garden.

Drumhead Savoy. Leaves are wrinkled, but not quite so much as the two foregoing kinds. It grows to a good size with large roundish heads.

St. Denis, or Chou Bonneuil. This was, at one time, one of the most popular varieties grown for this market, but during the past few years has not done so well as formerly, and is, therefore, planted very little now. It wants good ground and high cultivation. It does better for spring than for fall. Should be sown in November.

Excelsior. There are several varieties called by this name. What I offer is a second early variety; light green color, but few outside leaves and a large roundish head. It is not as hardy as the Superior Flat Dutch, and does excellently when planted for the spring. Seeds sown last season as late as January, produced fine, large heads. It stands the heat better than the Brunswick. This variety, the Brunswick and Early Summer, are the best to plant for shipping in the spring.

CAULIFLOWER.
CHOUFLEUR (Fr.), BLUMENKOHL (Ger.), COLIFLOR (Sp.).

Extra Early Paris.   Early Italian Giant.
Half Early Paris.   Late Italian Giant.
Early Erfurt.   Imperial.
Le Normands (short-stemmed).   Large Algiers.

This is one of the finest vegetables grown, and succeeds well in the vicinity of New Orleans. Large quantities are raised on the sea-coast in the neighborhood of Barataria Bay. The two Italian varieties are of excellent quality, growing to large size, and are considered hardier than the German and French varieties. I have had specimens brought to my store, raised from seed obtained from me, weighing sixteen pounds. The ground for planting Cauliflower should be very rich. They thrive best in rich, sandy soil, and require plenty of moisture during the formation of the head. The Italian varieties should be sown from April till July; the latter month and June is the best time to sow the Early Giant. During August, September and October, the Le Normands, Half Early Paris and Erfurt can be sown. The Half Early Paris is very popular, but the other varieties are just as good. For spring crop the Italian kinds do not answer, but the Early French and German varieties can be sown at the end of December and during January, in a bed protected from frost, and may be transplanted into the open ground during February and as late as March. If we have a favorable season, and not too dry, they will be very fine; but if the heat sets in soon, the flowers will not attain the same size as those obtained from seeds sown in fall, and which head during December and January.

Le Normands short-stemmed Cauliflower.

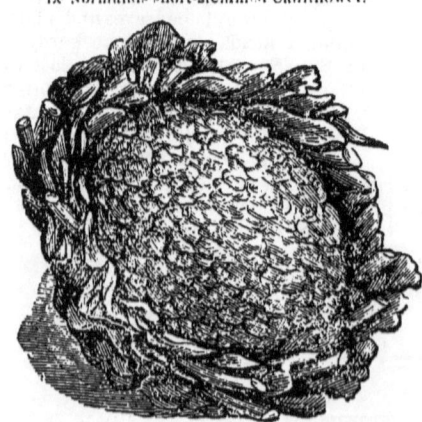

Large Algiers.

Extra Early Paris. The earliest variety; heads small, very tender.

Half Early Paris. The most popular in the New Orleans market. Heads of good size, white and compact.

Early Erfurt. This variety is of more dwarfish growth than the two former. Heads white and of good size. Heads with certainty.

Le Normands is a French variety, and largely cultivated here. It stands more dry weather than the other varieties, and has large and pure white heads. Not so popular as the Half Early Paris in this market, but there is no good reason why it should not be, as it is an excellent variety in every respect; stands the heat better than any other.

Large Algiers. A French variety of the same season as the Le Normands, but a surer producer. It is one of the best kinds, and has taken the place of other second early varieties since it has been introduced.

Early Italian Giant. Very large fine sort, not quite so late as the Late Italian, and almost as large. The heads are quite large, white and compact, and of delicious flavor. I recommend it to all who have not tried it. When sown at

Early Italian Giant Cauliflower.

the proper season, it will head with certainty, and will not fail to give satisfaction.

Late Italian Giant. This is the largest of all the Cauliflowers. It is grown to a considerable extent in the neighborhood of New Orleans. It is very large and compact; should not be sown later than June, as it takes from seven to nine months before it heads.

Imperial. A variety from France, very similar to the Le Normands, perhaps a little earlier; very good. I recommend it highly.

CARROT.

CAROTTE (Fr.), MOEHRE OR GELBE RUEBE (Ger.), ZANAHORIA (Sp.)

Early Scarlet Horn.
Half Long Scarlet French.
Improved Long Orange.
Long Red without core.

St. Valerie.
Half Long Luc.
Danver's Intermediate.

Requires a sandy loam, well manured the previous year, and deeply spaded up. Should be sown in drills ten to twelve inches apart, so the plants can be worked after they are up. Gardeners here generally sow them broad-cast, and often the roots are small from being crowded too much together.

Early Scarlet Horn. A short, stump-rooted variety of medium size, very early and of fine flavor. Not cultivated for the market.

Half Long French Scarlet. This is the most popular variety, and extensively grown for the market as well as for family use. It is a little later than the Early Horn, but much larger; bright scarlet in color, and of fine flavor.

Half Long Luc. This is a new variety from France. It is as early as any previously mentioned, but stump-rooted and larger. It is very smooth and of a fine color.

Improved Long Orange. This is an old variety; roots long and of deep orange color. It is not much cultivated in this section, and the flavor is not so fine as that of the two preceding kinds. Valuable for field culture.

Long Red, without core. A new variety from France, which is of cylindrical shape, very smooth, bright scarlet

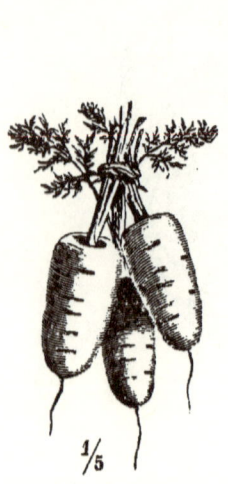
Early Scarlet Horn Carrot.

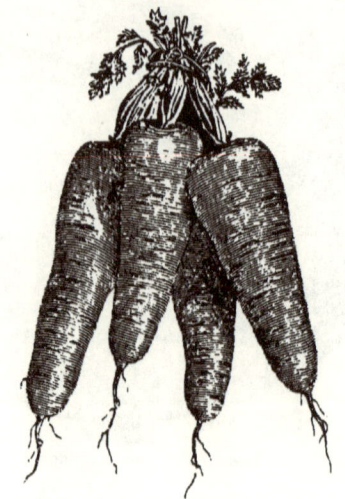
Half Long Luc Carrot.

Half Long French Scarlet Carrot.

Long Red Carrot without core.

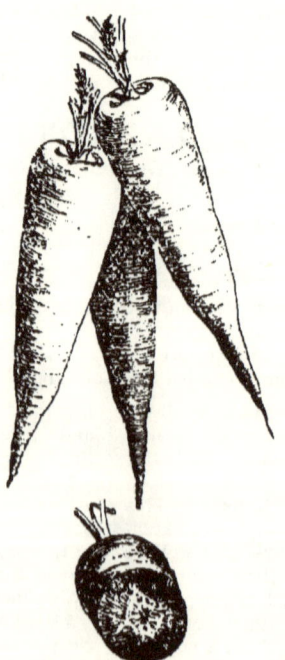
St. Valerie Carrot.

Danver's Intermediate.

color, and of fine flavor; has no heart or core. It is not quite so early as the Half Long, but more productive. Consider it a first-class variety for the table, and one that will come into general cultivation when better known.

St. Valerie. A new variety from France, bright red in color; a little larger and longer than the Half Long French, and stronger in the leaves.

This is one of the finest carrots, and will in the course of time take the place of the Half Long. It is very smooth.

Danver's. An intermediate American variety of recent introduction. It is of a bright orange color; very smooth; symmetrically formed; somewhat stump-rooted like the Half Long Luc. It will produce more in weight to the acre than any other Half Long variety.

CELERY.

CELERI (Fr.), SELLERIE (Ger.), APIO (Sp.).

Large White Solid.
Perfection Heartwell. (New.)
Turnip-Rooted.

Dwarf Large Ribbed.
Cutting or Soup.

Sow in May and June for early transplanting, and in August and September for a later crop. Sow thinly and shade during the hot months. When the plants are six inches high, transplant into trenches about four inches deep, nine wide

Dwarf, Large Ribbed Celery.

Large White Solid Celery.

and two and a half feet apart, made very rich by digging in rotten manure. Plants should be from 6 to 8 inches apart. When planted out during the hot months, the trenches require to be shaded, which is generally done by spreading cotton cloth over them; latanniers will answer the same purpose. Celery requires plenty of moisture, and watering with soapsuds, or liquid manure, will benefit the plants a great deal. When tall enough it should be earthed up to blanch to make it fit for the table.

Large White Solid. This variety used to be planted exclusively, but since the introduction of half dwarf and dwarf kinds has been dropped, more so by market gardeners. It is crisp, but not as fine flavored as the following kinds.

Perfection Heartwell. A new introduction from France. This variety is in size between the Large White Solid and Dwarf kinds; it is of excellent quality, very thick, and when blanched the heart is of a beautiful golden yellow color; preferable to the White Solid, and one of the best kinds ever introduced.

Celeriac or Turnip-Rooted Celery, is very popular in some parts of Europe, but hardly cultivated here. It should be sown in the fall of the year, and transplanted six inches apart, in rows one foot apart. When the roots have obtained a good size, they are boiled, scraped off, sliced and dressed with vinegar, etc., as a salad.

Dwarf Large Ribbed. This kind was brought here several years ago from France. It is short, but very thick-ribbed, solid and of fine flavor. The best dwarf variety for this section.

Celery for Soup. This is sown in the spring of the year, broad-cast, to be used for seasoning, the same as Parsley.

Celeriac or Turnip-Rooted Celery

CHERVIL.

CERFEUIL (Fr.), KERBELKRAUT (Ger.).

An aromatic plant, used a good deal for seasoning, especially in oyster soup, and is often cut between Lettuce when served as a salad. In the North this vegetable is very little known, but in this section there is hardly a garden where it is not found. Sow broad-cast during fall for winter and spring, and in January and February for summer use.

COLLARDS.

A kind of cabbage which does not head, but the leaves are used the same as other cabbage. Not so popular as in former years, and very little planted in this vicinity.

CORN SALAD.

MACHE. DOUCET (Fr.), ACKER SALAT (Ger.), VALERIANA (Sp.).

Broad-leaved Corn Salad is the variety generally cultivated. It is used as salad during the winter and early spring months. Should be sown broad-cast during fall and winter, or in drills nine inches apart.

CORN.
INDIAN.
Mais (Fr.), Welschkorn (Ger.), Maiz (Sp.).

Extra Early Dwarf Sugar.
Adam's Extra Early.
Early Sugar or Sweet.
Stowel's Evergreen Sugar.
Golden Dent Gourd Seed.
Early Yellow Canada.
Large White Flint.

Blunt's Prolific Field.
Improved Leaming.
Golden Beauty.
Champion White Pearl.
Mosby's Prolific.
Hickory King.

Plant in hills about three feet apart, drop four to five seeds and thin out to two or three. Where the ground is strong the Adam's Extra Early and Crosby's Sugar can be planted in hills two and a half feet apart, as these two varieties are more dwarfish than the other kinds. Plant for a succession from February to June.

Extra Early, or Crosby's Dwarf Sugar. This is a very early variety and of excellent quality. Ears small, but very tender. It is not so extensively planted as it deserves to be.

Adam's Extra Early, the most popular variety with market gardeners for first planting. It has no fine table qualities, but as it grows to a good size, and is matured in about forty days from time of planting, it meets with ready sale in the market, and for these reasons gardeners prefer it.

Early Sugar, or New England. A long eight-rowed variety, which succeeds the Extra Early sorts. Desirable variety.

Stowel's Evergreen Sugar. This is the best of all Sugar Corn. It is an early Corn, but the ears are of large size, and are well filled. It remains green longer than any other variety, and is quite productive. The cultivation of this excellent cereal, as well as all other Sugar Corn, is much neglected, yet why people will plant common field-corn for table use, considering size instead of quality, I can not understand.

Golden Dent Gourd Seed. A field variety which is very productive at the North. It makes a very fine Corn South, but has to be planted here several years in succession before it attains perfection as during the first year the ears are not well covered by the husk, which is the case with all Northern varieties. When selected and planted here for a few years, it becomes acclimated and makes an excellent Corn, with large, fine ears, grain deep and cob of medium size.

Early Yellow Canada. A long eight-rowed variety. It is very early, and is planted in both the field and garden. It does well here.

Large White Flint. A very popular variety with gardeners and amateurs. It is planted here for table use principally, but like the Golden Dent, makes an excellent kind for field culture after it has been planted here for two or three years.

Blunt's Prolific Field Corn. This is a very excellent variety, either for the field or for the table. It is very prolific, producing from four to six ears of corn. They are of medium size, but well filled and heavy. It is second early. This variety has done better than any other, and, being of Southern origin, it seems to be better adapted to our climate. I recommend it as an early yielding Corn for field culture.

Improved Leaming. An extra early variety, sold by me for the first time five years ago. It is not hard and flinty, but sweet and nutritious, making excellent feed and fine meal. The ears are large and handsome, with deep, large grains, deep orange color and small red cob. It is very productive. The shucks cover the ear better than any Northern or Western variety I have ever

Champion White Pearl Corn.

tried. It is adapted to a variety of soils, and produces well on heavy or light soil; it has shown itself as very reliable.

Golden Beauty. This variety is the handsomest of all yellow corn; the ears are of a perfect shape, long, and filled out to the extreme end of the cob. The grains are not of a flinty type, neither are they so soft as to be greatly shrivelled, as in the Golden Dent. Golden Beauty matures early, ripening in eighty days from planting, and surpasses all in size and beauty of grain.

Champion White Pearl. This is a very handsome white corn. The grain is pure white, exceedingly heavy and long, two of which will span the cob, which is small. Being medium in size of stalk it can be planted much thicker

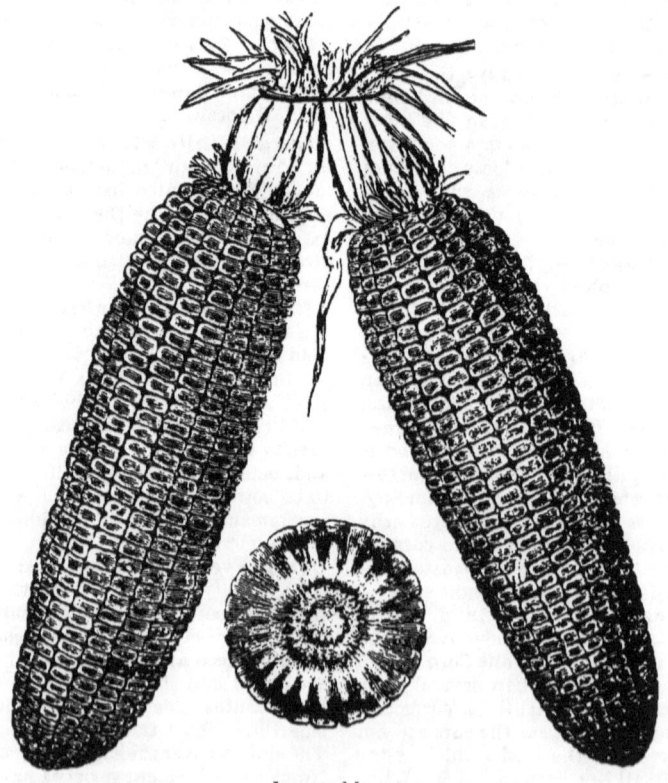

Improved Leaming.

than a large Corn, and at the same time bear a full sized ear. The originator has established in Champion White Pearl Corn a short, thick stalk, with the ear growing low upon it, which is an advantage in stormy weather.

Mosby's Prolific Corn. This is a Southern Corn, and is recommended for

Golden Beauty Corn.   Hickory King Corn.

Evergreen Sugar Corn.

Early Sugar, or New England Corn.

Extra Early Sugar Corn.

general crop. The originator of this variety says: "This corn is a cross between two widely different varieties. It is purely white, small cob, deep, full grain, neither too hard nor too soft. It will stand crowding in the drill as close again as any other variety. Ears of medium size, but long. It stands the drought better than ordinary corn." Should be planted early.

Hickory King. This New Field Corn was introduced here by me last year. It has proven itself all that was claimed for it. It is the largest grained and smallest White Dent Corn in the World. It is very early, and comes in succession to the Adams Early. The ears are from seven to nine inches in length, and are generally borne from three to five to a stalk, making it very productive. The ears are well covered by the shucks; a great consideration in Field Corn planted in the South.

CRESS.

CRESSON (Fr.), KRESSE (Ger.), BERRO (Sp.).

Used for salad during winter and spring. Sow broad-cast or in drills six inches apart.

Curled or Pepper Grass. Not much used in this section.

Broad-Leaved. This variety is extensively cultivated for the market. It is sown from early fall to late spring. The leaves resemble Water Cress; a variety which does not well succeed here. Is considered a very wholesome dish.

CUCUMBER.

CONCOMBRE (Fr.), GURKE (Ger.), PEPINO (Sp.).

Improved Early White Spine.
Early Frame.
Long Green Turkey.
Early Cluster.
Long Green White Spine.
Gherkin, or Burr (for pickling.)

Cucumbers need a rich soil. Plant in hills from three to four feet apart; the hills should be made rich with well decomposed manure, and eight to ten seeds should be planted in each hill, and covered about one-half inch deep; when well up, thin out to four plants in the hill till the vines meet. When the spring is dry the plants have to be watered, else they do not keep in bearing long. They can be planted from March till July. A great many cucumbers are planted here in February, or even sooner, and are protected by small boxes with a pane of glass on top. These boxes are removed during the day, and put back in the evening. When days are cloudy and cold, the plants are kept covered.

Improved Early White Spine. This is the most popular variety. It is of medium size, light green, covered with white spines, and turns white when ripe. The best kind for shipping. Of late years it is used by most gardeners for forcing as well as outdoor culture. It is very productive.

Early Frame. Another early variety, but not so popular as the fore-

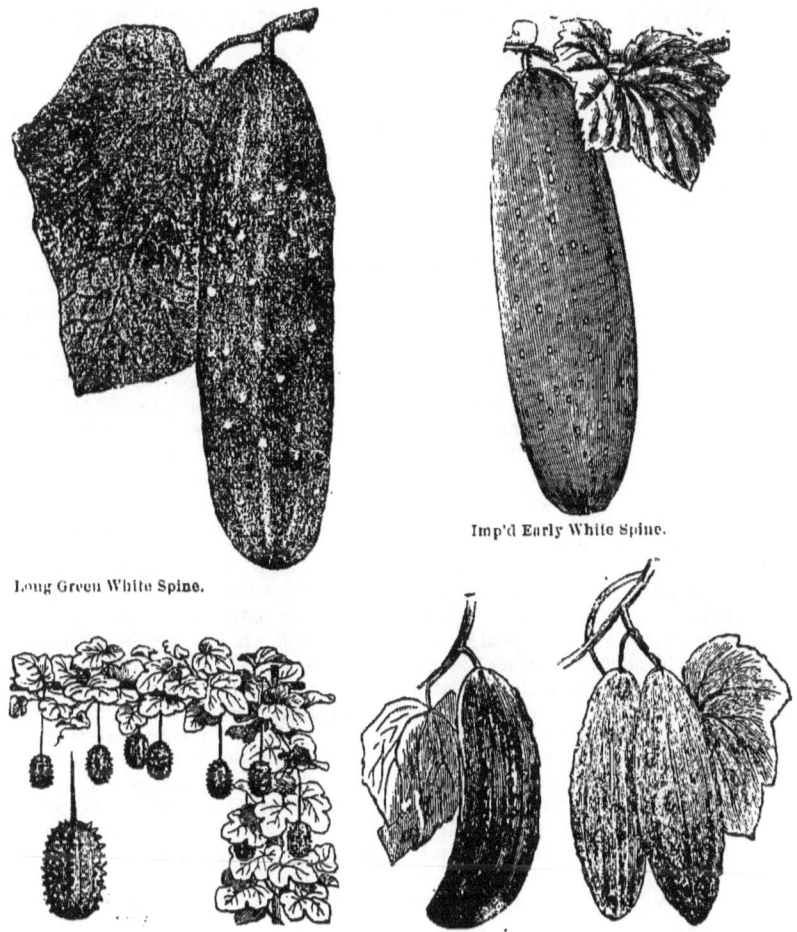

Imp'd Early White Spine.

Long Green White Spine.

West India Gherkin.

Early Frame

Early Cluster.

going kind. It is deep green in color, but turns yellow very quickly; therefore gardeners do not plant it much.

Long Green Turkey. A long variety attaining a length of from fifteen to eighteen inches when well grown. Very fine and productive.

Early Cluster. Early, short and prickly; it bears in clusters.

Long Green White Spine or New Orleans Market. This is a variety selected from an imported forcing cucumber introduced by me. It is good for forcing or open ground; very productive, keeps its green color, and has few vines. This kind can not be excelled for shipping, as it produces very perfect cucumbers and but few culls; the largest growers of cucumbers for shipping about here plant none but this variety. It is quite different from the Long White Spine offered by some.

West India Gherkin. This is an oval variety, small in size. It is used for pickling when young and tender. When grown to its full size it can be stewed with meat. In fact, this is the only use made of it about New Orleans.

The following may be of some importance to those who contemplate the raising of Cucumbers.

The **Cucumber** is a very important crop for the Southern Gardener and Truck-farmer. To give some information on the cultivation I publish the following letter which is written by one of the most extensive and successful growers of this vegetable in this neighborhood; he plants exclusively the Long Green White Spine or New Orleans Market.

NINE MILE POINT, JEFFERSON PARISH,
Sept. 17th, 1888.

Mr. RICHARD FROTSCHER,
NEW ORLEANS.

Dear Sir:

In compliance with your request, "to give you a description of my practice in growing Cucumbers," I send you this. Old growers will not find anything new in it, but to beginners it may be of some service.

There are three methods in general use by growers here. They are forcing in hot-beds, growing in cold frames, and the field crop. Of the first I have little to say here; it requires a plentiful supply of fresh stable manure, or other heating material, and so obliges one to be located where such can be had in abundance, and in my opinion, to be uniform and successful, requires also skilled labor.

My practice for growing in the cold frames is as follows. I make a good hot bed, (for doing this you have given clear, and ample instructions, in your Almanac and Garden Manual) make the beds large enough to hold three five inch pots for every sash you have in your cold frames; this will allow for one-third dying. The hot bed should be made the last week in December; in a week after, place your pots in the bed, fill the pots with a rich light soil, in this sow your seed, seven or eight in each pot, cover a little less than half an inch deep, let the ground on top of the pots get dry before watering, then water freely, close up the sash and keep it closed until the seed begins to come up, which it will do in less than three days. From this time on, the hot bed must be carefully watched, plenty of air given on bright days, even pulling the sash entirely off for a few hours in the middle of warm clear days. In cold cloudy weather keep them closed, the young plants are, at this stage, very liable to damp off. To prevent this, give plenty of air when the weather is good; if it is wet and cold, and the sash cannot be opened, sprinkle plenty of air slacked lime in the frame. Water only when dry, and then only in fair weather. When the plants are well up, thin out to three in a pot. After the second rough leaf is formed, pinch off the top bud, this will make them stocky. In four weeks after sowing the seeds, the plants should be fit to set out in the cold frames. The ground in the frames should be made rich and light, loose and well dug over with the spade. It is important to prepare the soil in the cold frames well, or a poor crop will be the result.

The transplanting from the hot-bed to the cold frame should be done on a warm calm day; knock the plants out of the pots carefully to avoid breaking the ball. Plant two hills under each sash, at about two feet apart, close up the sash as fast as planted, and do not water until next day; do not give any air till the plants recover the transplanting. As you will now have to depend on the heat of the sun to keep your plants growing, do not open your sashes too wide, open them only on fine days, and then open them late in the morning, and close them early in the evening. Two or three weeks of this treatment will bring the plants well forward, and as the weather gets warmer, give more air, stir the ground with a hoe to keep it loose, water plentifully when needed. By the first of March they should be setting fruit freely. From this time on, the sash can be pulled off entirely during the day, and put on again at night; as the weather gets warmer give plenty of water, in fact keep the ground almost wet. Cut off all cucumbers as fast as they get large enough for the market; do not leave any on the vines to get old, as it will have the effect of retarding the growth of the young fruit; thus making the vines less productive.

For the field crop, we plant the seed in strawberry boxes; in cold frames, the boxes are four inches each way, width, length and depth. This is the best size; they are without bottoms; they are packed in the frame close together, filled with a good soil and 5 or 6 seed planted in each box; water, shut the sash and keep it shut until the seed begins to come up. Then from this on give plenty of air in good weather, water freely when dry, and thin out to three in a box; in about four weeks they will be fit to plant out in the field. Have the ground where they are to be planted, well plowed, fine and in good order; open the rows eight feet apart with a plow. To take the plants out of the frames, run a sharp spade just under the bottom of the boxes to cut them loose from the bed, lift them on the spade and place them close together in a cart; pack them tight in the bottom of the cart to prevent jolting about in hauling to the field. Drive the cart on the ground to be planted, take the boxes one by one carefully out of the cart, and place them in the furrow already opened, about two feet apart; have a hand follow with a sharp knife, and cut down one corner of the box, and remove it in one piece, without breaking the ball of earth about the roots of the plants. Much depends upon this being carefully done; let hands enough follow with hoes to fill up the furrow with soil, drawing plenty of fine dirt to the roots of the plants. They must be watered if necessary. The after-treatment will be to keep the ground about the plants and between the rows loose and fine with the cultivator and hoe. Just before the vines begin to run, say in ten days after planting, bar off close to the plants with the plow, and in the furrow on both sides of the plants scatter a small handful of cotton seed meal or other good fertilizer; cover this with the plow, and plow out the middles; keep the ground loose around the plants, being careful not to disturb the vines at any time, and when the vines cover the ground no further cultivation is necessary. By this method we generally get fruit three weeks earlier than from seed planted in the field. I need not tell you that earliness in truck-farming is almost everything. The time for planting the seed in the boxes for the crop will depend on the season, locality, etc. This much is certain, you can keep the plants in the boxes for only four, or at the most five weeks after planting the seed. After that time they get too large to transplant safely. The only guide is to use our own judgment and plant the seed four weeks before we expect the last frost in the spring.

I have written this plainly, and described my practice so minutely, because I know from experience how hard it sometimes is to get from books, etc., a practical idea of how to do anything that we have little or no previous knowledge of.

Yours very respectfully,

WM. NELSON.

EGG-PLANT.

AUBERGINE (Fr.), EIERPFLANZE (Ger.), BERENGENA (Sp.).

The seed should be sown in hot-beds in the early part of January. When a couple of inches high they should be transplanted into another frame, so that the plants may become strong and robust. When warm enough, generally during March, the plants can be placed in the open ground, about two and a half feet apart. This vegetable is very popular in the South, and extensively cultivated.

Large Purple Egg-Plant.

Large Purple, or New Orleans Market. This is the only kind grown here; it is large, oval in shape and of a dark purple color and very productive. Southern grown seed of this, as of a good many other tropical or sub-tropical vegetables, it is preferable to Northern seed, as it will germinate more readily, and the plant will last longer during the hot season.

Early Dwarf Oval. This variety is very early and productive; the fruit is not so large as the New Orleans Egg-Plant, but equal in flavor. For market it will not sell as well as the former; desirable for family garden.

ENDIVE.

CHICOREE (Fr.), ENDIVIEN (Ger.), ENDIBIA (Sp.).

A salad plant which is very popular and much cultivated for the market, principally for summer use. It can be sown in drills a foot apart, and, when the plants are well up, thinned out till about eight inches apart. Or it can be sown broadcast thinly and transplanted the same as Lettuce. When the leaves are large enough, say about eight inches long, tie them up for blanching, to make them fit for the table. This can only be done in dry weather, otherwise the leaves are apt to rot. For summer use do not sow before the end of March, as if sown sooner, the plants will run into seed very early. Sow for a succession during the spring and summer months. For winter use sow in September and October.

Green Curled. Is the most desirable kind, as it stands more heat than the following sort, and is the favorite market variety.

Extra Fine Curled. Does not grow quite so large as the foregoing, and is more apt to decay when there is a wet summer. Better adapted for winter.

Broad-Leaved, or Escarolle. Makes a fine salad when well grown and blanched, especially for summer.

Green Curled Endive.

KOHL-RABI, or TURNIP-ROOTED CABBAGE.

CHOU NAVET (Fr.), KOHL-RABI (Ger.), COL DE NABO (Sp.).

This vegetable is very popular with the European population of this city, and largely cultivated here. It is used for soups, or prepared in the same manner as Cauliflower. For late fall and winter use it should be sown from the end of July till the middle of October; for spring use during January and February. When the young plants are one month old transplant them in rows one foot apart, and about the same distance in the rows. They also grow finely if sown broad-cast and thinned out when young, so that the plants are not too crowded; or, they may be sown in drills, and cultivated the same as Ruta Bagas.

Early White Vienna. The finest variety of all, and the only kind I keep. It is early, forms a smooth bulb, and has few small leaves. The so-called large White or Green is not desirable.

Early White Vienna Kohl-Rabi.

LEEK.

POIREAU (Fr.), LAUCH (Ger.), PUERO (Sp.).

A species of Onion, highly esteemed for flavoring soups. Should be sown broad-cast and transplanted, when about six to eight inches high, into rows a foot apart, and six inches apart in the rows. Should be planted at least four inches deep. They require to be well cultivated in order to secure large roots. Sow in October for winter and spring use, and in January and February, for summer.

Large London Flag. Is the most desirable kind, and the most generally grown.

Large Carentan. This is a new French variety which grows to a very large size.

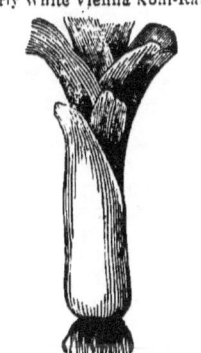

Large London Flag Leek.

LETTUCE.

LAITUE (Fr.), LATTICH (Ger.), LECHUGA (Sp.).

Early Cabbage, or White Butter-Head.
Improved Royal Cabbage.
Brown Dutch Cabbage.
Drumhead Cabbage.

White Paris Coss.
Perpignan.
Improved Large Passion.

Lettuce is sown here during the whole year by the market gardener. Of course it takes a great deal of labor to produce this vegetable during our hot summer months. For directions how to sprout the seed during that time, see "Work for June." The richer and better the ground the larger the head will be. No finer Lettuce is grown anywhere else than in New Orleans during fall and spring. The seed should be sown broad-cast, and when large enough, planted out in rows a foot apart, and from eight to ten inches apart in the rows. Some kinds grow larger than others; for instance, Butterhead will not require as much space as Drumhead or Perpignan.

Drumhead Cabbage Lettuce.

Early Cabbage or White Butter.

Improved Royal Cabbage Lettuce.

Perpignan Lettuce.

White Paris Coss Lettuce.

Early Cabbage, or White Butter. An early variety, forming a solid head, but not quite so large as some others. It is the best kind for family use, to sow during fall and early spring, as it is very early and of good flavor.

Improved Royal Cabbage. This is the most popular variety in this State. Heads light green, of large size, and about two weeks later than the White Butter. It is very tender and crisp; can be sown later in the spring than the foregoing kind, and does not run into seed so quickly.

Brown Dutch Cabbage. A very hard kind, forms a solid head; not so popular as many other kinds; good for winter.

Drumhead Cabbage. An excellent spring variety, forming large heads, the outer leaves curled.

White Paris Coss. This is very popular with the New Orleans market gardeners, as it is the favorite with the French population It grows to perfection and forms large, fine heads, particularly in the spring of the year.

Perpignan. A fine German variety which forms large, light green heads, and which stands the heat better than the Royal. It is much cultivated for the market, as it thrives well when sown during the latter end of spring.

Improved Large Passion. This is a large Cabbage Lettuce introduced by me from California; it attains a large size, grows slowly, but heads very hard. It does better here during late autumn and winter than in summer, as it cannot stand the heat. If sown late in the fall and transplanted during winter, it grows to very large heads, hard and firm. It is the kind shipped from here in the spring.

MELON.
MUSK OR CANTELOUPE.

Netted Nutmeg.
Netted Citron.
Pine Apple.

Early White Japan.
Persian or Cassaba.
New Orleans Market.

Melons require a rich sandy loam. If the ground is not rich enough, a couple of shovels full of rotted manure should be mixed into each hill, which ought to be from five to six feet apart; drop ten or twelve seeds, and when the plants have two or three rough leaves, thin out to three or four plants. Canteloupes are cultivated very extensively in the neighborhood of New Orleans; the quality is very fine and far superior to those raised in the North. Some gardeners plant during February and cover with boxes, the same as described for Cucumbers. When Melons are ripening, too much rain will impair the flavor of the fruit.

Note.—The above cut represents the New Orleans Melon; it has been taken from a common specimen grown by one of my customers, who raises the seed of this variety for me.

Netted Nutmeg Melon. Small oval melon, roughly netted, early, and of fine flavor.

Netted Citron Canteloupe. This variety is larger than the foregoing kind; it is more rounded in shape, of medium size and roughly netted.

Pine Apple Canteloupe. A medium sized early variety, oval in shape, and of very fine flavor.

Early White Japan Canteloupe. An early kind, of creamish white color, very sweet, and of medium size.

Persian or Cassaba. A large variety, of oval shape and delicate flavor. The rind of this kind is very thin, which is a disadvantage in handling, and prevents it from being planted for the market. Very fine for family use.

New Orleans Market. A large species of the citron kind. It is extensively grown for this market; large in size, very roughly netted and of luscious flavor; different altogether from the Northern Netted Citron, which is earlier, but not so fine in flavor, and not half the size of the variety grown here. The New Orleans Market cannot be excelled by any other variety in the world. In a favorable season it is a perfect gem. I have tried it alongside of varieties praised at the North, such as are brought out every year,—but none of them could compare with the New Orleans Market. As for some years past the seeds were scarce I had some grown North, but they lost their fine qualities, size and flavor. It requires a Southern sun to bring the seed to perfection. Small varieties of melons will improve in size if cultivated here for a number of years, and if care is taken that no Cucumbers, Squashes, Gourds or Pumpkin are cultivated in the vicinity. If the best and earliest specimens are selected for seed, in three or four years the fruit will be large and fine.

MELON.
WATER.
MELON D'EAU (Fr.), WASSERMELONE (Ger.), SANDIA (Sp.).

Mountain Sweet.
Mountain Sprout.
Ice-Cream (White Seeded.)
Orange Water.
Rattle Snake.
Cuban Queen.

Mammoth Iron Clad.
Pride of Georgia.
Kolb Gem.
Florida's Favorite.
Oemler's Triumph.

Water Melon will grow and produce in places where Canteloupe will not do well. The soil for this plant should be light and sandy. Plant in hills about eight feet apart, eight to twelve seeds in a hill; when the plants are well up thin out to three. The plants should be hoed often, and the ground between the hills kept clean till the vines touch.

Mountain Sweet Water. This was once a very popular variety; it is of oblong shape, flesh bright scarlet, and of good flavor. It is very productive.

Mountain Sprout Water. This is similar in the shape to the foregoing variety, but rather later. It

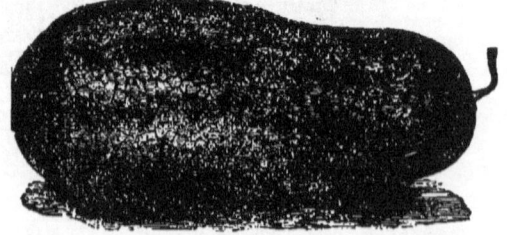

Mountain Sweet Water Melon.

is light green with irregular stripes of dark green. Flesh bright scarlet.

Ice-Cream. (WHITE SEEDED.) A medium sized variety of excellent quality. It is early and very productive. Being thin in the rind it is not so well adapted for the market as the other kinds; notwithstanding this, it is grown exclusively by some for that, on account of its earliness. It has come into general cultivation more and more every year, as it is very sweet, and sells readily in the market.

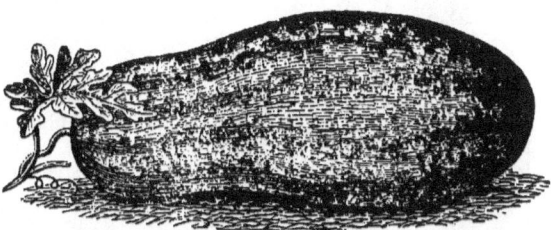

Mountain Sprout Melon.

Orange Water. Quite a distinct variety from the others. The rind can be peeled off the same as the skin of an orange. It is of medium size, fair quality. Very little cultivated.

Cuban Queen.

Rattle Snake. An old Southern variety which has come into notice of late years. It is of large size, light green, with large dark stripes, and is identical with the Gipsey. Fine market variety. It stands transportation better than most other kinds; has been the standard market variety till the Kolb's Gem was introduced. However, it always will remain a favorite with market-gardeners. The seed I offer of this variety, is grown for me by one of the best growers in Georgia. It is of the purest strain that can be found.

Cuban Queen. A striped variety; highly recommended by Northern seedsmen; said to reach from fifty to seventy pounds. Sweet and of delicate flavor; it does not grow as large here as said it does North.

Mammoth Iron Clad. A new variety; highly recommended North. It did not do as well as Southern raised seed. I have the seed now grown in Florida, and, no doubt, it will give better satisfaction.

Pride of Georgia. A new Melon from Georgia, of excellent quality; attains a large size when well cultivated. A very good variety for family use.

The Kolb Gem. Only a few years since this variety has been introduced, but the shipping qualities are so good, that the bulk of melons raised for the market are of that kind. Flesh crimson, very thin but tough rind; fine flavor and full of flesh, no hollow in the middle. It is the heaviest melon for its size. What I offer are Southern grown seeds, which stand the sun better and produce larger and more Melons than Northern grown seeds.

Florida's Favorite. This variety was introduced two years ago. It originated with W. M. Girardeau, of Monticello, Fla. It is an excellent variety, very prolific, earlier than the Kolb Gem, Rattlesnake or Pride of Georgia, and very fine for the table. It is not as good for shipping as the Kolb Gem, or Rattlesnake; it is of medium size, colored with

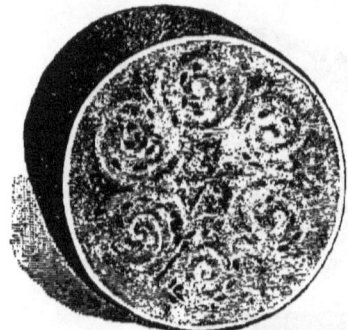

Oemler's Triumph Water Melon.

light and dark green stripes alternately, flesh deep red, deliciously sweet, very firm and crisp. Best Melon for family use.

Oemler's Triumph Water Melon. This new Melon originated on the borders of the Black Sea, in Russia. The seeds are so diminutive that a No. 6 thimble will hold 55 of them, whereas it holds only 7 of those of our ordinary water melon seeds, hence they can be swallowed without inconvenience. It is very curly and very productive. In shape it is a short oval, weighing about 15 lbs., more or less. The color is a

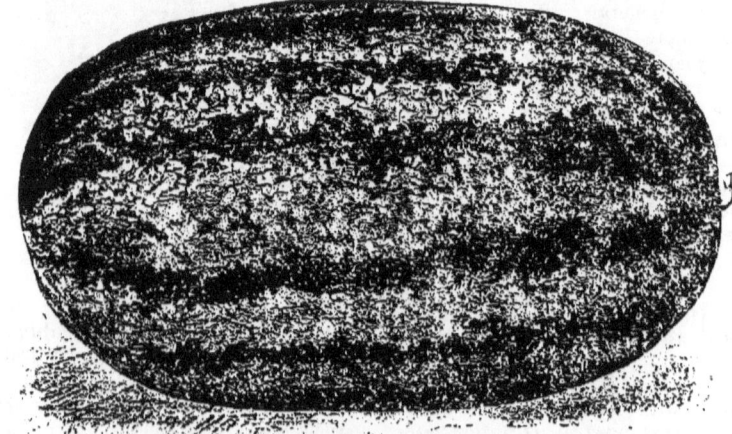

Mammoth Iron Clad Melon.

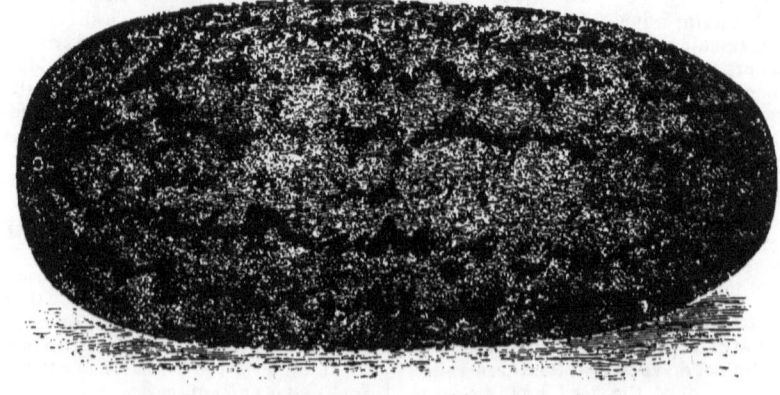

Florida's Favorite Melon.

dark mottled green, and that of the flesh a dark red with an edging of orange yellow. It has no light colored or tasteless core. Its flavor is very sweet. Good for family use.

Pride of Georgia Melon.

Kolb Gem Melon.

MUSTARD.

MOUTARDE (Fr.), SENF (Ger.), MOSTAZA (Sp.).
White or Yellow Seeded. | Large-Leaved Curled.
Chinese very large Cabbage-Leaved.

This is grown to quite an extent in the Southern States, and is sown broad-cast during fall, winter and spring. It may be used the same as spinach, or boiled with meat as greens. The White or Yellow Seeded is very little cultivated, and is used chiefly for medical purposes, or pickling. The large-leaved or Curled has black seed, a distinct kind from the Northern or European variety. The seed is raised in Louisiana. It makes very large leaves; cultivated more and more every year.

Large-Leaved Curled. This is the favorite kind here, sown largely for the market. Leaves are pale green, large and curled or scalloped on the edges.

Chinese Very Large Cabbage-Leaved. This is a European variety, with light green, very large leaves. It has not the same taste as the large-leaved or the large curled, but will stand longer before going to seed.

NASTURTIUM.

CAPUCINE (Fr.), INDIANISCHE-KRESSE (Ger.), CAPUCHINA (Sp.).
Tall | Dwarf.

Planted here only for ornament. (For description, see List of Climbing Plants.)

OKRA.

Green Tall-Growing. | Dwarf Green. | New Velvet.

This is a highly esteemed vegetable in the South, and no garden, whether small or large, is without it. It is used in making "Gumbo," a dish the Creoles of

New Velvet.

Tall Growing Okra.

Louisiana know how to prepare better than any other nationality. It is also boiled in salt and water, and served with vinegar as a salad, and is considered a very wholesome dish. Should not be planted before the ground is warm in spring as the seeds are apt to rot. Sow in drills, which ought to be two to three feet apart, and when up, thin out, and leave one or two plants every twelve or fifteen inches.

Tall Growing. This is the variety most cultivated here. The pods are long, round towards the end, and keep tender longer than the square podded kind.

Dwarf Green. This is a very early and prolific variety, and remains tender longer than any other. It has come into general cultivation, planted much more than the tall. It may be said here, that all dwarf varieties, when cultivated here in this locality for some years, will grow taller every year.

New Velvet. A new variety; dwarf, round, smooth pods, free from ridges and seams, and not prickly to the touch; very prolific and early. I tried this variety the last two years, and sold a good deal of the seed last year. It has come up to what is claimed for it. I recommend it to all who have not tried it.

ONION.

OGNON (Fr.), ZWIEBEL (Ger.), CEBOLLA (Sp.).

Louisiana or Creole.   *New White Queen.*

The Onion is one of the most important vegetables, and is grown to a large extent in Louisiana. It is one of the surest crops to be raised, and always sells. Thousands of barrels are shipped in Spring from here to the Western and Northern States. There is one peculiar feature about raising Onions here, and that is, they can only be raised from Southern or so-called Creole seed. No seed from North, West, or any part of Europe, will produce a merchantable Onion in the South. When the crop of Creole seed is a failure, and they are scarce, they will bring a good price, having been sold as high as ten dollars a pound, when at the same time Northern seed could be had for one-fourth of that price. Northern raised seed can be sown to be used green, but as we have Shallots here which grow during the whole autumn and winter, and multiply very rapidly, the sowing of seed for green Onions is not profitable. Seed ought to be sown from the middle of September to the end of October; if sown sooner, too many will throw up seed stalks. When the month of September has been dry and hot, the beds where the seeds are sown ought to be covered with moss. Where this cannot be had, palmettos can be used, but they should be taken off in the evening and replaced in the morning. When the seeds are well up, this is no longer necessary, but watering should be continued. —They are generally sown broad-cast, and when the size of a goose quill should be transplanted into rows one to two feet apart, and about five inches in the rows. Onions are different, in regard to rotation, from other vegetables. They do best if raised on the same ground for a succession of years. Onions did not bring very high prices, owing to the very heavy yield, the largest ever made in Louisiana upon the same acreage. The crop of seed has been short the past season, and prices so high that it was impossible to sow any for sets. Could not fill orders received in the latter part of the season; seeds were sold out.

Louisiana or Creole Onion. This is generally of a light red color, darker than the Strassburg, and lighter in color than the Wethersfield. The seed I have been selling of this kind, for a number of years, has been raised on Bayou Lafourche, and has never failed to make fine large Onions.

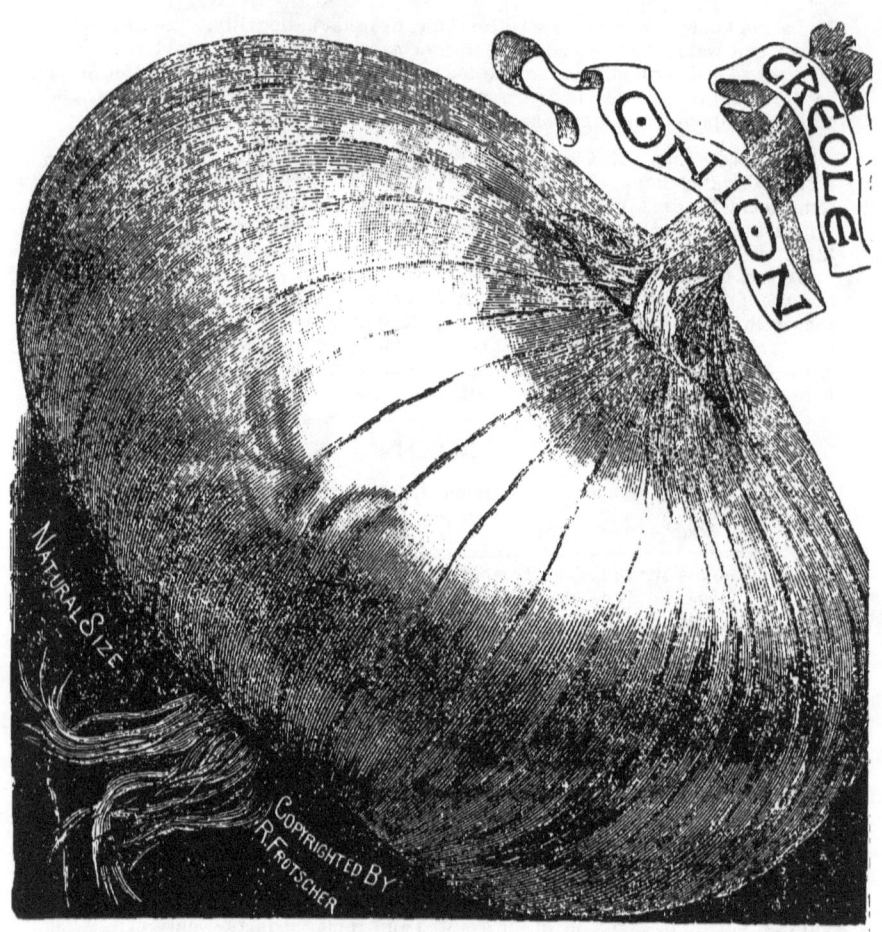

The crop of Creole Onion seed having failed some years ago, I sold a good deal of Italian seed and ha l ample opportunity to see the results The Giant Roca I have discarded; it takes too long to bulb and is very spongy. The Bermuda and Red Tripoli have done fairly, but the Onions do not mature as early as the Creole, and do not keep so well, although attaining a very large size, and more so the Bermuda. They are of mild flavor, and well adapted to be used up in spring; but I would not recommend them to be raised for shipping, except the White Queen.

NEW ITALIAN ONIONS.

New Queen. This is a medium sized, white variety from Italy, very early and flat; can be sown as late as February, and good sized bulbs will yet be obtained. It is of mild flavor and very fine when boiled and dressed for the table. It can not be too highly recommended.

SHALLOTS.

ECHALLOITE (Fr.), SCHALOTTEN (Ger.).

A small sized Onion which grows in clumps. It is generally grown in the South, and used in its green state for soups, stew, etc. There are two varieties, the Red and White; the latter variety is the most popular. In the fall of the year the bulbs are divided and set out in rows a foot apart, and four to six inches in the rows. They grow and multiply very fast, and can be divided during winter, and set out again. Late in spring, when the tops become dry, they have to be taken up, thoroughly dried, and stored in a dry airy place.

PARSLEY.

PERSIL (Fr.), PETERSILIE (Ger.), PERJIL (Sp.).

Plain Leaved. | *Improved Garnishing.*
Double Curled.

Parsley can be sown during the fall from August to October, and during spring, from the end of January to the end of April. It is generally sown broad-cast.

Plain Leaved. This is the kind raised for the New Orleans market.

Double Curled. The leaves of this variety are curled. It has the same flavor as the other kind, but is not so popular.

Improved Garnishing. This is the best kind to ornament a dish; it has the same flavor as the other kinds.

PARSNIP.

PANAIS (Fr.), PASTINAKE (Ger.), PASTINAÇA (Sp.).

Hollow Crown, or Sugar.

Should be sown in deep, mellow soil, deeply spaded, as the roots are long, in drills twelve to eighteen inches apart; when the plants are three inches high, thin out to three inches apart in the row. Sow from September to November for winter, and January to March for spring and summer crops.

The Hollow Crown, or Sugar, is the kind generally cultivated; it possesses all the good qualities for which other varieties are recommended.

PEAS.

POIS (Fr.), ERBSE (Ger.), GUISANTE (Sp.).

EARLIEST.

Cleveland's Alaska, 2½ *feet.* | *Early Tom Thumb, 1 foot.*
Extra Early, or First and Best, 2½ *feet.* | *Laxton's Alpha, 3 feet.*
Early Washington, 3 feet. | *American Wonder,* 1½ *feet.*

SECOND CROP.

Bishop's Dwarf Long Pod, 1½ *feet.* | *McLean's Little Gem,* 1½ *feet.*
Champion of England, 5 feet. | *Laxton's Prolific Long Pod, 3 feet.*
McLean's Advancer, 3 feet. | *Eugenie, 3 feet.*
Carter's Stratagem, 2½ *feet.* | *Carter's Telephone, 5 feet.*

GENERAL CROP.

Dwarf Blue Imperial, 3 feet. | *Large White Marrowfat, 4 feet.*
Royal Dwarf Marrow, 3 feet. | *Dwarf Sugar,* 2½ *feet.*
Black Eyed Marrowfat, 4 feet. | *Tall Sugar, 6 feet.*

Peas are a fine vegetable, and therefore are very generally cultivated. It is best to plant in ground manured the previous year, else they will make more vines than peas. As a general thing the dwarf kinds require richer ground than the tall growing varieties. Marrowfat Peas planted in rich ground will not bear well, but they produce finely in sandy light soil.

The Extra Early, Tom Thumb, or Laxton's Alpha will not produce a large crop without being in rich ground. Peas have to be planted in drills two inches deep and from two to three feet apart, according to the height they may grow. Tom Thumb can be planted one foot apart, whereas White Marrowfat or Champion of England require three feet. The Extra Early, Alpha and Tom Thumb can be planted during August and September for fall. During November and December we plant the Marrowfats; January and February, as late as March, all kinds can be planted, but for the latter month only the earliest varieties should be used, as the late varieties will get mildewed before they bring a crop. Peas will bear much better if some brush or rods are stuck in the drills to support them, except the very dwarf kinds.

Cleveland's Alaska. This is an extra early Pea, blue in color, the earliest by a few days of any other kind; very pure and prolific, the best flavored pea among the Extra Early smooth podded kinds. Recommend it highly.

Extra Early, or First and Best. This was the earliest Pea cultivated, until the Alaska was introduced; very popular with the small market gardeners here, who have rich grounds. It is very productive and good flavored. The

stock I sell is as good as any sold in the country, not surpassed by any, no matter whose name is put before "Extra Early."

Early Washington, Early May or Frame, which are all nearly the same thing; is about ten days later than the Extra Early. It is very productive and keeps longer in bearing than the foregoing kind. Pods a little smaller. Very popular about New Orleans.

Tom Thumb. Very dwarfish and quite productive. Can be cultivated in rows a foot apart; requires no branches or sticks.

Laxton's Alpha. This is a variety of recent introduction; it is the earliest wrinkled variety in cultivation; of delicious flavor and very prolific. This variety deserves to be recommended to all who like a first-class pea. It will come into general cultivation when better known.

American Wonder. A wrinkled pea of dwarf growth, 10 to 12 inches; it is prolific, early, and of fine quality; it comes in after the Extra Early.

Bishop's Dwarf Long Pod. An early dwarf variety; very stout and branching; requires no sticks but simply the earth drawn around the roots. It is very productive and of excellent quality.

Champion of England. A green, wrinkled variety of very fine flavor; not profitable for the market, but recommended for family use.

McLean's Advancer. This is another green, wrinkled variety, about two weeks earlier than the foregoing kind.

McLean's Little Gem. A dwarf, wrinkled variety of recent introduction. It is early, very prolific and of excellent flavor. Requires no sticks.

Laxton's Prolific Long Pod. A green marrow pea of good quality. Pods are long and well filled. It is second early, and can be recommended for the use of market gardeners, being very prolific.

Eugenie. A white wrinkled variety, of fine flavor; it is of the same season as the Advancer. Cannot be too highly recommended for family use.

Carter's Stratagem. This is a new wrinkled variety from England, sold by me for the first time two years ago. It is very distinct in vine and foliage, growing thick and large, does not need any support. It is the latest variety ever brought out, pods 4—5½ inches long, which cannot be surpassed in flavor, and is very productive. Recommend it highly.

Carter's Telephone. Another wrinkled English late variety; grows about from 4½ to 5 feet high. The pods are very long containing from 8—12 fine flavored Peas. It is productive; will bear twice as much as the Champion of

Carter's Stratagem.

Carter's Telephone. Extra Early, or First and Best.

England which is about of the same season.

Dwarf Blue Imperial. A very good bearer if planted early, pods are large and well filled.

Royal Dwarf Marrow. Similar to the large Marrowfat, but of dwarf habit.

Black-eyed Marrowfat. This kind is planted more for the market than any other. It is very productive, and when young, quite tender. Grows about four feet high.

Large White Marrowfat. Similar to the last variety, except that it grows about two feet taller, and is less productive.

Dwarf Sugar. A variety of which the whole pod can be used after the string is drawn off from the back of the pod. Three feet high.

Tall Sugar. Has the same qualities as the foregoing kind, only grows taller, and the pods are somewhat larger. Neither of these two varieties are very popular here.

THE PEA BUG.

All peas grown near Philadelphia have small holes in them, caused by the sting of the Pea Bug, while the pod is forming, when it deposits its egg in it. Later the insect perfects itself and comes out of the dry pea, leaving the hole.

The germ of the pea is never destroyed, and they grow equally as well as those without holes. Market gardeners in this neighborhood who have been planting the Extra Early Peas for years, will not take them without holes, and consider these a trade mark.

FIELD OR COW PEAS.

There are a great many varieties of Cow Peas, different in color and growth. They are planted mostly for fertilizing purposes, and are sown broad-cast; when in a good stand, and of sufficient height, they are plowed under. The Clay Pea is the most popular. There are several varieties called crowders, which do not grow as tall as the others, but produce a great many pods, which are used green, the same as snap-beans, and if dried, like dried beans, make a very good dish. The crowders are of an oblong shape, almost pointed at one end; they are on an average larger than the other Field Peas. Lady Peas are small, white, with a black eye; they are generally planted between corn, so that they can run up on it. Dry, they are considered the very best variety for cooking.

PEPPER.

PIMENT (Fr.), SPANISCHER PFEFFER (Ger.), PIMENTO (Sp.).

Bell or Bull Nose.
Sweet Spanish Monstrous.
Sweet Ruby King.
Golden Dawn Mango.
Long Red Cayenne.

Red Cherry.
Bird Eye.
Chili.
Tabasco.

Peppers are tender and require to be raised in the hot-bed. Seed should be sown in January, and when large enough transplanted into the ground in rows from one and a half to two feet apart, and a foot to a foot and a half in the rows. There are more Peppers raised here than in other sections of the country; the hot varieties are used for seasoning and making pepper sauce; the mild variety is highly esteemed for salad. Care should be taken not to grow different kinds close together, as they mix very readily.

Sweet Spanish or Monstrous. A very popular variety, much cultivated. It is very mild, grows to a large size, tapering towards the end, and, when green, is used as a salad. Superior for that purpose to any other kind.

Sweet Pepper, Ruby King. This variety grows to a larger size than the Sweet Spanish Monstrous, and is of different shape. The fruit is from 5 to 6 inches long by about 3 to 4 inches in diameter, and of a bright red color. It is remarkably mild and pleasant in flavor, and can be sliced and eaten as a salad, the same as the Spanish Monstrous. Single plants ripen from 8 to 10 fruits, making this variety both productive and profitable. A decided acquisition.

Golden Dawn Mango. This sweet pepper attracted much attention for the last three years, and was admired by all who saw it. I believe it to be all the originator claims for it. In shape and size it resembles the Bell. Color, a bright waxy golden yellow; very brilliant and handsome. Single plants ripen from twelve to twenty-four fruits, making them productive and profitable. They are entirely exempt from any fiery taste or flavor, and can be eaten as readily as an apple.

Bell or Bull Nose. Is a large oblong variety which is not sweet or mild, as thought by some people. The seeds are very hot. Used for pickling.

Long Red Cayenne. Is very hot and pungent. Cultivated here and used for pepper sauce and seasoning purposes. There are two varieties; one is long and straight, and the other like shown in cut, which is the only kind I keep.

Red Cherry. A small roundish variety, very hot and productive.

Bird Eye. Small, as the name indicates. It is very hot and used principally for pepper vinegar.

Sweet Pepper Ruby King.

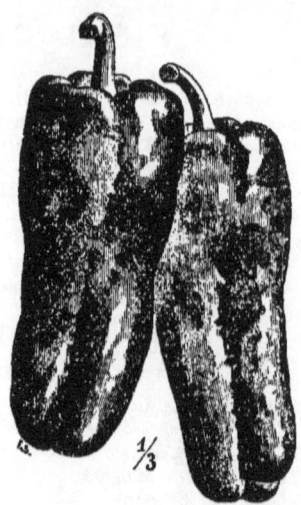

Sweet Spanish, or Monstrous Pepper

Long Red Cayenne Pepper.

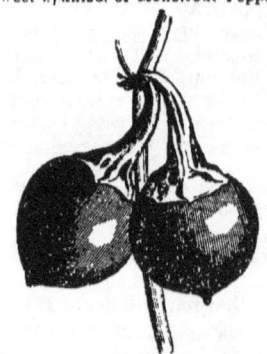

Red Cherry Pepper.

Chili. A small variety, from three-fourths to an inch long. It is strong, and used for pepper sauce; very prolific.

Tabasco. True. Another small variety, used more for pepper sauces than any other kind; the fruit is easily gathered, growing almost erect on the branches.

POTATOES.

POMME DE TERRE (Fr.), KARTOFFEL (Ger.).

Early Rose.
Breese's Peerless.
Russets.
Extra Early Vermont.

Snowflake.
Beauty of Hebron.
White Elephant.
Rural Blush.

Potatoes thrive and produce best in a light, dry but rich soil. Well decomposed stable manure is the best, but if not to be had, cotton seed meal, bone dust, or any other fertilizer should be used to make the ground rich enough. If the ground was planted the fall previous with Cow Peas, which were plowed under, it will be in good condition for Potatoes. Good sized tubers should be selected for planting, which can be cut in pieces not too small; each piece ought to contain at least three eyes. Plant in drills from two to three feet apart, according to the space and how to be cultivated afterwards. Field culture two and a half to three feet apart; for garden, two feet will answer. We plant potatoes here from end of December to end of March, but the surest time is about the first of February. If planted early they should be planted deeper than if planted late, and hilled up as they grow. If potatoes are planted shallow and not hilled soon, they will suffer more, if caught by a late frost, than if planted deep and hilled up well. Early potatoes have not the same value here as in the North, as the time of planting is so long, and very often the first planting gets cut down by a frost, and a late planting, which may just be peeping through the ground, will escape and produce in advance of the first planted. A fair crop of potatoes can be raised here if planted in August; if the autumn is not too dry, they will bring nice tubers by the end of November. They should not be cut if planted at this time of the year, but planted whole. They should be put in a moist place before planting, so they may sprout. The early varieties are preferable for this time of planting.

I have been handling several thousand barrels of potatoes every season for planting, and make Seed Potatoes a specialty. The potatoes I sell are Eastern grown, which, as every one interested in potato culture knows, are superior and preferable to Western grown.

I have tried and introduced all new kinds here; but of late so many have come out that it is almost impossible to keep up with them. New varieties of potatoes come out with fancy prices, but these prices for new potatoes do not pay here, as we can keep none over for seed, and any person raising for the market would not realize a cent more for a new fancy variety per barrel, than for a barrel of good Peerless or Early Rose. Earliness is no consideration, as we plant from December to end of March. Somebody may plant Early Rose in December and another in February, and those planted in February come to the market first; it depends entirely upon the season. If late frosts set in, early planted potatoes will be cut down, and those just coming out of the ground will not be hurt. The Jackson White has given but little satisfaction the last four years, except in cases where planted very early. The yield was very good, but the quality poor and very knotty. Perhaps this was the fault of the season. It is hardly planted any more for the market. Up to now the Peerless is the standard variety. Among the new kinds I have tried, I find the White Elephant to be a fine potato. It is a very strong grower, tubers oblong, very productive, good quality and flavor. It is late, and will come in at the end of the season, if planted with the earlier varieties. The Extra Early Vermont, Beauty of Hebron, Snowflake and Early Rose for early, and Peerless and White Elephant for late, are as good varieties as exist, and it is not likely that we will have anything better by new introductions. The Rural Blush, which I introduced two years ago, may be added to the late varieties; it is of excellent quality, strong grower, and yields heavily. Most people are not careful enough in selecting their seed. Some of the potatoes sold in this market for seed are not fit for planting.

Early Rose. This is, without any doubt, the best potato for the table. It is oval, very shallow-eyed, pink-skinned, very dry, and mealy when boiled. It has not become so popular as it deserves as a market variety, as pink or red potatoes do not sell so well here as the white kinds. This variety should not be planted too soon, from the fact that they make small stalks, and cut down by frost, they suffer more than other varieties; but they want rich, light soil to grow to perfection.

Breese's Peerless. Fifteen years ago this variety was introduced, yet at present it is the leading variety for mar-

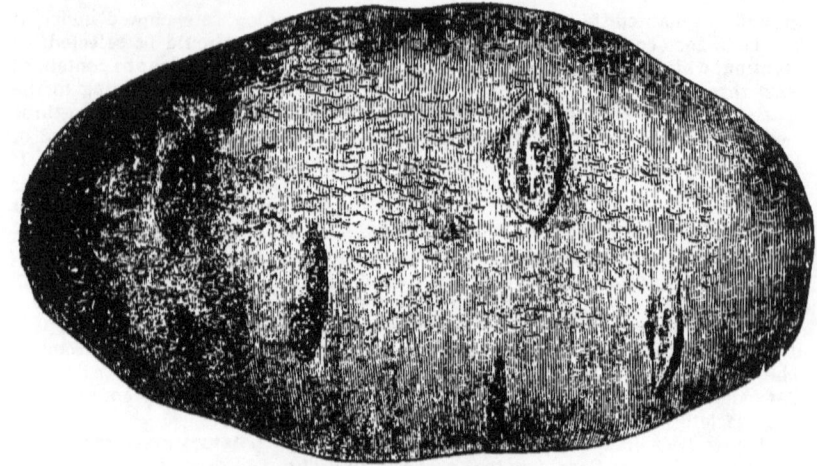

Extra Early Vermont.

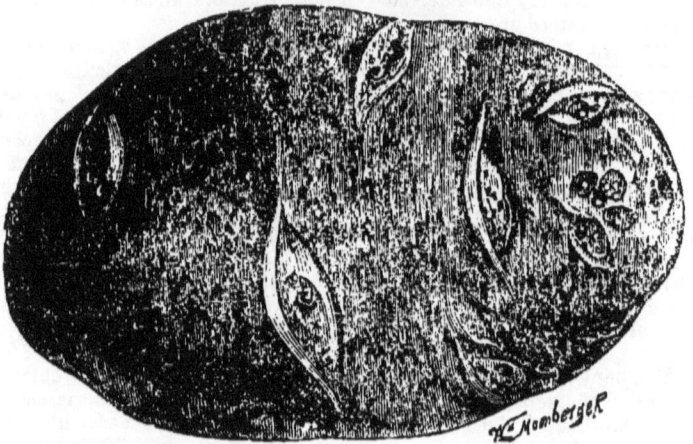

Snowflake.

ket as well as for family use. Skin dull white, sometimes slightly russetted; eyes few and shallow, round, occasionally oblong; grows to a large size; very productive and earlier than the Jackson White. As white potatoes are more suitable than pinkish kinds, and as this variety is handsome in appearance, and of good quality, it has become the general favorite in this section.

Russets. This kind is still planted by some. It is round, reddish and slightly russetted. Eyes deep and many. Very productive, but not so fine a quality as some others. Does best in sandy soil, such as we have along the lake coast. If the season is dry it will do well, but in a wet season, this variety will rot quicker than any other.

Extra Early Vermont. Very similar to the Early Rose, but of a stronger growth; a little earlier, and the tubers are more uniform and larger. It is an excellent table variety.

Snowflake. This is a very early variety. Tubers good medium size, elongated, very uniform and quite productive. Eyes flat on the body of the tuber, but compressed on the seed end. Skin white, flesh very fine grained, and when boiled, snow-white.

Beauty of Hebron. I have tried this variety thoroughly and found it in every particular as has been represented. It is earlier than the Early Rose, which resembles it very much, being a little lighter and more russetted in color. It is very productive and of excellent table quality; more mealy than the Early Rose, but smaller.

White Elephant. This variety has again given entire satisfaction the past season. The tubers are large and of excellent quality; planted alongside of the Peerless, it produced fully one third more than that variety.

Rural Blush. Second early, tubers roundish flattened, blush skin, flesh slighted with pink. Very dry and of excellent quality. A heavy yielder.

THE SWEET POTATO.
Convolvulus Batatas.

The sweet Potato is next to corn the most important food crop in the South. They are a wholesome and nutritious diet, good for man and beast. Though cultivated to a limited extent on the sandy lands of New Jersey and some of the middle States, it thrives best on the light rich lands of the South, which bring their red and golden fruits to greatest perfection under the benign rays of a southern sun. It is a plant of a warm climate, a child of the sun, much more nutritious than the Irish Potato on account of the great amount of saccharine matter it contains, and no southern table should be found without it from the first day of August till the last day of May. Some plant early in spring the potato itself in the prepared ridges, and cut the vine from the potato when large enough, and plant them out; others start the potatoes in a bed prepared expressly for that purpose, and slip off the sprouts as they come up, and set these out. The latter method will produce the earliest potatoes; others who set the vines, say that they make the largest tubers. In preparing the land the soil should be thoroughly pulverized, the ridges laid off about five feet apart, well drawn up and rather flat on top. If everything is ready, and time for planting has arrived, do not wait for a rain, make a paste of clay and cow manure; in this dip the roots of the slips and press the earth firmly around them. Old slips are more tenacious of life than young ones, and will under circumstances answer best. Watering afterwards, if dry weather continues, of course will be beneficial. Otherwise plant your vines and slips just before or after a rain. Two feet apart in the rows is considered a good distance. The ridges should never be disturbed by a plow from the time they are made until the potatoes are ready to be dug.

Scrape off the grass and young weeds with the hoe, and pull up the large ones by hand. Crab grass is peculiarly inimical to the sweet potato, and should be carefully kept out of the patch. The vines should never be allowed to take root between the rows. Sweet potatoes should be dug before a heavy frost occurs; a very light one will do no harm. The earth should be dry enough to keep it from sticking to the potatoes. The old fashioned potato bank is the best arrangement for keeping them, the main points being a dry place and ventilation.

Varieties generally cultivated in the South.

The Yam. Taking into consideration quality and productiveness, the Yam stands at the head of the list. Frequently, when baked, the saccharine matter in the shape of candy will be seen hanging to them in strings. Skin and flesh yellow and very sweet. Without a doubt, the best potato for family use.

Southern Queen. Very similar to the former, but smoother, the tubers having no veins or very few; it is earlier.

Shanghai or California Yam. This is the earliest variety we have, frequently, under favorable circumstances, giving good sized tubers two months after planting the vine. Very productive, having given 300 bushels per acre when planted early and on rich land. Is almost the only kind cultivated for the New Orleans market. Skin dull white or yellow, flesh white, dry and mealy, in large specimens frequently stringy.

There are some other varieties of Sweet Potatoes highly prized in the West, but not appreciated here. The Red and Yellow Nansemond are of a fine quality and productive, but will not sell so well as the California Yam, when taken to market. For home consumption they are fine, and deserve to be cultivated.

PUMPKIN.

POTIRON (Fr.), KÜRBISS (Ger.), CALABAZA (Sp.).

Kentucky Field.
Large Cheese.
Cashaw Crook Neck. (Green Striped.)
Golden Yellow Mammoth.

Are generally grown in the field, with the exception of the Cashaw, which is planted in the garden; but great care must be taken not to plant them close to Squashes or Melons, as they will mix and spoil their quality. Plant in hills from eight to twelve feet apart.

Golden Yellow Mammoth.

Kentucky Field. Large round, soft shell, salmon color; very productive; best for stock.

Large Cheese. This is of a bright orange, sometimes salmon color, fine grained, and used for table or for stock feeding.

Cashaw Crook Neck. This is very extensively cultivated in the South for table use. There are two kinds, one all yellow and the other green striped with light yellow color. The latter is the preferable kind; the flesh is fine grained, yellow and very sweet. It keeps well. This variety takes the place here of the Winter Squashes, which are very little cultivated.

Golden Yellow Mammoth. This is a very large Pumpkin. Flesh and skin are of a bright golden color, fine grained and of good quality. I had some brought to the store weighing one hundred to one hundred and fifty pounds, raised on land which was not manured or fertilized,

RADISH.

Radies, Rave (Fr.), Radies, Rettig (Ger.), Rabano (Sp.).

Early Long Scarlet.
Chartier's Long.
Early Scarlet Turnip.
Golden Globe.
Early Scarlet Olive-shaped.
White Summer Turnip.

Scarlet Half Long French.
Scarlet Olive-shaped, White-Tipped or French Breakfast.
Black Spanish (Winter).
Chinese Rose (Winter).

This is a very popular vegetable, and grown to a large extent. The ground for radishes should be rich and mellow. The early small varieties can be sown broadcast among other crops, such as beets, peas, spinach, or where lettuce has been transplanted. Early varieties are sown in this section the whole year, but during summer they require frequent watering to make them grow quickly. The Golden Globe and White Summer Turnip are best for planting during the summer months. The Half Long Scarlet French is the only red kind raised for the New Orleans market, and all the other cities in the United States taken together do not use as many of that one variety as New Orleans does. I have sold nearly two thousand pounds of the seed per annum for the last twelve years.

Early Long Scarlet. This is a very desirable variety; it is of a bright scarlet color; short top and very brittle.

Chartier's Long Radish. A new long Radish, described as deep crimson colored at the top, shading off lighter, until at the bottom it becomes white. My trials with this variety have not been satisfactory; the roots are larger, but not very symmetrical, and not better in flavor than the long scarlet. Never will become a favorite here.

Early Scarlet Turnip. A small, round variety, the favorite kind for family use. It is very early, crisp and mild when young.

Golden Globe. This stands the heat better than the foregoing kinds. It is of an oblong shape, and of a beautiful bright yellow color. It should be sown very thinly. Best adapted for summer and fall sowing. The variety I keep is of the finest strain, and as good as any ever sold.

Early Scarlet Olive-shaped. This is similar to the Half Long French, but shorter, and not quite so bright in color. It is early and of good quality. Top short.

White Summer Turnip. This is a summer and fall variety. Oblong in shape, skin white, stands the heat well, but not much used.

Scarlet Half Long French. This is the most popular Radish for the market. It is of a bright scarlet color, and when well grown, from two to three inches long, very brittle and tender.

Scarlet Olive-shaped. White tipped, or **French Breakfast.** A handsome Radish of the same shape as

Early Long Scarlet.

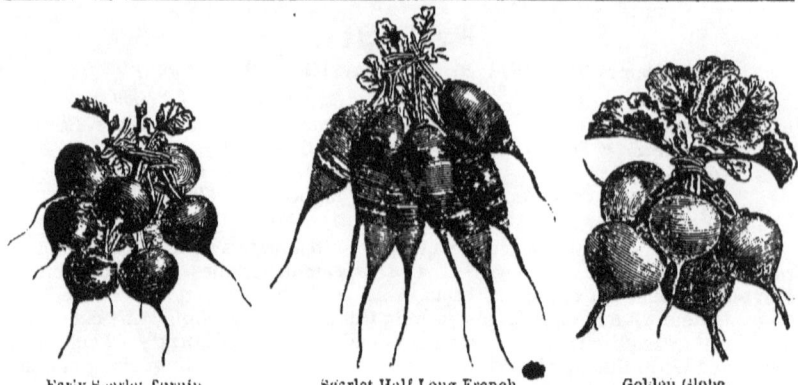

Early Scarlet Turnip.   Scarlet Half Long French.   Golden Globe.

the foregoing kind, with end and root white. Quite tender.

Black Spanish. (WINTER.) This is sown during fall and early winter. It is oval in shape, very solid, and stands considerable cold weather without being hurt. It can be sown broad-cast between Turnips, or planted in rows a foot apart, thinned out from three to four inches in the rows.

Chinese Rose. (WINTER.) This is of a half long shape, bright rose color. It is as hardy as the last described kind, not so popular, but superior to the foregoing kind. Consider it the best winter variety.

New White Strasburgh. A new variety, of an oblong, tapering shape; the skin and flesh are pure white, firm, brittle and tender, and has the tendency of retaining its crispness even when the roots are old and large. It is a very good kind for summer use, as it withstands the severe heat, and grows very quickly. The seed can be planted throughout the summer, and fine large roots will be rapidly formed. It is an excellent variety for family use, as well as for the market.

ROQUETTE.

ROQUETTE (Fr).

Sown from September to March. It is used as a salad, resembling the Cress in taste.

SALSIFY,

OR OYSTER PLANT.

SALSIFIS (Fr.), HAFERWURZEL (Ger.), OSTRA VEGETAL (Sp.).

New Sandwich Island (Mammoth).

A vegetable which ought to be more cultivated than it is. It is prepared in different ways. It partakes of the flavor of oysters. It should be sown in the fall

Salsify, or Oyster Plant.

of the year; not later than November. The ground ought to be manured the spring previous, deeply spaded, and well pulverized. Sow in drills about ten inches apart, and thin out from three to four inches in the rows.

New Sandwich Island Salsify. (Mammoth.) This is a new sort which grows much quicker than the old varieties, it attains a large size; can be called with right mammoth.

SPINACH.

EPINARD (Fr.), SPINAT (Ger.), ESPINAGO (Sp.).

Extra Large Leaved Savoy. | *Broad Leaved Flanders.*

A great deal of this is raised for the New Orleans Market. It is very popular. Sown from September to end of March. If the fall is dry and hot, it is useless to sow it, as the seeds require moisture and cool nights to make them come up. The richer the ground the larger the leaves.

Extra Large Leaved Savoy. The leaves of this variety are large, thick and a little curled. Very good for family use.

Broad Leaved Flanders. This is the best standard variety, both for market and family use. Leaves large, broad and very succulent.

SORREL.

OSEILLE (Fr.), SAUERAMPFER (Ger.), ACEDERA (Sp.).

Planted in drills a foot apart, during the fall of the year, and thinned out from three to four inches in the drills. Sorrel is used for various purposes in the kitchen. It is used the same as Spinach; also in soups and as a salad.

SQUASH.

COURGE (Fr.), KÜRBISS (Ger.), CALABAZA TONTANERA (Sp.).

Early Bush, or Patty Pan.   *The Hubbard.*
Long Green, or Summer Crook Neck. | *Boston Marrow.*
London Vegetable Marrow.

Sow during March in hills from three to four feet apart, six to eight seeds. When well up, thin them out to three of the strongest plants. For a succession

Early Bush or Patty Pan.

Long Green or Summer Crook Neck.

The Hubbard.

they can be planted as late as June. Some who protect by boxes, plant as soon as the first of February, but it is best to wait till the ground gets warm. When it is time to plant Corn, it is also time to plant Squash.

Early Bush, or Patty Pan. Is the earliest and only popular kind here. All other varieties are very little cultivated, as the Cashaw Pumpkin, the striped variety, takes their place. It is of dwarfish habit, grows bushy, and does not take much room. Quality as good as any.

Long green, or Summer Crook-Neck. This is a very strong grower, and continues in bearing longer than the first named kind. It is of good quality, but not so popular.

London Vegetable Marrow. A European variety, very little cultivated here. It grows to a good size and is very dry. Color whitish with a yellow tinge.

The Hubbard. This is a Winter Squash, very highly esteemed in the East, but hardly cultivated here. It is, if planted here, inferior to the Southern striped Cashaw Pumpkin which can be kept from one season to another, and is superior in flavor to the former kind.

Boston Marrow. Cultivated to a large extent North and East for winter use, where it is used for custards, etc. It keeps for a long time and is of excellent quality, but not esteemed here, as most people consider the Southern grown Cashaw Pumpkin superior to any Winter Squash.

TOMATO.

TOMATE (Fr.), LIEBESAPFEL (Ger.), TOMATE (Sp.).

King of the Earlies.
Extra Early Dwarf Red.
Early Large Smooth Red.
Tilden.
Trophy, (Selected.)
Large Yellow.
Acme.
Paragon.
Livingston's Perfection.
Livingston's Favorite.
Livingston's Beauty.

Seed should be sown in January, in hot-beds, or in boxes, which must be placed in a sheltered spot, or near windows. In March they can be sown in the open ground. Tomatoes are generally sown too thick and become too crowded when two or three inches high, which makes the plants too thin and spindly. If they are transplanted when two or three inches high, about three inches apart each way, they will become short and sturdy, and will not suffer when planted into the open ground. Plant them from three to four feet apart. Some varieties can be planted closer; for instance, the Extra Early, which is of very dwarfish habit, two and a half feet apart is enough.

They should be supported by stakes. When allowed to grow up wild, the fruit which touches the ground will rot. For a late or fall crop the seed should be sown towards the latter part of May and during June.

King of the Earlies. This variety was introduced here by me last year. It is very early and productive; color bright red, of good size and quite solid. The vine is medium, stout and branching The buds appear soon, blossoms as a rule adhere and produce fruit. It is so much earlier than the Livingston varieties, that it should be planted for the first. The latter varieties are so very handsome in shape, that they will sell better than any other, when the market is once well supplied.

Extra Early Dwarf. This is the earliest in cultivation. It is dwarfish in habit; fruit larger than the following kind, and more flat; bright scarlet in color and very productive. For an early market variety it cannot be surpassed.

FOR THE SOUTHERN STATES. 73

King of the Earlies.

Livingston's Favorite.

Extra Early Dwarf.

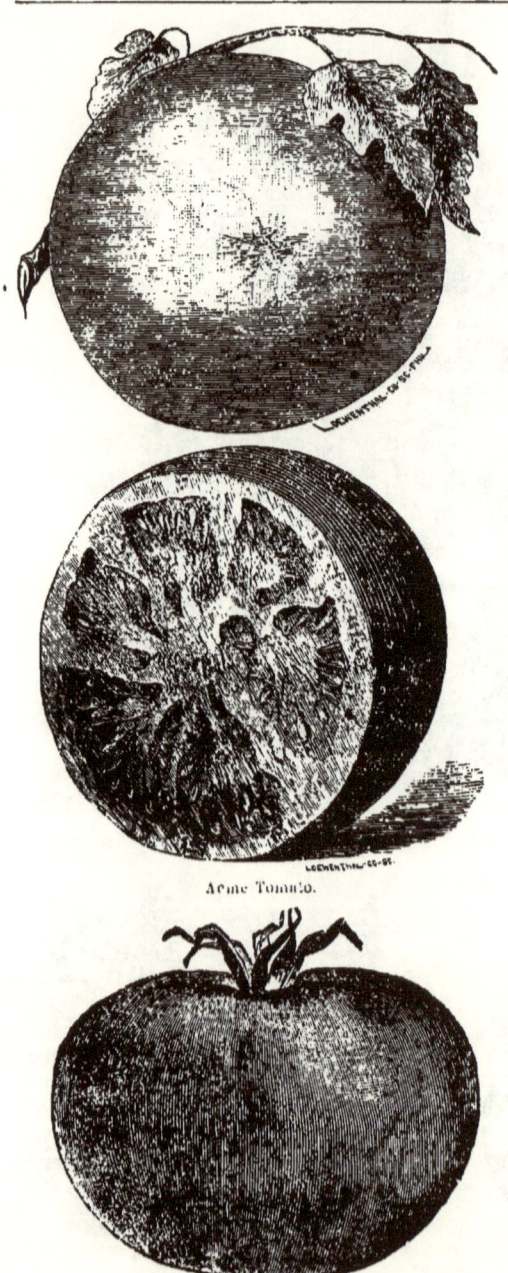

Acme Tomato.

Paragon.

Early Large Smooth Red. An early kind of medium size; smooth and productive.

Tilden. This has been the standard variety for family gardens as well as market, but has been supplanted to a great extent by later introductions. It is of a good shape, brilliant scarlet, and from above medium to large in size, and keeps well.

Selected Trophy. A very large, smooth Tomato, more solid and heavier than any other kind. It is not quite as early as the Tilden. Has become a favorite variety.

Large Yellow. This is similar in shape to the large Red, but more solid. Not very popular

Acme. This is one of the prettiest and most solid Tomatoes ever introduced. It is of medium size, round and very smooth, a strong grower, and a good and long bearer. They are the perfection of Tomatoes for family use, but will not answer for shipping purposes; the skin is too tender, and cracks when fully ripe. Of all the varieties introduced, none has yet surpassed this kind when all qualities are brought into consideration. It does well about here where the ground is heavy.

Paragon. This variety has lately come into notice. It is very solid, of a bright reddish crimson color, comes in about the same time as the Tilden, but is heavier in foliage, and protects its fruit. It is productive and keeps long in bearing. Well adapted for shipping.

Selected Trophy.

Livingston's Beauty.

Livingston's Perfection. Very similar to the foregoing in shape and color.

Livingston's Favorite. This novelty was introduced only a few years ago; it is as perfect in shape and as solid as the Acme, but much larger, and of a handsome dark red color. I had some sent to me by a customer, and they surely were the finest specimen of tomatoes I ever saw, and were admired by everybody who saw them. They will keep well, and do not crack.

Livingston's Beauty. A new variety, offered for the first time three years ago. It is quite distinct in color, being a very glossy crimson with a light tinge of purple, (lighter than the Acme). It ripens with the Acme or Paragon, but keeps longer. It is very perfect in shape and does not crack, like some of the thin skinned sorts.

The seeds of the last five varieties are raised for me by the originators, Messrs. Livingston's Sons, and can be relied upon as being true to name and of superior quality.

TURNIP.

NAVET (Fr.), RÜBE (Ger.), NABO COMUN (Sp.).

Early Red or Purple Top (strap-leaved).
Early White Flat Dutch, strap-leaved.
Purple Top Globe.
Large White Globe.
Pomerian Globe.
White Spring.
Yellow Aberdeen.

Golden Ball.
Amber Globe.
Early Purple Top Munich.
Extra Early Purple Top.
Purple Top Ruta Baga.
Improved Ruta Baga.
Extra Early White French, or White Egg Turnip.

Turnips do best in new ground. When the soil has been worked long, it should receive a top dressing of land-plaster or ashes. If stable manure is used the ground should be manured the spring previous to sowing, so it may be well incorporated with the soil. When fresh manure is used the turnips are apt to become speckled. Sow from end of July till October for fall and winter, and in January, February and March for spring and summer use. They are generally sown broad-cast, but the Ruta Baga should be sown in drills, or rather ridges, and should not be sown later than the end of August; the Golden Ball and Aberdeen, not later than the end of September. The White Flat Dutch, Early Spring and Pomerian Globe are best for spring, but also good for autumn.

Early Red or Purple Top. (STRAP LEAVED.) This is one of the most popular kinds. It is flat, with a small tap-root, and a bright purple top. The leaves are narrow and grow erect from the bulb. The flesh is finely grained and rich.

Early White Flat Dutch. (STRAP-LEAVED.) This is similar to the above in shape, but considered about a week earlier. It is very popular.

Purple Top Globe. A variety of recent introduction; same shape as the Pomerian Globe, but with purple top. Fine variety for table or for stock. It is not quite so early as the Early Red or Purple Top. I recommend it very highly.

Large White Globe. A very large variety, mostly grown for stock. It can be used for the table when young. Flesh coarse, but sweet; tops very large.

Pomerian Globe. This is selected from the above. It is smoother and handsomer in shape; good to plant early in spring. When pulled before it is too large it is a very salable turnip in the market.

White Spring. This is similar to the White Flat Dutch; not quite so large, but rounder in shape. The tops are larger; it is early, a good quality, and best adapted for spring planting.

Yellow Aberdeen. This is a variety very little cultivated here. It is shaped

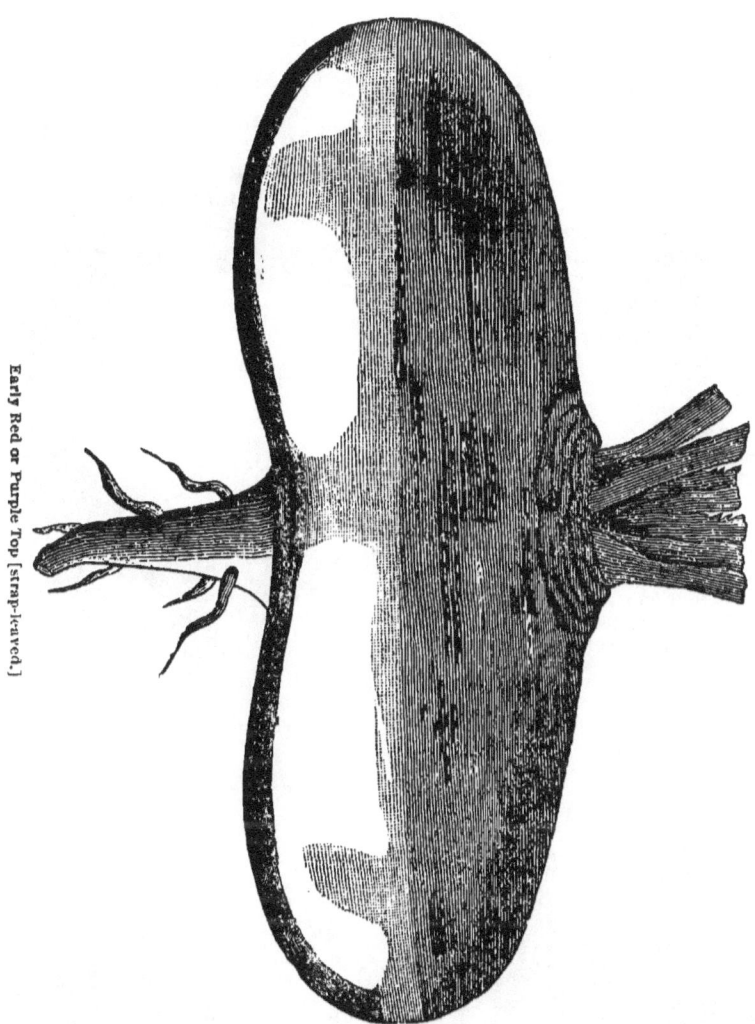

Early Red or Purple Top [strap-leaved.]

like the Ruta Baga, color yellow with purple top. Good for table use or feeding stock.

Robertson's Golden Ball, is the best of the yellow Turnips for table use. It is very smooth, oval in shape, and of a beautiful orange color. Leaves are small. Should be sown in the fall of the year, and always in drills, so that the plants can be thinned out and worked. This kind ought to be more cultivated.

Amber Globe. This is very similar to the above kind.

Early Purple Top Munich. A new variety from Germany; flat, with red or purple top; same as the American variety, but fifteen days earlier to mature. It is very hardy, tender, and of fine flavor.

Purple Top Ruta Baga or Swede. This is grown for feeding stock, and also for table use. It is oblong in shape, yellow flesh, very solid. Should always be sown in rows or ridges.

Improved Purple Top Ruta Baga. Similar to the above; but smoother, and with few fibrous roots.

Extra Early White French or White Egg Turnip. This is a lately introduced variety; is said to be very early, tender and crisp. The shape of it is oblong, resembling an egg. Having tried it, I found it as represented, quickly growing, tender and sweet. It will never become a favorite market variety, as only flat kinds sell well in this market. It has to be pulled up soon, as it becomes pithy shortly after attaining maturity.

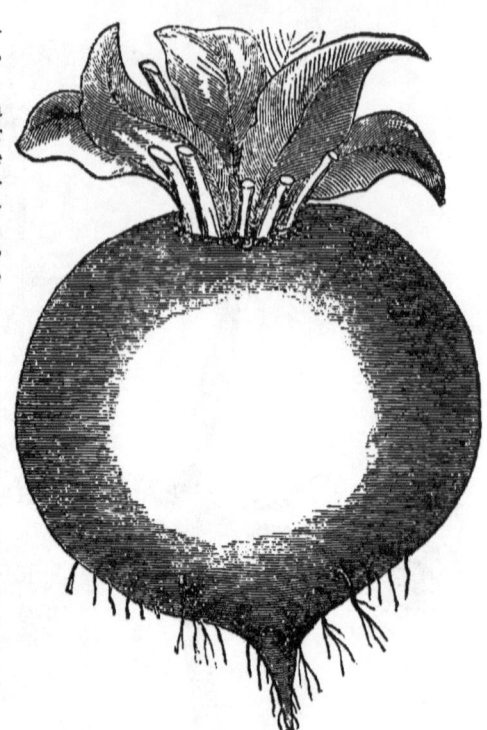

Pomerian Globe.

Early White Flat Dutch [strap-leaved].

Milan Extra Early Purple Top.

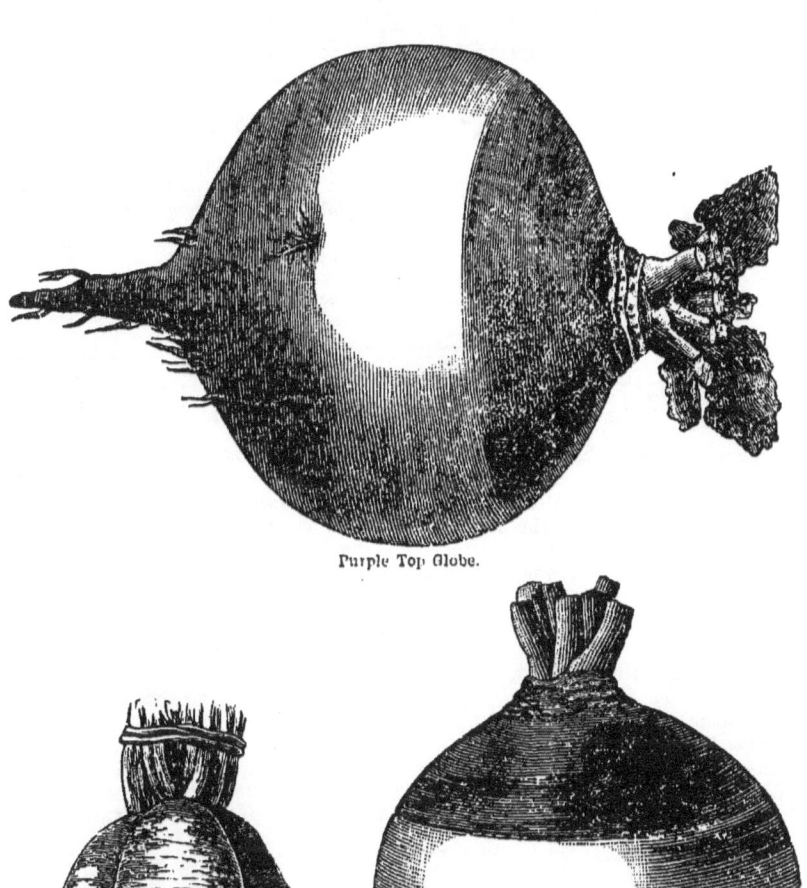

Purple Top Globe.

Extra Early White French, or White Egg Turnip.   Improved Purple Top Ruta Baga.

TOBACCO SEEDS.

Imported Havana. I imported from one of the principal growers, the finest and purest strain of Vuelto Abajo; which is considered the best of the Havana varieties.
Price, 10 cts. per package,—40 cts. per oz., $4.00 per lb.
Connecticut Seed Leaf. A well-known American variety.
Price, 10 cts. per package,—25 cts. per oz.,—$2 50 per lb.

SWEET AND MEDICINAL HERBS.

Some of these herbs possess culinary as well as medicinal properties. Should be found in every garden. Ground where they are to be sown should be well prepared and pulverized. Some of them have very fine seed, and it is only necessary, after the seed is sown, to press the ground with the back of the spade; if covered too deep they cannot come up. Early spring is the best time to sow them—some, such as Sage, Rosemary, Lavender and Basil, are best sown in a frame and afterwards transplanted into the garden.

Anise, *Pimpinelle Anisum*.
Balm, *Melissa Officinalis*.
Basil, large and small leaved. *Ocymum Basilicum*.
Bene, *Sesamum Orientale*.
Borage, *Borago Officinalis*.
Caraway, *Carum Carui*.
Dill, *Anethum Graveolens*.
Fennel, sweet, *Anethum Foeniculum*.

Lavender, *Lavendula Vera*.
Majoram, sweet, *Origanum Majoram*.
Pot Marigold, *Calendula Officinalis*.
Rosemary, *Rosemary Officinalis*.
Rue, *Ruta Graveolens*.
Sage, *Salvia Officinalis*.
Summer Savory, *Satureja Hortensis*.
Thyme, *Thymus Vulgaris*.
Wormwood, *Artemisia Absinthium*.

GRASS AND FIELD SEEDS.

I have often been asked what kind of Grass Seed is the best for this latitude, but so far I have never been able to answer this question satisfactorily. For hay I do not think there is anything better than the Millet. For permanent grass I have almost come to the conclusion that none of the grasses used for this purpose North and West will answer. Barley, Rye, Red Oats and Rescue Grass will make winter pasturage in this latitude. Different kinds of Clover answer very well during spring, but during the hot summer months I have never found anything to stand and produce, except the Bermuda and Crabgrass, which are indigenous to the South.

Of late years the Lespedeza Striata, or Japan Clover, has been sown extensively, a description of which will be found on page 87.

The Bermuda, in my opinion, is better suited for pasturage than hay, as it is rather short and hard when cured. Having tried Guinea Grass I have come to the conclusion that it will not answer here, from the fact that it will freeze out every year. It will produce a large quantity of hay or green fodder, but has to be resown every spring. The seeds that are raised here are light, and do not germinate freely. To import seed every year is rather troublesome. The Johnson Grass advertised by some as Guinea Grass, is not Guinea Grass; it is much coarser, and can hardly be destroyed after having taken hold of a piece of ground. Some are enthusiastic about Alfalfa or Lucerne; others, whose opinion ought also to be respected, say it will not do here. There exists a great difference of opinion in regard to which grass seed is most suitable for the South.

Red Clover. Should be sown either during fall or early in spring. Six to eight pounds to an acre.

White Dutch Clover. A grass sown for pasturage at the rate of four to six pounds to the acre. Should be sown in fall and early spring.

Alfalfa or Chili Clover, or French Lucerne. This variety does well here, but the ground has to be well prepared and deeply plowed. It will not do in low wet ground. Should be sown in the fall of the year, or January and February; eight to ten pounds per acre. This being of special value I refer to the letter written by E. M. Hudson on the subject. (See latter part of this Almanac.)

Kentucky Blue Grass. (EXTRA CLEANED.) Should be sown in dry soil. Two bushels per acre.

Mendow Fescue, *Festuca pratensis*. As a pasture grass I consider this one of the most valuable. It is not affected by dry weather, as its roots penetrate the earth 12 to 15 inches; it is much relished by all kinds of stock on account of its long and tender leaves. It yields a very superior hay when cured. It has been grown very little in this country and is deserving of much more attention. Sow in spring or fall. Two bushels to the acre. In some sections it is called Randall Grass. This should not be confounded with the English Rye Grass, offered by some dealers as the same variety.

Orchard Grass. This is one of the best grasses for pasturing. It grows quickly, much more so than the Blue Grass. Can be sown either in fall or spring. Sow one to one and a half bushels per acre. (See extract from "Farmers' Book of Grasses.")

Rescue Grass. A forage plant from Australia. It grows during winter. Sow the seed in the fall of the year, but not before the weather gets cool, as it will not sprout so long as the ground is warm. Sow 1½ bushels seed to the acre.

Hungarian Grass. This is a valuable annual forage plant, and good to make hay. Sow three pecks to the acre. It should be cut when in bloom.

German Millet. Of all the Millets this is the best. It makes good hay, and produces heavily. Three pecks sown to the acre broad-cast secures a good stand. Can be sown from April till June but the former month is the best time. Should be cut the same as the foregoing kind.

Rye. Is sown during the fall months as late as December, for forage; and for pasturage, during winter and spring.

Barley, Fall. Can be sown fall and winter, but requires strong, good soil. Used here for forage during its green state.

Red or Rust Proof Oats. It is only a few years since these oats have come into general cultivation. They are very valuable, and will save a great deal of corn on a farm. The seed of this variety has a reddish cast, and a peculiar long beard, and is very heavy. It is the only kind which will not rust in the Southern climate. They can be sown as early as October, but should be pastured down as soon as they commence to joint, till February. When the ground is low, or the season wet, this cannot well be done without destroying the whole crop. During January and February is the proper time, if no pasturing can be done. One to one and a half bushels per acre is sufficient. These oats have a tendency to stool, and therefore do not require as much per acre as common oats. Those who have not already tried this variety should do so.

Sorghum. Is planted for feeding stock during the spring and early summer. For this purpose it should be sown as early in spring as possible in drills about two to three feet apart; three to four quarts per acre. It makes excellent green fodder.

Dhouro, or Egyptian Corn. Sorghum vulgare. This is a well known cereal. It produces a large quantity of seed, of which fowls and animals are fond.—Can also be sown broad-cast, for soiling or in drills for fodder and seed. If sowed in drills, one peck of seed per acre is ample. If sown broad-cast, one bushel per acre. For grain, the stalks should not be nearer than 10 inches in the drill, but if to be cut repeatedly for soiling, it is better to sow quite thickly in the hills. Seed should not be sown too early, and covered from one half to one inch. If too much rain in the Spring, the seed will not come well; - they require more heat than the other Sorghums. Rural Branching Sorghum or Millow Maize produces the seed heads upright in a vertical position, while the others are dropping. The seeds are smaller, but will keep longer than the other varieties. The stalk grows very large and produces a good many large leaves. It suckers and tillers more and more the oftener it is cut. It exceeds greatly in yield of green fodder any of the familiar fodder plants, except the "Teosinte."—It should be planted exclusively in drills four feet apart, 18 to 20 inches in the drills.

Broom Corn. Can be planted the same as corn, put the hills closer together in the row. Six quarts will plant an acre.

The following extracts have been taken, by permission, from the author, Dr. D. L. Phares, from his book "Farmers' Book of Grasses." It is the most valuable work of the kind ever published in the South, and should be in the hands of every one who takes an interest in the cultivation of grasses.

Copies for sale at publisher's price. Paper covers, 50 cents; Cloth, 75 cents; postage paid.

ORCHARD GRASS.
(Dactylis Glomerata.)

Of all the grasses this is one of the most widely diffused, growing in Africa, Asia and every country in Europe and all our States. It is more highly esteemed and commended than any other grass, by a larger number of farmers in most countries—a most decided proof of its great value and wonderful adaptation to many soils, climates and treatments. Yet, strange to say, though growing in England for many centuries it was not appreciated in that country till carried here from Virginia in 1764. But, as in the case of Timothy, soon after its introduction from America, it came into high favor among farmers, and still retains its hold on their estimation as a grazing and hay crop.

Nor is this strange when its many advantages and points of excellence are considered. It will grow well on any soil containing sufficient clay and not holding too much water. If the land be too tenacious, drainage will remedy the soil; if worn out, a top dressing of stable manure will give it a good send-off, and it will furnish several good mowings the first year. It grows well between 29° and 48° latitude. It may be mowed from two to four times a year, according to the latitude, season and treatment; yielding from one to three tons of excellent hay per acre on poor to medium land. In grazing and as hay, most animals select it in preference among mixtures in other grasses. In lower latitudes it furnishes good winter grazing, as well as for spring, summer and fall. After grazing, or mowing, few grasses grow so rapidly (three or six inches per week), and are so soon ready again for tooth or blade. It is easily cured and handled. It is readily seeded and catches with certainty. Its long, deeply penetrating, fibrous roots enable it to sustain itself and grow vigorously during droughts that dry up other grasses, except tall oat grass, which has similar roots and characteristics. It grows well in open lands and in forests of large trees, the underbrush being all cleared off. I have had it grown luxuriantly even in beech woods, where the roots are superficial, in the crotches of roots and close to the trunks of trees. The hay is of high quality, and the young grass contains a larger per centage of nutritive digestable matter than any other grass. It thrives well without any renewal on the same ground for thirty-five, nay forty years; how much longer, I am not able to say. It is easily exterminated when the land is desired for other crops. Is there any other grass for which so much can be said?

RED TOP GRASS.
(Agrosis Vulgaris.)

This is the best grass of England, the herd grass of the Southern States; not in honor of any man, but probably, because so well adapted to the herd. It is called also Fine Top, Burden's and Borden's Grass. Varying greatly in characters, according to soil, location, climate and culture, some botanists have styled it *A. Polymorpha*. It grows two to three feet high, and I have mown it when four feet high. It grows well on hill tops and sides, in ditches, gullies and marshes, but delights in moist bottom land. It is not injured by overflows, though somewhat prolonged. In marshy land it produces a very dense, strong network of roots capable of sustaining the weight of men and animals walking over it.

It furnishes considerable grazing during warm "spells" in winter and in spring and summer an abundant supply of nutrition. It has a tendency, being very hardy, to increase in density of growth and extent of surface, and will continue indefinitely, though easily subdued by the plow.

Cut before maturing seed, it makes a good hay and large quantity. It seems to grow taller in the Southern States than it does further North, and to make more and better hay and grazing. Red Top and Timothy, being adapted to the same soil and maturing at the same time do well together, and produce an excellent hay. But the Red Top will finally root out Timothy, and if pastured much it will do so sooner.

Sow about two bushels (28 lbs.) per acre, if alone, in September, October, February, or March; if with Timothy for hay, from 6 to 10 pounds; if with other grasses for pasture, 3 to 5 pounds. It is an excellent pasture grass, and will grow on almost any kind of soil.

KENTUCKY BLUE GRASS.
(Poa Pratensis.)

This is also called smooth meadow grass, spear grass, and green grass, all three very appropriate, characteristic names. But Blue is a misnomer for this grass. It is not blue, but green as grass, and the greenest of grasses. The *P.compressa*, flat-stalked meadow grass, wire grass, blue grass is blue, 'the true blue' grass from which the genus received its trivial name.

Kentucky blue grass, known also in the Eastern States as June grass, although esteemed in some parts of America as the best of all pasture grasses, seems not to be considered very valuable among English farmers except in mixtures. It is certainly a very desirable pasture grass however. Its very narrow leaves, one, two or more feet long, are in such profusion, and cover the ground to such depth with their luxuriant growth, that a mere description could give no one an adequate idea of its beauty, quantity, and value; that is on rich land. On poor, sandy land, it degenerates sadly, as do other things uncongenially located.

Perennial, and bearing cold and drought well, it furnishes grazing a large part of the year. It is specially valuable as a winter and spring grass for the South. To secure the best winter results, it should be allowed a good growth in early fall, so that the ends of the leaves, being killed by the frost, afford an ample covering for the under-part which continue to grow all winter, and afford a good bite whenever required by sheep, cattle, hogs and horses. In prolonged summer drought it dries completely, so that, if fired, it would burn off clean. But this occurs in Kentucky, where indeed it has seemed without fire, to disappear utterly; yet, when rain came, the bright green spears promptly recarpeted the earth.

With its underground stems and many roots, it sustains the heat and drought of the Southern States as well as those of Kentucky, where indeed it is subjected to severer trials of this kind than in the more Southern States. In fact, it bears the vicissitudes of our climate about as well as Bermuda grass, and is nearly as nutritious.

Blue grass grows well on hill tops, or bottom lands, if not too wet and too poor. It may be sown any time from September to April, preferably perhaps in the latter half of February, or early in March. The best catch I ever had was sown the 20th of March, on unbroken land, from which trash, leaves, etc., had just been burned. The surface of the land should be cleaned of trash of all kinds, smooth, even; and if recently plowed and harrowed, it should be rolled also. The last proceeding is for compacting the surface in order to prevent the seed from sinking too deep in the ground. Without harrowing or brushing in, many of them get in too deep to come up, even when the surface of the land has had the roller over it. The first rain after seeding will put them in deep enough, as the seeds are very minute, and the spears of grass small as fine needles, and therefore unable to get out from under heavy cover. These spears are so small as to be invisible, except to close examination; and in higher latitudes, this condition continues through the first year. Thus, some who have sown the blue grass seed, seeing the first year no grass, imagine they have been cheated, plant some other crop, and probably lose what close inspection would have shown to be a good catch. This, however, is not apt to occur in the Southern tier of States, as the growth here is more rapid. The sowing mentioned above, made on the 20th of March, came up promptly, and in three months the grass was from six to ten inches high. One year here gives a finer growth and show than two in Kentucky, or any other State so far North.

Sown alone, 20 to 26 pounds, that is 2 bushels, should be used; in mixtures, 4 to 6 pounds.

ENGLISH OR PERENNIAL RYE GRASS.
(Lolium Perenne.)

This is the first grass cultivated in England over two centuries ago, and at a still more remote period in France. It was long more widely known and cultivated than any other grass, became adapted to a great variety of soils and conditions, and a vast number (seventy or more) of varieties produced, some of which were greatly improved, while others were inferior and became annuals. Introduced into the United States in the first quarter of the current century, it has never become very popular, although shown by the subjoined analysis of Way not to be deficient in nutritive matter. In 100 parts of the dried grass cut in bloom were albuminoids 11.85, fatty matters 3.17, heat-producing principles 42.24, wood fibre 35.20, ash 7.54. The more recent analysis of Wolff and Knopp, allowing for water, gives rather more nutritive matter than this.

It grows rapidly, and yields heavy crops of seed; makes good grazing, and good hay. But, as with all the Rye grasses, to make good hay, it must be cut before passing the blossom stage, as after that it deteriorates rapidly. The roots being short, it does not bear drought well, and exhausts the soil, dying out in a few years. In these respects it is liable to the same objections as Timothy. The stem, one to two feet high, has four to six purplish joints and as many dark green leaves; the flexious spiked panicle, bearing two distant spikelets, one in each bend.

It should be sown in August or September, at the rate of twenty-five or thirty pounds, or one bushel seed per acre.

TALL MEADOW OAT GRASS.
(Arrhenatherum Avenaceum.)

Evergreen grass in Virginia, and other Southern States, and it is the Tall Oat (*Avena elatior*) of Linnæus. It is closely related to the common oat, and has a beautiful open panicle, leaning slightly to one side. "Spikelets two flowered, and a rudiment of a third, open; lowest flower staminate or sterile, with a long bent awn below the middle of the back." —Flint.

It is widely naturalized and well adapted to a great variety of soils. On sandy, or gravelly soils, it succeeds admirably, growing two or three feet high. On rich, dry upland it grows from five to seven feet high. It has an abundance of perennial, long fibrous roots, penetrating deeply in the soil, being, therefore, less affected by drought or cold, and enabled to yield a large quantity of foliage, winter and summer. These advantages render it one of the very best grasses for the South, both for grazing (being evergreen) and for hay, admitting of being cut twice a year. It is probably the best winter grass that can be obtained.

It will make twice as much hay as Timothy, and containing a greater quantity of albuminoids and less of heat-producing principles, it is better adapted to the uses of the Southern farmer, while it exhausts the surface soil less, and may be grazed indefinitely, except after mowing. To make good hay it must be cut the instant it blooms, and, after being cut, must not get wet by dew or rain, which damages it greatly in quality and appearance.

For green soiling, it may be cut four or five times with favorable seasons. In from six to ten days after blooming, the seeds begin to ripen and fall, the upper ones first. It is, therefore, a little troublesome to save the seed. As soon as those at the top of the panicle ripen sufficiently to begin to drop, the heads should be cut off and dried, when the seeds will all thresh out readily and be matured. After the seeds are ripe and taken off, the long abundant leaves and stems are still green, and being mowed make good hay.

It may be sown in March or April, and mowed the same season; but for heavier yield, it is better to sow in September or October. Along the more southernly belt, from the 31° parallel southward, it may be sown in November and onward till the middle of December. Whenever sown it is one of the most certain grasses to have a good catch. Not less than two bushels (24 pounds) per acre should be sown. Like Timothy, on inhospitable soils, the root may sometimes become bulbous. The average annual nutrition yielded by this grass in the Southern belt, is probably twice as great as in Pennsylvania and other Northern States.

JOHNSON GRASS.
(*Sorghum halapense.*)

This has been called Cuba grass, Egyptian grass, Means grass, Alabama and Guinea grass, etc.

It seems pretty well agreed now. however, to call it Johnson grass, and leave the name Guinea grass for the *Panicum jumentorum*, to which it properly belongs.

It is true that in Mr. Howard's pamphlet, as well as in many periodicals and books, and in letters and common usage, this grass has been far more generally called Guinea grass than the trueGuinea grass itself, thus causing vast confusion. It is, therefore, assuredly time to call each by its right name. Johnson grass is perennial and has cane-like roots, or more properly, underground stems, from the size of a goose-quill to that of the little finger. These roots are tender, and hogs are fond of and thrive on them in winter. The roots literally fill the ground near the surface, and every joint is capable of developing a bud. Hence the grass is readily propagated from root cutting. It is also propagated from the seeds, but not always so certainly; for in some localities many faulty seeds are produced, and in other places no seeds are matured. Before sowing the seeds, therefore, they should be tested, as should all grass seeds indeed, in order to know what proportion will germinate, and thus what quantity per acre to sow. One bushel of a good sample of this seed is sufficient for one acre of land.

The leaf, stalk and panicle of this grass resemble those of other sorghums. It grows on any land where corn will grow; and like the latter, the better the land the heavier the crop. On rich land the culms attain a size of over half an inch in diameter, and a height of seven feet. It should be cut while tender, and then all live stock are fond of it; for a few weeks are sufficient to render it so coarse and hard that animals refuse it, or eat sparingly.

A few testimonials are here quoted to give an idea of the productiveness and value of this plant. In a letter published in the *Rural Carolinian* for 1874, Mr. N. B. Moore, who had for more than forty years grown crops, speaks of this grass under the name of Guinea grass.

"My meadow consists of one hundred acres of alluvial land, near Augusta. * * * In winter I employ but four men, who are enough to work my packing-press; in summer, when harvesting, double that number. In autumn I usually scarify both ways with sharp, steel-toothed harrows, and sow over the stubble a peck of red clover per acre, which, with volunteer vetches, comes off about the middle of May. The second yield of clover is uniformly eaten up by grasshoppers. The top root remains to fertilize the then coming Guinea grass, which should be but from two to three feet high. * * * On such land as mine, it will afford three or four cuttings if the season is propitious. I use an average of five tons of gypsum soon after the first cutting, and about the same quantity of the best commercial fertilizers, in March and April. * * * The grass, which is cut before noon, is put up with horse sulky rakes, in cocks, before sun-down."

Mr. Moore's income from this field was from seven thousand to ten thousand dollars a year.

Mr. Goelsel, of Mobile, says: "It is undoubtedly the most profitable soiling plant yet introduced, and also promises to be *the plant* for our Southern hay stacks, provided it can be cut every three or four weeks."

Note.—Recognizing all the above, I would say, that great care must be taken not to sow this grass near cultivated lands. If done, it should not be allowed to go to seed, as the wind will blow them off from the stalks, and when it gets amongst cane or other crops it causes a great deal of trouble. It is almost impossible to get it out of the land.

RESCUE GRASS.

(Ceratochloa australis or Bromus Schraderi.)

It is an annual winter grass. It varies in the time of starting growth. I have seen it ready for mowing the first of October and furnish frequent cuttings till April. Again, it may not start before January, nor be ready to cut till February. This depends upon the moisture and depression of temperature. When once started, its growth, after the successive cuttings or grazings, is very rapid. It is tender, very sweet, and stock eat it greedily. It makes also a good hay. It produces an immense quantity of leaves. On loose soil some of it may be pulled out by animals grazing it. I have seen it bloom as early as November when the season had favored it, and no grazing or cutting were permitted. Oftener it makes little start before January. But whether late or early starting, it may be grazed or mowed frequently, until April, it still will mature seed. It has become naturalized in limited portions of Texas, Louisiana, Mississippi, Alabama, and perhaps other States. It is a very pretty grass in all its stages; and especially so when the culms, two or three feet high, are gracefully bending the weight of the diffuse panicle with its many pedicelled flattened spikelets, each an inch or more long and with twelve to sixteen flowers.

I would not, however, advise sowing this grass on poor land with the expectation of getting a remunerative return. It tillers abundantly under favorable conditions.

JAPAN CLOVER.
(*Lespedeza Striata.*)

There is now so much enquiry about this plant, so much confusion, lack of knowledge and confounding with or mistaking for it another worthless native species, and also the same errors in regard to a small genuine clover, that it is deemed proper to give some correct information on the subject.

HISTORY.

To botanists this plant has been known for many generations in its native habitat in China and other eastern parts of Asia. Finding its way to Japan it encountered congenial climate and soil, and rapidly spread over the entire country occupying all waste places, which it has continued to possess and improve for much more than a century. Here as on the continent, it was of dwarfish habit and received a name indicative of the fact.

Finally a few seeds, arriving in the United States, germinated, contested, a few feet of soil with other native and exotic plants that had long pre-occupied the land.

It gained strength and increased in yield of seed till becoming somewhat abundant, it commenced its westward invasion, simultaneously extending its conquests northward and southward, firmly holding all conquered territory. Since 1870 its strides westward have been immense. It now extends from the Atlantic seaboard across the Mississippi, and its out-posts are pushed far towards the western border of Texas.

Denuded, soil-less hill tops, sandy plains, gravelly slopes, bottoms and banks of washes and gullies, pine thickets, open woods, fields, dry and damp soils, all seem as if specially created for its home. It seizes upon all with equal facility.

It maintains its dwarfish habit on sands, gravels and other spots too poor to produce any other vegetation, densely covering the surface with its green robe and affording delighted live stock with delicious nutritious grazing for four to eight months of the year. But on richer soil it doffs the dwarf and dons the tree style justifying the American name of "bush clover," sending its long tap root deep down in the subsoil and its stem two to three feet up into the light and air, with its many branches thickly set with leaves, inviting tooth and blade.

It attains here on rich or medium soil protected from live stock a magnitude that could not have been imagined by one seeing it in its far eastern home. It takes possession not only of unoccupied land and pine thickets but grows among sedges, grasses, briers and weeds, completely eradicating many species of noxious grasses and weeds. It subdues even broom grass and holds equal contest with Bermuda grass: in some localities one yielding, in other localities the other succumbing, while in other spots both maintain equal possession; or one year one may seem to rule, and the next year the other.

VALUE.

On sands, gravels, or denuded clay hill tops no other plant known to me is so valuable for grazing. Taking a succession of ten years, the same assertion would not be far out of the way for rich lands while few forage plants on these would yield so much or so valuable hay. The analysis of red clover gives 16 per cent albuminoids and 41 carbohydrates. The average of two analyses of Japan clover gives 13.85 albuminoids and 56 carbohydrates, placing it above red clover in nutritive value. It is SUPERIOR TO OTHER FORAGE PLANTS, in several important particulars not generally observed by the careless stock-man. 1. The growing plant contains less moisture than any other very valuable forage plant with perhaps a single exception. Hence we never hear of animals having hoven or bloat or scours from eating this plant as when they have free access to red clover, peas and many grasses. 2. We have never yet found on the Japan clover any fungous growths which are so common on other plants as to cause many deaths annually among animals grazing on them or fed with the hay. 3. Heavy grazing for a few weeks destroys the clovers, lucerne and most of the grasses, while this plant may be grazed however closely, whether the season be wet or prolonged drouth prevail, without damage. 4. There is less difficulty of obtaining a catch with this plant than most others. The seed may be scattered on bare, poor, barren ground, rich soil, among weeds and dead grass or in March on small grain sown the previous autumn or winter and a catch will be obtained. 5. The grain being harvested when ripe does not injure the Lespedeza; which is ready for the mower through September and October. 6. It is more easily cured than the clovers, pea vines and many grasses. 7. It does not lose the foliage in curing as do clovers, peas and some other plants. 8. It furnishes good grazing from May, some years last of March till killed by frost in October or November.

PRODUCT OF HAY.

On medium to good land it ranges from one to three tons per acre; and this may be obtained after having during the summer harvested from the same land a good crop of grain and straw.

QUALITY.

Some of our farmers, who have been mowing Lespedeza striata for five to ten years regard it as the soundest, best, most wholesome and palatable hay they ever used. These mowings have ranged from two to three hundred tons on single farms in one season. Yet no complaint as to quality, or relish of animals for it, or as to its nutritive value and good effect on the stock has ever reached us. Those who have used it longest and in largest quantities and kept animals—cattle, sheep, horses and mules—in best condition commend it most. We have now before us a beautiful sample of this hay from Louisiana being from a crop of perhaps 300 tons mowed last autumn.

SEEDING.

A measured half bushel of seed per acre may be sown broad-cast the first week in March south of parallel 32° of latitude, a few days later as we proceed northward for each degree or two. Sown in the fall or winter it springs up, but freezes often throw it out and destroy it. As already stated it germinates and grows well on land in any condition, if the surface is not so loose as to let the seed sink too deep. When land has been prepared for or sown in grain, the winter rains put it in about the best condition for growing this plant for heavy crops of hay.

All our remarks on this plant, as found in our Southern States, are based on what we have seen and learned of it in a belt lying between $30\frac{1}{2}°$ and 34° of latitude.

The only

COMPLETE PROOF

of the value of a forage plant is found in the concurrence of chemical analysis and the observation and experience of the stockman. When the relish of an animal for the forage is keen, the health preserved and improved, growth promoted, a maximum quantity of excellent beef or mutton or pork, and, if superior milk and butter, are obtained, we certainly have an admirable food plant. The judgment of the cow, the convictions of the farmer arising from his experiences independent of, and indeed in utter ignorance of any chemical analysis, confirming the decisions of the chemist, give us the best of all evidences of the value of forage. And all these we have in this case. Japan clover is also a great

AMELIORATOR AND FERTILIZER.

Its abundant, long tap-roots decaying render the soil porous and leave in it much nitrogenous material and humus. It releases and brings up from the subsoil valuable plant food; the ashes containing nearly 40 per cent. potash, 29.-60 oxide lime, 7.82 sulphuric acid, 7.54 phosphoric acid - all most valuable elements in plant life and growth. Soils are thus renovated, slopes prevented from washing, gullies filled, moisture solicited and retained, atmospheric fertilizers gathered and garnered; bald, barren wastes covered with living green to fill the stomach, delight the eye and cheer the heart.

It should have been stated that this plant has eradicated over large areas the much detested helenium or bitter weed, which so often damages the flavor of the milk of cows eating it while grazing. It is believed that it exterminates also two or three plants that are fatally poisonous to cattle and horses.

Price, per bushel of 25 lbs., $5; ½ bush., $3.00; per pound, 30 cts.

BURR CLOVER.

(Medicago Maculata.)

This variety of clover was brought from Chili to California, and thence to the States, under the name of California Clover. It is often taken for Lucerne, which name is wrongly applied. The Burr Clover has only two or three yellow blossoms in each cluster, while Lucerne has many blue blossoms in an elongated head. It furnishes good grazing from February till April or May. It is good for grazing and hay. As there is no way for removing the seeds from the pods of spotted medic, it is necessary to sow the burr like pods, say one-half bushel per acre. The planting should be done early in fall, so the pods may have time to rot and release the seeds. Should be covered very lightly.

BERMUDA GRASS.

(Cynodon Dactylon.)

Almost everybody living in this section of the country knows this grass; it is planted as a Lawn grass, and nothing will stand the sun better, or will make a prettier carpet, when kept short, than this grass. It is also very valuable as a pasture and hay grass. It is only lately that I have been able to obtain the seed of this grass, which heretofore had to be propagated by the roots. Six pounds will sow an acre. Should be planted in spring, but can also be sown later. Under the most favorable circumstances it takes from 20 to 25 days to sprout; requires damp weather and hot sun; but when once up it grows very rapidly.

DIRECTIONS FOR PLANTING.

The directions given here are for the Southern part of Louisiana. If applied to localities North of here, the time of planting will not be quite so early in spring, and earlier in fall. For instance: the directions for January will answer for February in the Northern part of this State, and Southern part of Mississippi or Arkansas. In autumn, directions for September can be followed in August. In those sections, very little can be planted in November and December.

JANUARY.

Sow Spinach, Mustard, Carrots, Beets, Parsnips and Leeks, the early varieties of Radish, and for the last crop, the Black Spanish.

Sow Spring and Purple Top Turnip. Ruta Baga may also be sown, for table use later in spring.

Sow Lettuce, Endive, Cabbage, Broccoli, Kohlrabi, and early Cauliflower; the best sown in a frame to be transplanted next month.

Cress, Chervil, Parsley and Celery for cutting, should be sown this month. Sow Roquette and Sorrel.

If the hot-bed has not been prepared already, make it at once to sow Egg-Plant, Pepper and Tomatoes.

All kinds of Herb seed may be sown during this month. Plant Peas for a general crop, towards the end of the month the Extra Early varieties may be planted.

Plant Potatoes, but the Early Rose should not be planted before the latter end of this month.

Divide and transplant Shallots. Transplant Cabbage plants sown in November. Onions, if not already set out, should be hurried with now, so they may have time to bulb. Those who desire to raise Onion sets, should sow the seed towards the end of this month, as they may be used for setting out early in the fall, and can be sold sooner than those raised from seed. Creole seed is the only kind which can be used to raise sets from. Northern seed will not make sets. This I know from experience. Asparagus roots should be set out this month.

Red Oats can be sown. I consider these and the German Millet the two best annual forage plants for Louisiana. —Cucumbers can be planted in the hot-bed; they are mostly planted here during November and December, but if the hot-bed is properly made, those planted in this month will bear better than those planted in November.

FEBRUARY.

All winter vegetables can be sown this month, such as Spinach, Mustard, Carrots, Beets, Parsnips and Leeks. Also, the early varieties of Radishes and Spring and Purple Top Turnip, Swiss Chard and Kohlrabi.

Sow, for succession, Lettuce, Cabbage and early Cauliflower; if the season is favorable, and the month of April not too dry, the latter may succeed.

Cauliflower and Cabbage plants should be transplanted; Shallots divided and set out again.

Sow Sorrel, Roquette, Chervil, Parsley, Cress and Celery for seasoning.

Peas of all kinds can be planted, especially the early varieties. The late kinds should be sown in January, but they may be planted during this month.

This is the time to plant the general crop of Potatoes. On an average they will succeed better when planted during this, than during any other month.

Herb seeds should be planted; tender varieties best sown in a frame, and transplanted into the open ground afterwards.

Asparagus roots should be planted; this is the proper month to sow the seed of this vegetable.

Plants in the hot-bed will require attention; give air when the sun shines, and the weather is pleasant. If too thick, thin out, so they may become sturdy.

Bush Beans can be commenced with this month; Cucumbers, Squash and Melons may be tried, as they often succeed; if protected by small boxes, as most gardeners protect them, there is no risk at all.

Corn can be planted towards the end of this month. For market, the Adams Extra Early and Early White Flint are planted. I recommend the Sugar varieties for family use; they are just as large as those mentioned, and Stowel's Evergreen is as large as any variety grown.

Mangel Wurzel and Sugar Beet should be sown in this month for stock. Sweet Potatoes can be put in a bed for sprouting, so as to have early slips.

MARCH.

Sow Beets, Radish, Cabbage, early varieties; Kohlrabi, Lettuce, Spinach Mustard, Carrots, Swiss Chard and Leek.

Also, Celery for cutting, Parsley, Roquette, Cress and Chervil. The latter part of the month sow Endive. Of Lettuce, the Royal Cabbage and Perpignan; the White Coss is a favorite variety for spring; the Butterhead will run into seed too quickly, and should not be sown later than the middle of February in this latitude.

Plant a full supply of Bush and Pole Beans. For Lima Beans better to wait till towards the end of the month, as they rot easily when the ground is not warm enough, or too wet.

Squash, Cucumbers, Melons and Okra can be planted. The remark in regard to Lima Beans holds good for Okra. Early varieties of Peas may still be planted.

Tomatoes, Egg Plants and Peppers can be set out in the open ground, and seed sown for a later crop. Plant Sweet Corn.

Potatoes can be planted; all depends upon the season. Some years they do as well as those planted during last month.

Beans are hard to keep in this climate, and therefore very few are planted for shelling purposes. With a little care, however, they can be kept, but they ought not to be planted before the first of August, so that they may ripen when the weather gets cooler. When the season is favorable leave them out till dry; gather the pods and expose them a few days to the sun. It is best to shell them at once, and after they are shelled put them to air and sun again for a few days longer. Sacks are better to keep them in than barrels and boxes. The Red and White Kidney are generally the varieties used for drying. Beans raised in spring are hard to keep, and if intended for seed they should be put up in bottles, or in tin boxes, and a little camphor sprinkled between them.

Sweet Potatoes should be planted.

APRIL.

Sow Bush, Pole and Lima Beans, Sweet Corn, Cucumbers, Squash, Melons and Okra.

Beets Carrots, Swiss Chard, Radish, Lettuce, Mustard, Endive, Roquette, Cress, Parsley, Chervil and Celery for cutting.

Sow Tomatoes, Egg Plants and Pepper for succession. It is rather late to sow Cabbage seed now, but if sown, the early varieties only can be successfully used. Kohlrabi can still be sown, but it is best to sow it thinly in drills a foot apart, and thin out to four inches in the rows.

Towards the end of this month a sowing of the late Italian Giant Cauliflower can be made. It is very large, and takes from eight to nine months before it matures, so it has to be sown early. It is always best to make a couple of sowings, so that in case one should fail the other may be used. This variety is hardier than the French and German kinds. A good plan is to sow the seed in boxes, elevated two feet or more above the ground, as it will keep the cabbage-fly of. The plants should be overlooked daily, and all green cabbage worms or other vermin removed.

Sweet Potato Slips, for early crop, can be planted out. Early Irish Potatoes will be fit to dig now, and the ground they are taken out of may be planted with Corn, Beans, Squash, etc.

Sow Pumpkins of both kinds. the Field and the Cashaw.

German Millet should be sown this month. The ground ought to be well plowed and harrowed. Three pecks of seed is the quantum to be sown per acre. It will be well to roll the ground after sowing, and the seed will require no other covering. If no roller is handy, some brush tied together ought to be passed over the ground sown. For hay, it should be cut when in flower. Every planter should give it a trial.

MAY.

Very few varieties of vegetables can be sown during this month. Many of the winter varieties will not do well if sown now. The ground should now be occupied with growing crops.

Where Potatoes and Onions are taken up, Corn, Melons, Cucumbers, Squash and Pumpkins may be planted. Nothing of the Cabbage kind, except the Creole Cabbage seed, can be sown this month. It is supposed to stand the heat better than other varieties, but it makes only loose heads and runs up to seed as early as the end of November.

Yellow and white summer Radish and Endive should be sown. Lettuce requires much water during hot weather, and, if neglected, will become hard and tasteless. The Perpignan is the best kind for summer use. Okra can still be sown.

The first sowing of White Solid Celery is to be made this month. The seed requires to be shaded, and, if the weather is dry, should be regularly watered. Late Italian Cauliflower should be sown.

Cow Peas can be planted between the corn, or the crowders in rows; the latter are the best to be used green. If they are sown for fertilizing purposes, they are sown one bushel per acre, and plowed under when the ground is well covered; or sometimes they are left till fall, when they commence to decay and then plowed down.

Sweet Potato Slips can be set out, taking advantage of an occasional rain; if it does not rain they have to be watered. The top of Shallots will commence to get dry; this indicates that they are fit to take up. Pull them up and expose to the sun for a few days, and then store them away in a dry, airy place, taking care not to lay them too thick, as they are liable to heat. Lima or Pole Beans can be planted; the Southern Prolific is the best variety for late planting.

JUNE.

This month is similar to the last, that is, not a great deal can be sown. The growing crops will require attention, as weeds grow fast. Plant Corn for the last supply of roasting ears. A few Water and Musk Melons may be planted. Cucumbers, Squash and Pumpkins planted this month generally do very well, but the first requires an abundance of water if the weather is dry.

Southern Prolific Pole Beans may be planted during this month. Continue to set out Sweet Potato vines.

Sow Yellow and White Summer Radish; sow Endive for Salad; this is raised more easily than the Lettuce.

Lettuce can be sown, but it requires more care than most people are willing to bestow. Soak the seeds for half an hour in water, take them out and put them in a piece of cloth, and place in a cool spot—under the cistern, or, if convenient, in an ice box. Keep the cloth moist, and in two or three days the seeds will sprout. Then sow them; best to do so in the evening, and give a watering.

If the seed is sown without being sprouted, ants will be likely to carry it away before it can germinate, and the seedsman be blamed for selling seeds that did not grow. This sprouting has to be done from May to September, depending upon the weather. Should the weather be moist and cool in the fall, it can be dispensed with. Some sow late Cabbage for winter crop in this month, saying the plants are easier raised during this than the two following months. I consider this month too soon; plants will become too hard and long-legged before they can be planted out.

This is the last month to sow the Late Italian Cauliflower; towards the end the Early Italian Giant Cauliflower can be sown. Some cultivators transplant them, when large enough, at once into the open ground; others plant them first into flowerpots and transplant them into the ground later. If transplanted at this time, they will require to be shaded for a few days, till they commence to grow.

Sow Tomatoes for late crop during the latter part of this month.

JULY.

Plant Pole Beans; also, Bush Beans, towards the end of the month. Sow Tomatoes in the early part for the last crop. Some Corn for roasting ears may still be planted. Cucumbers can be planted for pickling. Early Giant Cauliflower can be sown. Sow Endive, Lettuce, Yellow and White Summer Radish. Where the ground is new, some Turnips and Ruta Bagas can be sown. Cabbage should be commenced with after the 15th of this month; Superior Flat Dutch, Improved Drumhead, St. Denis, or Bonneuil and Brunswick are the leading kinds. It is hard to say which is the best time to sow, as our seasons differ so much—some seasons we get frost early, other seasons not before January. Cabbage is most easily hurt by frost when it is half grown; when the plants are small, or when they are headed up, frost does not hurt much. It is always good to make two or three sowings. As a general thing, plants raised from seeds sown in July and August, give the most satisfaction; they are almost certain to head. September, in my experience, is the most ticklish month; as the seed sown in that month is generally only half grown when we have some frosts, and therefore, more liable to be hurt. But there are exceptions. Some years ago the seed sown in September turned out best. Seed sown at the end of October and during November generally give good results. November is the proper month to sow for shipping. The surest way to sow is in a cold frame, to protect the plants from frosts which sometimes occur in December and January. January, and the early part of February, is early enough to set out. Brunswick and Excelsior are the earliest of the large growing kinds, and it should be sown in July and August, so that it may be headed up when the cold comes, as it is more tender than the Flat Dutch and Drumhead. The same may be said in regard to the St. Denis. All cabbages require strong, good soil; but these two varieties particularly. Brunswick makes also a very good spring cabbage when sown at the end of October. The standard varieties, the Superior Flat Dutch and Improved Drumhead, should be sown at the end of this month and during next. It is better to sow plenty of seeds than to be short of plants. I would prefer one hundred plants raised in July and August, to four times that amount raised in September. It is very hard to protect the young plants from ravages of the fly. Strong tobacco water is as good as anything else for this purpose, or tobacco stems cut fine and scattered over the ground will keep them off to some extent. As the plants have to be watered, the smell of the tobacco will drive the flies away.

AUGUST.

This is a very active month for gardening in the South. Plant Bush Beans, Extra Early and Washington Peas. Sow late Cabbages and Drumhead Savoy, also Broccoli, Brussels Sprouts and Kale. The Early Italian Giant Cauliflower may still be sown; but now is the proper time to sow the Half Early Paris, Asiatic and other early varieties.

Sow Parsley, Roquette Chervil, Lettuce, Endive and Sorrel; but, in case of dry weather, these seeds will have to be watered frequently.

Continue to sow Yellow Turnip Radishes, and commence to sow red varieties, such as Scarlet Turnip, Half Long French and Long Scarlet.

Towards the end of the month the Black Spanish Radish can be sown; also, Swiss Chard.

Sow Mustard and Cress; the former will generally do well. All kinds of Turnips and Ruta Bagas should be sown; also, Kohlrabi.

The seed of all kinds of Beets should be put in the ground.

Towards the end of the month Carrots can be sown; but the sowing of all vegetables at this time of the year depends much upon the season. If we should have hot and dry weather, it is useless to do much, as seed cannot come up without being watered. White Solid Celery should be sown for a succession, and the Dwarf kinds for spring use.

Shallots can be set out during this month; also, Onion Sets especially if they are raised from Creole seed. The early part of the month is the proper time to plant Red and White Kidney Beans, for shelling and drying for winter use.

Early Rose and other varieties of Potatoes should be planted early this month for a winter crop, and the latest of Tomato plants should be set out, if not done last month. If Celery plants are set out during this month, they require to be shaded.

SEPTEMBER.

Most of the seeds recommended for last month can be sown this month, and some more added.

In the early part, Bush Beans can be planted, as they will bear before frost comes. Plant Extra Early and early varieties of Peas. Sow Radishes of all kinds, Carrots, Beets, Parsnip, Salsify, Roquette, Chervil, Parsley, Sorrel, Cress, Lettuce, Endive, Leek, Turnips, Kohlrabi, Broccoli, Early Cauliflower, Kale, Celery, Corn Salad and Mustard.

After the 15th of this month, Creole Onion seed can be sown. This is an important crop, and should not be neglected. If it is very dry, cover the bed, after the seed has been sown, with green moss; it will keep the ground moist, and the seed will come up more regularly. The moss has to be taken off as the young plants make their appearance.

Celery plants may be set out in ditches prepared for that purpose. Cauliflower and Cabbage plants can be transplanted if the weather is favorable.

If the weather is not too hot and dry, Spinach should be sown; but it is useless to do so if the weather is not suitable.

Cabbage can be sown, but it is much better to sow in August and transplant during this month.

Set out Shallots. Sorrel should be divided and replanted.

Sow Turnip-rooted Celery.

OCTOBER.

Artichokes should be dressed, the suckers or sprouts taken off and new plants made.

Onion seed can still be sown; but it is better to get the seed into the ground as soon as possible, so the plants get to be some size before the cold weather comes.

Towards the end of the month Black Eye Marrowfat Peas can be planted; also, English or Windsor Beans.

Sow Cabbage, Cauliflower, Broccoli, Brussels Sprouts, Kale, Spinach, Mustard, Swiss Chard, Carrots, Beets, Salsify, Leek, Corn Salad, Parsley, Roquette, Chervil, Kohlrabi, Radish, Lettuce, Endive and Parsnip. Shallots from the first planting can be divided and set out again. Salsify does very finely here, but is generally sown too late; this is the proper month to sow the seed. The ground should be mellow and have been manured last spring. It should be spaded up very deeply, as the size and smoothness of the roots depend upon the preparation of the soil.

Water the Celery with soap suds, and if the season has been favorable by the end of this month, some may be earthed up.

Sow Rye, Barley and Red Oats, Orchard Grass, Red and White Clover, and Alfalfa Clover. Strawberry plants should be transplanted; they cannot be left in the same spot for three or four years, as is done North. The Wilson's Albany, and Sucker State, are the favorite varieties for the market.

The Wilson's Albany do not make many runners here, but they form a stool, something like the plants of violets, and these stools have to be taken up and divided.

NOVEMBER.

Continue to sow Spinach, Corn Salad, Radish, Lettuce, Mustard, Roquette, Parsley, Chervil, Carrots, Salsify, Parsnips, Cress and Endive, also Turnips and Cabbage. Superior Flat Dutch and Improved Drumhead, sown in this month, make fine Cabbage in the spring. —Artichokes should be dressed, if not already done last month.

Sow Black Eye and other late varieties of Peas. Frost does not hurt them as long as they are small, and during this time of the year they will grow but very slowly. English Beans can be planted; frost does not hurt them, and,

if not planted soon, they will not bear much.

Manure for hot-beds should be looked after, and ought not to be over one month old. It should be thrown together in a heap, and, when heated, forked over again, so the long and short manure will be well mixed. The first vegetables generally sown in the hot-beds are Cucumbers; it is best to start them in two or three inch pots, and when they have two rough leaves, transplant them to their place; two good plants are sufficient under every sash.

DECEMBER.

Not a great deal is planted during this month, as the ground is generally occupied by the growing crops.

Plant Peas for a general crop; some Potatoes may be risked, but it is uncertain whether they will succeed or not.

Sow Spinach, Roquette, Radish, Carrots, Lettuce, Endive and Cabbage.

Early varieties of Cauliflower can be sown in a frame or sheltered situation, to be transplanted in February into the open ground. Early Cabbages, such as York, Oxheart and Winningstadt, may be sown.

To those who wish to force Tomatoes I will say that this is the month to sow them. The best kind for that purpose is the Extra Early Dwarf Red. It is really a good acquisition; it is very dwarfish, very productive, and of good size, and bears the fruit in clusters, but will sell only for the first, as the fruit is not so large as the Livingston varieties, which come in later.

FLOWER SEEDS.

The following list of Flower seeds is not very large, but it contains all which is desirable and which will do well in the Southern climate. I import them from one of the most celebrated growers in Prussia, and they are of the best quality. There are very few or no flower seeds raised in this country, and Northern houses, which publish large lists and catalogues, get them from just the same sources as myself; but they, on an average, sell much higher than I do. Some varieties, which are bi-ennial in Europe or North, flower here the first season; in fact, if they do not, they generally do not flower at all, as they usually are destroyed by the continued long heat of summer. Some kinds grow quicker here and come to a greater perfection than in a more Northern latitude.

Flower seeds require a little more care in sowing than vegetable seeds. The ground should be well pulverized and light enough not to bake after a rain. Some of the more delicate and finer varieties are better sown in boxes or seed pans, where they can be better handled and protected from hard rains or cold weather; the other kinds do not transplant well, and are better sown at once where they are to remain, or a few seeds may be sown in small pots to facilitate transplanting into the garden without disturbing the plants, when large enough. Some have very fine seeds, which the mere pressing of the hand or spade to the soil will cover; others may be covered one-fourth of an inch, according to their size. Watering should be done carefully, and if not done with a syringe, a watering pot, where the holes of the spout are very fine, should be used.

By setting the plants out, or sowing the seeds in the border, consideration should be taken of the height, so that the taller varieties may be in the middle and the dwarf kinds on the edge of the bed.

The seeds are put up at ten cents a package, fifteen packages for one dollar, except a few rare or costly kinds, where the price is noted. All flower seeds in packages are mailed free of postage to the purchaser. Where there is more than one color, I generally import them mixed, as I find that most of my customers do not wish to purchase six packages, or more, of one variety, in order to get all the colors. One package of Asters, Zinnia, Phlox, Chinese Pink, German Stocks, Petunia, Portulaca, and others, will always contain an equal mixture of the best colors.

Althea Rosen. Hollyhock. This flower has been much improved of late years, and is very easily cultivated. Can be sown from October till April. Very hardy; from four to six feet high.

Alyssum maritimum. Sweet Alyssum. Very free flowering plants, about six inches high, with white flowers; very fragrant. Sow from October till April.

Antirhinum majus. Snapdragon. Choice mixed. Showy plant of various colors. About two feet high. Should be sown early, if perfect flowers are desired. Sow from October till March.

Aster. Queen Margaret. German Quilled. Perfect double quilled flower, of all shades, from white to dark purple and crimson. One and a half feet high.

Aster. Trufaut's Pæony-Flowered Perfection. Large double pæony-shaped flowers, of fine mixed colors; one of the best varieties. Two feet high; sow from December till March. Asters should be sown in a box or in pots, and kept in a green-house, or near a window; when large enough, transplant into the border. Take a shovel of compost and mix with the ground before planting. Put three to four plants together and they will show better. They can be cultivated in pots.

Adonis autumnalis. Flos Adonis or Pheasant's Eye. Showy crimson

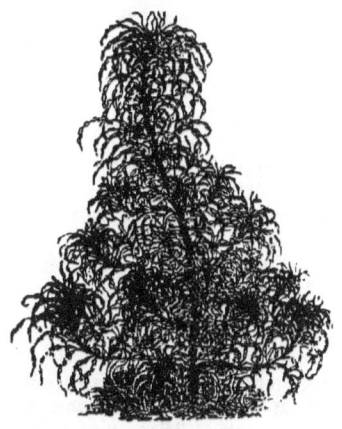
Amaranthus Salicifolius, Fountain Plant.

Truffaut's Pæony-Flowered Aster.

Althæa Rosea.

German Quilled Aster.

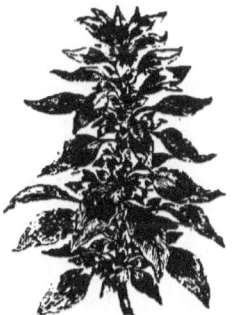
Amaranthus Tricolor.

Amaranthus Caudatus.

Double Daisy.

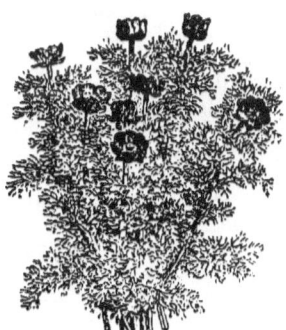
Adonis autumnalis.

flower, of long duration. One foot high. Sow from November till April.

Amaranthus caudatus. Love Lies Bleeding. Long red racemes with blood red flowers. Very graceful; three feet high.

Amaranthus tricolor. Three-colored Amaranth. Very showy; cultivated on account of its leaves, which are green, yellow and red. Two to three feet high.

Amaranthus bicolor. Two-colored Amaranth. Crimson and green variegated foliage; good for edging. Two feet high.

Amaranthus Salicifolius. Fountain Plant. Rich colored foliage, very graceful. Five to six feet high. Sow from February till June.

Aquilegia. Columbine. A showy and beautiful flower of different colors; two feet high. Sow from October till March. Should be sown early if flowers are wished; if sown late will not bloom till next season.

Balsamina Hortensis. Lady Slipper. A well known flower of easy culture. Requires good ground to produce double flowers.

Balsamina. Improved Camelia-flowered. Very double and beautiful colors. The strain which I offer of this variety is very fine; but to have them perfect, they should not be sown too soon. In rich ground and during dry weather they require plenty of water.

Balsamina camellia flora alba, Pure white flowers, used for bouquets; about two feet high. Sow from February till August.

Bellis Perennis. Daisy. Finest double mixed variety; four inches high. From October till January.

Cacalia coccinea. Scarlet Tassel Flower. A profuse flowering plant, with tassel-shaped flowers in cluster; one and a half feet. Sow February till May.

Calendula officinalis. Pot Marigold. A plant which, properly speaking, belongs to the aromatic herbs, but sometimes cultivated for the flowers, which vary in different shades of yellow; one and a half feet high. From January till April.

Celosia cristata. Dwarf Cock's-comb. Well known class of flowers which are very ornamental, producing large heads of crimson and yellow flowers; one to two feet high. Sow from February till August.

Cheiranthus Cheiri. Wall Flower. This flower is highly esteemed in some parts of Europe, but does not grow very perfectly here, and seldom produces the large spikes of double flowers which are very fragrant. Two feet high. November till March.

Campanula Speculum. Bell-Flower, or Venus' Looking-Glass. Free flowering plants of different colors, from white to dark blue; one foot high. Sow December till March.

Centaurea cyanus. Bottle Pink. A hardy annual of easy culture, of various colors; two feet high.

Centaurea suavolens. Yellow, Sweet Sultan. December to April.

Cineraria hybrida. A beautiful green-house plant. Seed should be sown in October or November, and they will flower in spring. Per package, 25 cents.

Cineraria Maritima. A handsome border plant, which is cultivated on account of its silvery white leaves. Stands our summer well.

Coleus. A well known and beautiful bedding plant, which can he easily propagated by seeds which produce different shades of colored plants.

Dianthus Barbatus. Sweet William. A well known plant which has been much improved of late years. Their beautiful colors make them very showy. Should be sown early, otherwise they will not flower the first spring; one and a half feet high. October till April.

Dianthus Chinensis. Chinese Pink. A beautiful class of annuals of various colors, which flower very profusely in early spring and summer; one foot high. From October till April.

Dianthus Heddewiggii. Japan Pink. This is the most showy of any of the annual pinks. The flowers are very large and of brilliant colors; one foot high. Sow from October till April.

Dianthus plumaris. Border Pink. A fragrant pink used for edging. The

FOR THE SOUTHERN STATES.

Aquilegia, or Columbine.   Cheiranthus Cheiri.

Dianthus Chinensis, Double.   Centaurea Cyanus.   Dianthus Barbatus.

Celosia Cristata.   Balsamina Camellia-Flowered.   Calendula officinalis.

flowers are tinged, generally pink or white, with a dark eye. Does not flower the first year; two feet high. Sow from January till April.

Dianthus caryophyllus. Carnation Pink. This is a well known and highly esteemed class of flowers. They are double, of different colors, and very fragrant; can be sown either in fall or spring; should be shaded during midsummer and protected from hard rains; three to four feet high. November till April.

Dianthus Picotee. Finest hybrids. Stage flowers saved from a collection of over 500 named varieties; per package, 50c.

Dianthus pumila. Early dwarf flowering Carnation. If sown early, this variety will flower the first season. They are quite dwarfish and flower very profusely. November till April.

Delphinium Imperialis, fl. pl. Imperial flowering Larkspur. Very handsome variety of symmetrical form. Mixed colors; bright red, dark blue and red stripes; 1½ feet high.

Delphinium ajacis. Rocket Larkspur. Mixed colors; very showy; two and a half feet.

Delphinium Chinensis. Dwarf China Larkspur. Mixed colors; very pretty; one foot high. November till April.

NOTE—None of the above three varieties transplant well, and are better sown at once where they are intended to remain.

Dahlia. Large flowering Dahlia. Seed sown in the spring will flower by June. Very pretty colors are obtained from seed; the semi-double or single ones can be pulled up as they bloom; but those seeds which are saved from fine double varieties will produce a good percentage of double flowers. February till June.

Eschscholtzia Californica. California Poppy. A very free flowering plant, good for masses. Does not transplant well. One foot high. December till April.

Gaillardia bicolor. Two-colored Gaillardia. Very showy plants, which continue to flower for a long time. Flowers red, bordered with orange yellow. One and a half feet high. January till April.

Gillia. Mixed Gillia. Dwarf plants which flower freely, of various colors. One foot. December till April.

Gomphrena alba and purpurea. White and Crimson Batchelor Button or Globe Amaranth. Well known variety of flowers; very early and free flowering; continue to flower for a long time. Two feet high. From February till August.

Geranium Zonale. Zonale Geranium. Seed saved from large flowering varieties of different colors; should be sown in seed pans, and when large enough transplanted into pots, where they can be left, or transplanted in spring into the open ground.

Geranium pelargonium. Large flowering Pelargonium. Spotted varieties, 25 cents per package.

Geranium odoratissima. Apple-scented Geranium. Cultivated on account of its fragrant leaves; 25 cents per package. Both of these kinds are pot plants, and require shade during hot weather. Should be sown during fall and winter.

Gypsophila paniculata. Gypsophila. A graceful plant with white flowers, which can be used for bouquets. One foot high. From December to April.

Heliotropium. Mixed varieties with dark and light shaded flower. A well known plant, esteemed for the fragrance of its flowers, which are produced during the whole summer in great profusion. This plant is generally propagated by cuttings, but can also be raised from seed. Should be sown in a hot-bed if sown early.

Helichrysum monstrosum album. White Everlasting Flower. Very showy double flowers. One and a half feet high.

Helichrysum monstrosum rubrum. Red Everlasting Flower. Very ornamental. One and a half feet high. December till April. Does not transplant well.

FOR THE SOUTHERN STATES.

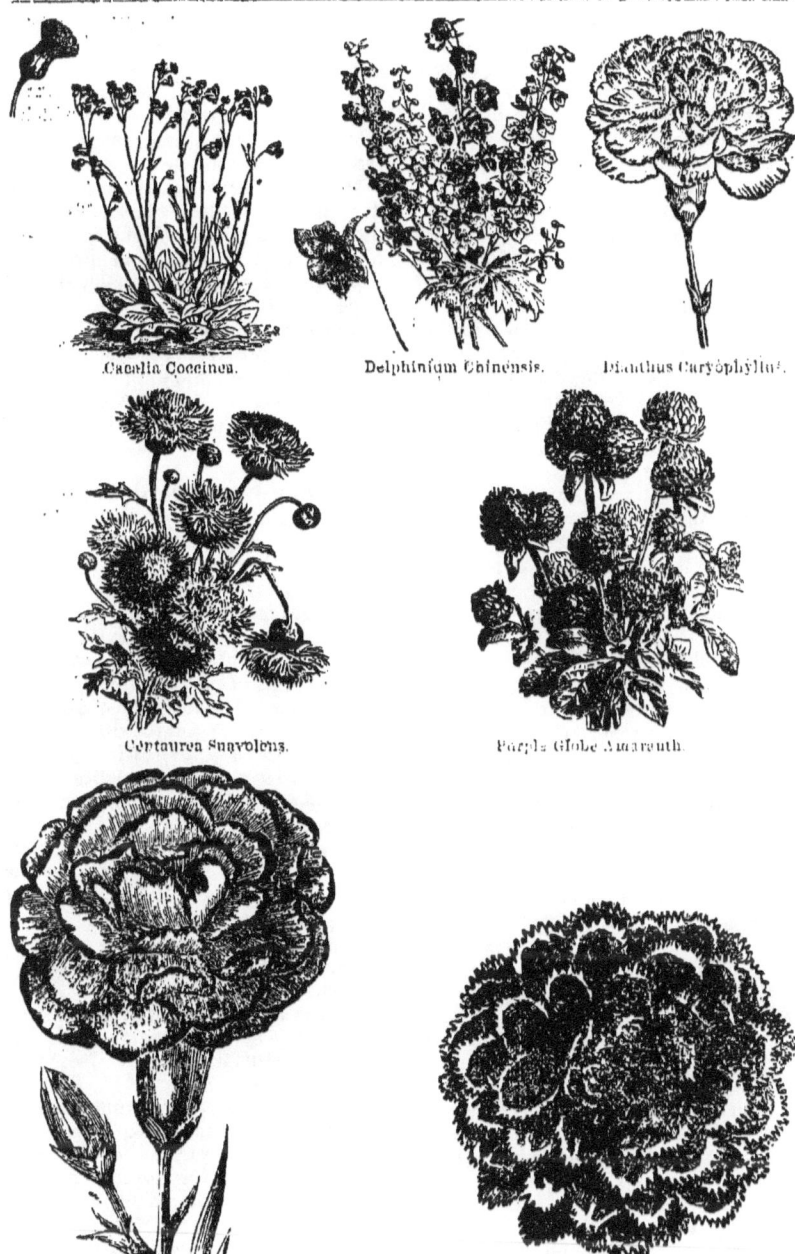

Cacalia Coccinea.　　Delphinium Chinensis.　　Dianthus Caryophyllus.

Centaurea Suavolens.　　Purple Globe Amaranth.

Dianthus Picotee.　　Dianthus Heddewiggii.

Helianthus fl. pl. Double Flowering Sunflower. A well known plant, with showy yellow flowers. The double is often cultivated in the flower garden. The single varieties are cultivated mostly for the seed. They are said to be anti-malarious. Four feet high. February till May.

Iberis amara. White Candytuft. A well known plant raised a good deal by florists for bouquets. Can be sown at different times to have a succession of flowers. One foot high.

Iberis umbelata rosea. Purple Candytuft. One foot. October till April.

Linum grandiflorum rubrum. Scarlet Flax. A very pretty plant for masses or borders, with bright scarlet flowers, dark in the centre. One foot. January till April.

Lobelia erinus. Lobelia. A very graceful plant with white and blue flowers, well adapted for hanging baskets or border. Half foot. October till March.

Lychnis chalcedonica. Lychnis. Fine plants with scarlet, white and rose flowers. Two feet. December till April.

Lupinus. Lupinus. Plants with spikes of flowers of various colors. Should be sown soon. Does not transplant well. Two feet. October till March.

Mathiola annua. Ten weeks stocks. This is one of the finest annuals in cultivation. Large flowers of all colors, from white to dark blue or crimson. Should be sown in pots or pans, and when large enough transplanted into rich soil. One and a quarter feet. October till March.

Mesembryanthemum crystallinum. Ice plant. Neat plant with icy looking foliage. It is of spreading habit. Good for baskets or beds. One foot. February till March.

Mimulus tigrinus. Monkey flower. Showy flowers of yellow and brown. Should be sown in a shady place. Does not transplant well. Half foot. December till March.

Matricaria capensis. Double Matricaria. White double flowers, resembling the Daisy, but smaller; are fine for bouquets; blooms very nearly the whole summer. Two feet. December till March.

Mimosa pudica. Sensitive Plant. A curious and interesting plant which folds up its leaves when touched. One foot. February till June.

Mirabilis jalapa. Marvel of Peru. A well known plant of easy culture; producing flowers of various colors. It forms a root which can be preserved from one year to another. February till June. Three feet.

Myosotis palustris. Forget-me-not. A fine little plant with small, blue, star-like flowers. Should have a moist, shady situation. Does not succeed so well here as in Europe, of which it is a native. Half foot high. December till March.

Nemophila Insignis. Blue Grove Love. Plants of easy culture, very pretty and profuse bloomers. Bright blue with white centre. One foot high.

Nemophila maculata. Large white flowers spotted with violet. One foot high. December till April.

Nigella damascena. Love in a Mist. Plants of easy culture, with light blue flowers. Does not transplant well. One foot high. December till April.

Nierembergia gracilis. Nierembergia. Nice plants with delicate foliage, and white flowers tinted with lilac. One foot high. November till April.

Œnothera Lamarckiana. Evening Primrose. Showy, large yellow flowers. December till April. Two feet high.

Papaver Somniferum. Double flowering Poppy. Of different colors; very showy.

Papaver ranunculus flowered. Double fringed flowers; very showy. Cannot be transplanted. Two feet high. October till March.

Petunia hybrida. Petunia. Splendid mixed hybrid varieties. A very decorative plant of various colors, well known to almost every lover of flowers. Plants are of spreading habit, about one foot high. January till May.

Petunia flora pleno. Large double flowering varieties. They are hybridized with the finest strains, and will give from 20 to 25 per cent. of double flowers. Very handsome; 25 cents per package. January till March.

Phlox Drummondii. Drummond's Phlox. One of the best and most popular annuals in cultivation. Their various colors and length of flowering,

Early Dwarf Double Carnation Pink.   Gaillardia Bicolor.   Lobelia Erinus.

Heliotropium

Mathiola Annua.    Geranium Zonale.

Blue Grove Love.

Petunia Hybrida.

Nigella Damascena.

with easy culture, make them favorites with every one." All fine colors mixed. One foot high. December till April.

Phlox Drummondii grandiflora. This is an improvement on the above; flowers are larger, with white centre, different colors mixed. Very beautiful. One foot high. December till April.

Phlox Drummondii grandiflora alba. Pure White, some with purple or violet eye.

Phlox Drummondii grandiflora, stellata splendens. (New.) This is admitted to be the richest colored and most effective of all large-flowered Phloxes. It combines all the good qualities of the Splendens, with the addition of a clearly defined, pure white star, which contrasts strikingly with the vivid crimson of the flowers.

Portulaca. A small plant of great beauty, and of the easiest culture. Does best in a well exposed situation, where it has plenty of sun. The flowers are of various colors, from white to bright scarlet and crimson. The plant is good for edging vases or pots; or where large plants are kept in tubs, the surface can be filled with this neat little genus of plants. Half foot high. February till August.

Portulaca grandiflora fl. pl. Double Portulaca. The same variety of colors with semi-double and double flowers. Half foot high. February till August.

Primula veris. Polyanthus. An herbaceous plant of various colors, highly esteemed in Europe. Half foot high. December till April.

Primula chinensis. Chinese Primrose. A green-house plant, which flowers profusely and continues to bloom for a long time; should be sown early to insure the plant flowering well. Different colors; mixed, per package, 25 cents. One and a half feet high. October till February.

Pyrethrum aureu. Golden Feather. The flowers resemble Asters. It has bright yellow leaves which make it very showy as a border if massed with plants, such as Coleus, etc.

Lychnis Chalcedonica.

Geranium Pelargonium.

Ice Plant.

Double Matricaria.

Helichrysum Monstrosum Album.

Œnothera Lamarckiana.

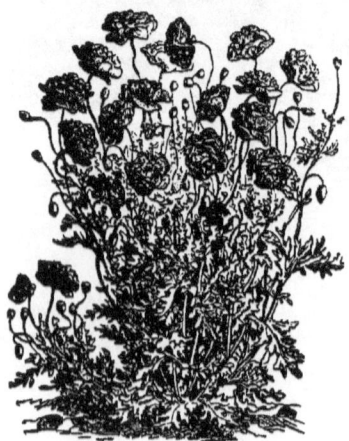

Papaver Ranunculus Flowered.

Portulaca.

Reseda odorata. Sweet Mignonette. A fragrant plant and a favorite with everybody. One foot high.

Reseda grandiflora. Similar to the above plant and flower, spikes larger. Fifteen inches. December till April.

Scabiosa nana. Dwarf Mourning Bride. Plants of double flowers of various colors. One foot high. December till April.

Saponaria calabrica. Soapwort. A very free flowering annual, of easy culture, resembling somewhat in leaves the Sweet William. One and a half feet high. December till April.

Salvia coccinea splendens. Scarlet Salvia or Red Flowering Sage. A pot or green-house plant, but which can be grown as an annual, as it flowers freely from seed the first year. Two to three feet high. February till April.

Silene Armeria. Lobel's Catchfly. A free blooming plant of easy culture; flowers almost anywhere. Red and white. One and a half feet high.

Tagetes erecta. African or Tall-growing Marigold. Very showy annuals for borders, with bright yellow flowers growing upright. One and a half feet high.

Tagetes patula. French or Dwarf Marigold. A very compact dwarf growing variety, covered with yellow and brown flowers. One and a half feet high. January till April.

Torenia Fournieri. A plant from Mexico of recent introduction, but which has become very popular in a short time. It stands the heat well, is well adapted to pot culture, and makes one of the most valuable bedding plants we have. The flowers are of a sky blue color, with three spots of dark blue. The seeds are very fine and take a good while to germinate. It transplants very easily.

Verbena hybrida. Hybridized Verbena. A well known and favorite flower for borders. Their long flowering and great diversity of color make them valuable for every garden, however small. All colors mixed. One and a half feet high. January till April.

Phlox Drummondii Grandiflora.

Phlox Drummondii Grandiflora Stellata Splendens. [New.]

Scabiosa nana.

Primula Veris.   Petunia Hybrida, Double.   Tagetes Erecta.

Tagetes Patula.   Vinca Rosea and Alba.   Reseda Odorata.

Verbena Striped Italian. These are beautiful striped kinds of all colors with large eyes.

Verbena Niveni. White Verbena. Pure white Verbena of more or less fragrance. One and a half feet high. January till April.

Vinca rosea and alba. Red and White Periwinkle. Plants of shining foliage, with white and dark rose colored flowers, which are produced the whole summer and autumn. Two feet high. February till April.

Viola odorata. Sweet Violet. Well known edging plant, which generally is propagated by dividing the plants; but can also be raised from seed. Half foot high. Sown from January till March.

Viola tricolor maxima. Large flowering choicest Pansy. This is one of the finest little plants in cultivation for pots or the open ground. They are of endless colors and markings. When planted in the garden, they will show better if planted in masses, and a little elevated above the level of the garden. Half foot high. October until March.

Large Trimardeau Pansy. This is the largest variety in cultivation; the flowers are well formed, generally three spotted; quite distinct; the plants grow compact.

Zinnia elegans fl. pl. Double Zinnia. Plants of very easy culture, flowering very profusely through the whole summer and fall; producing

FOR THE SOUTHERN STATES. 109

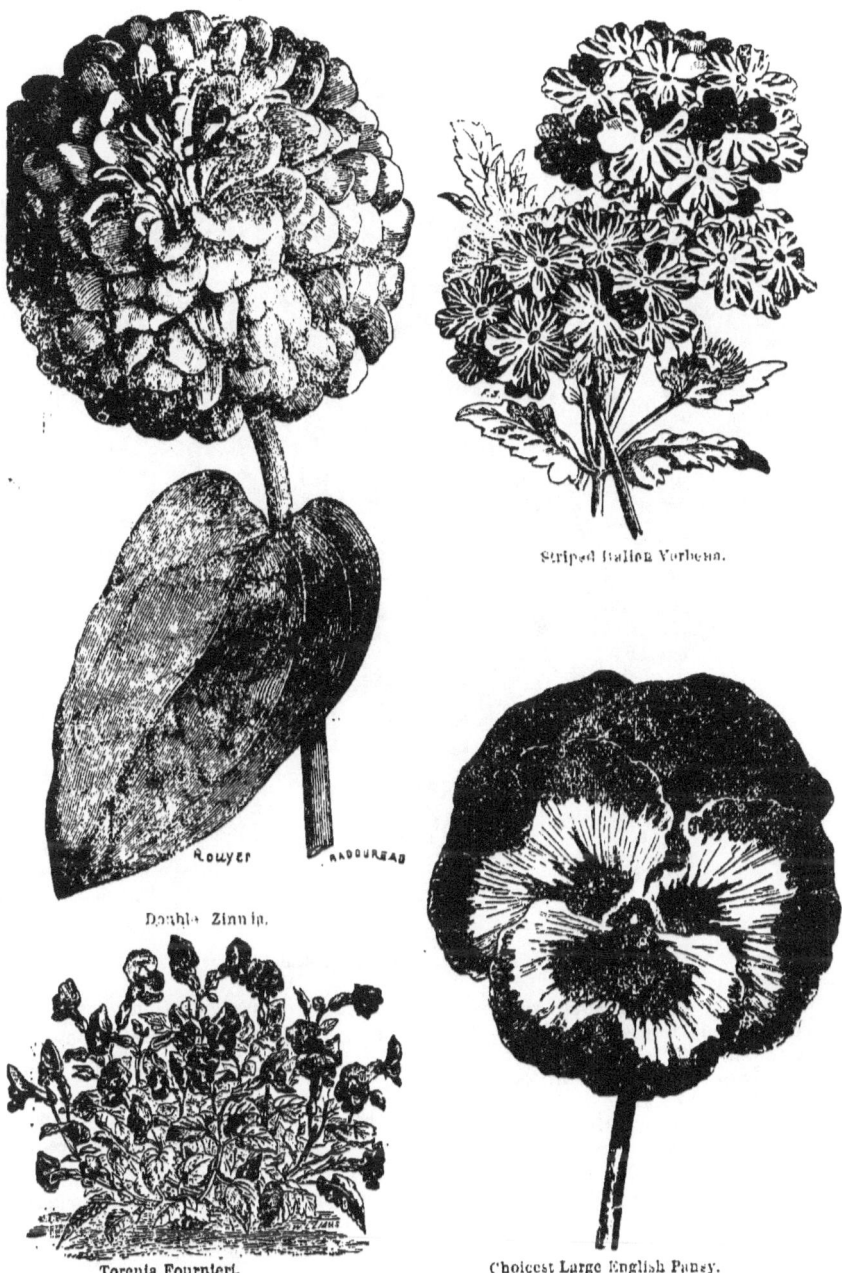

Striped Italian Verbena.

Rouyer   RADOUREAU

Double Zinnia.

Torenia Fournieri.

Choicest Large English Pansy.

Zinnia Elegans, Grandiflora Robusta Plenissima.

double flowers of all colors, almost as large as the flower of a Dahlia. Three feet high. February till August.

Zinnia elegans pumila fl. pl. Dwarf Double Mixed. A new dwarf section, especially desirable. The compact, bushy plants rarely grow over two feet high, and are covered with large, double Dahlia like flowers of great beauty.

Zinnia elegans, grandiflora robusta plenissima. A new variety recently introduced here from Germany. The plants of this new class of showy and attractive annuals are of very robust growth and produce very large and extremely double flowers; measuring from 4 to 5 inches in diameter. The seeds I offer for sale, come direct from the originator, and contain about eight different beautiful colors, mostly very bright.

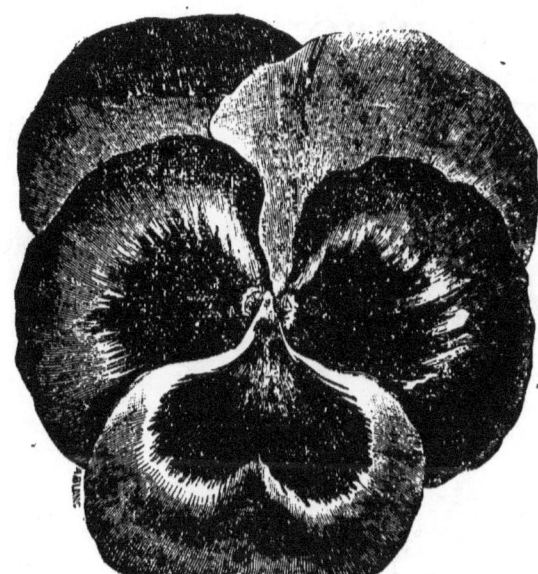

Large Trimardeau Pansy.

Double Portulaca.

Hybridized Verbena.

CLIMBING PLANTS.

Balloon Vine.

Climbing Cobæa.

Morning Glory.

Mixed Thunbergia.

Benincasa cerifera. Wax Gourd. A strong growing vine with long shaped dark crimson fruit, which looks very ornamental. It is used for preserves.

Cardiospermum. Balloon Vine. A quick-growing climber, the seeds of which are in a pod, shaped like a miniature balloon, therefore the name.

Cobæa Scandens. Climbing Cobæa. Large purple bell-shaped flowers. Should be sown in a hot-bed, and not kept too moist. Place the seed edgewise in the ground. Twenty feet high. January till April.

Convolvulus major. Morning Glory. Well known vine with various handsomely colored flowers, of easy culture. Grows almost anywhere. Ten feet high. February till July.

Curcurbita. Ornamental Gourd. Mixed varieties or Ornamental Gourds of different shapes and sizes. February till May.

Curcurbita lagenaria dulcis. Sweet Gourd. A strong growing vine of which the young fruits are used like Squash. February till April.

Dolichos Lablab. Hyacinth Beans. Free growing plant, with purple and white flowers. March till April.

Ipomæa Quamoclit rosea. Red Cypress Vine. Very beautiful, delicate foliage, of rapid growth, with scarlet flowers.

Hyacinth Bean.

Maurandia Barclayana.

Ipomæa Quamoclit alba. White Cypress Vine. The same as the red variety.

Ipomæa Bona Nox. Large Flowering Evening Glory. A vine of rapid growth, with beautiful blue and white flowers which open in the evening. Twenty feet high. February till June.

This is the Moon flower advertised in Northern catalogues as a novelty, notwithstanding the fact that it has been known here for the past century.

Lathyrus odoratus. Sweet Peas. Beautiful flowers of all colors, very showy. Good for cut flowers. Six feet high. December till April.

Maurandia Barclayana. Mixed Maurandia. A slender growing vine of rapid growth. Rose purple and white colors mixed. Ten feet high. February till April.

Mina Lobata. This novelty, which is supposed to have first originated in Mexico, is one of the most beautiful climbing vines for ornamenting the garden. It closely resembles in growth and its three-lobed foliage the several species of the family of Ipomæa; but the flowers are altogether different. The flowers appear on fork-like racemes bearing themselves upright or almost erect out of the dense and luxuriant foliage, and with their bright colors they present an extraordinary striking aspect. The buds are at first bright red, but change to orange yellow, and when in full bloom, to yellowish white. The most singular feature of this plant is, that it retains the racemes developed at first during the whole flowering season, the buds continuing to grow successively at the top of the racemes, while the lower flowers, after blooming for some time, fade, bearing thus continually clusters of flowers from the bottom up to the highest vine of the

Mina Lobata.

plant. The oldest racemes attain a length of 15 to 18 inches, and at the end of the time of blooming they have produced from 30 to 40 individual flowers on each raceme, of which 6 to 10 had been in full bloom at a time. This plant is a very rapid growing climber; within three months the vine attains a height of 18 to 20 feet. It does well on sunny situations, and cannot be surpassed for covering arbors, trellises, etc., on account of its rapid growth and great dimensions. I have flowered this beautiful climber, the past season, and can substantiate all what is stated above. It should be sown early, in order to get it to perfection.

Do not fail to give it a trial.

Price, per packet, 25c.

Mamordica Balsamina. Balsam Apple. A climbing plant of very rapid growth, producing cucumber-like fruits, with warts on them. They are believed to contain some medicinal virtues. They are put in jars with alcohol, and are used as a dressing for cuts, bruises, etc.

Luffa acutangula. Dish Rag Vine. A very rapid growing vine of the Gourd family. When the fruit is dry, the fibrous substance, which covers the seeds, can be used as a rag. February till April.

Sechium edule. Vegetable Pear or Mirliton. A rapid growing vine with grape-like leaves, of which the fruit is eaten; there are two varieties, white and green. It has only one seed, and the whole fruit has to be planted.

Tropæolum majus. Nasturtium. Trailing plants with elegant flowers of different shades, mostly yellow and crimson, which are produced in great abundance. Four feet high. February till April.

Thunbergia. Mixed Thunbergia. Very ornamental vines, with yellow bell-shaped flowers, with dark eye. Six feet high. February till May.

BULBOUS ROOTS.

Anemones. Double flowering. Planted and treated the same as the Ranunculus. They are of great varieties in color.

Double Dutch, 40 cts. per dozen.

Dahlias. Fine double-named varieties. Plants so well known for their brilliancy, diversity of colors and profuse flowering qualities, that they require no recommendation. They can be planted from February till May; they thrive best in rich loamy soil. They should be tied up to stakes, which ought to be driven into the ground before or when planting them. To have them flower late in the season they should be planted late in the spring, and the flower buds nipped off when they appear; treated in this way, they will produce perfect flowers during fall. Undivided roots, $3.00 per dozen.

The roots I offer are of the very best type, having taken special pains to discard varieties which did not flower well here.

Gladiolus. Hybrid Gladiolus. One of the best summer flowering bulbs; they have been greatly improved of late years, and almost every color has been produced; is tinged and blotched in all shades from delicate rose to dark vermillion. When planted at intervals during spring, they will flower at different times, but those that are planted earliest produce the finest flowers. The roots should be taken up in the fall.

Hybrids mixed, first choice, 10c. each; 75c. per dozen.

Hybrids, white ground, 1st choice, 10c each; 75c. per dozen.

Gloxinias. These are really bulbous green house plants, but they can be cultivated in pots and kept in a shady place in the garden, or window. They are very beautiful; color from white to dark violet and crimson. The leaves are velvety, and on some varieties very large. They should be planted early in spring; require sandy ground and a good deal of moisture during flowering time. French Hybrids, strong bulbs, $3.00 per dozen.

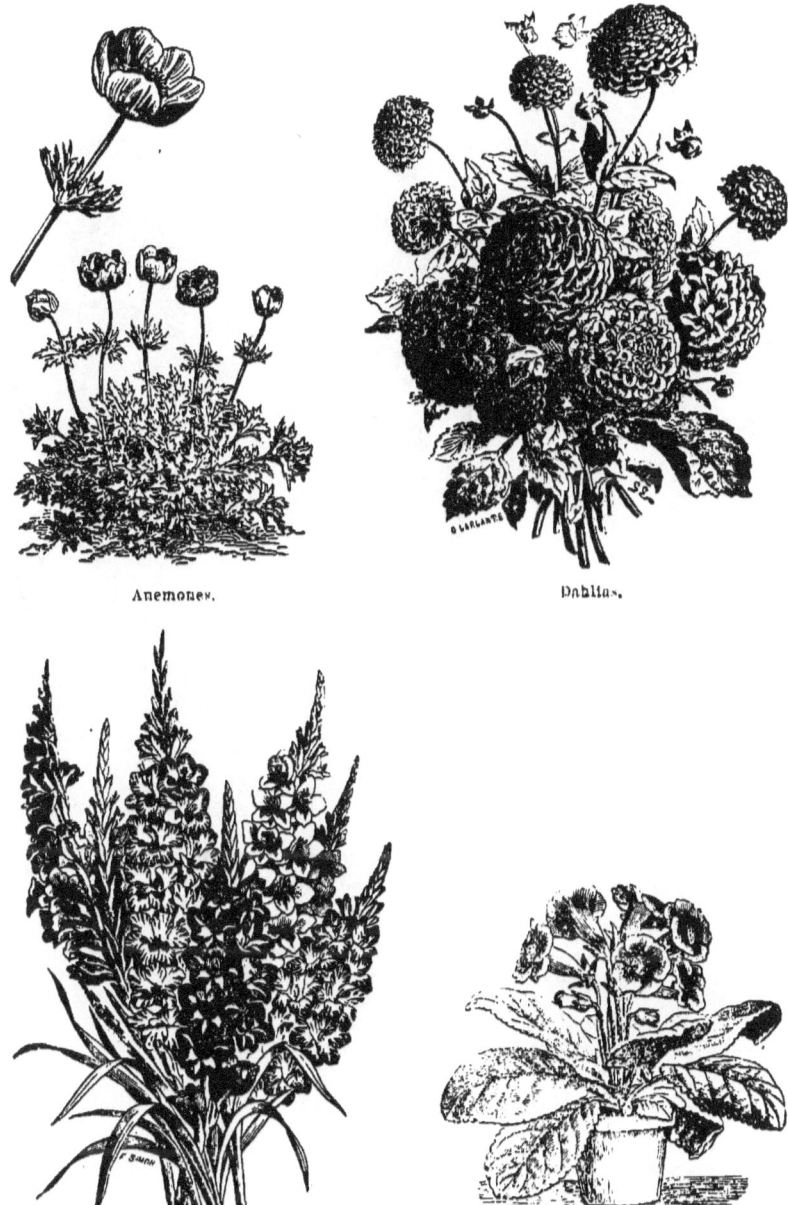

Anemones. Dahlias.

Hybrid Gladiolus. Gloxinias.

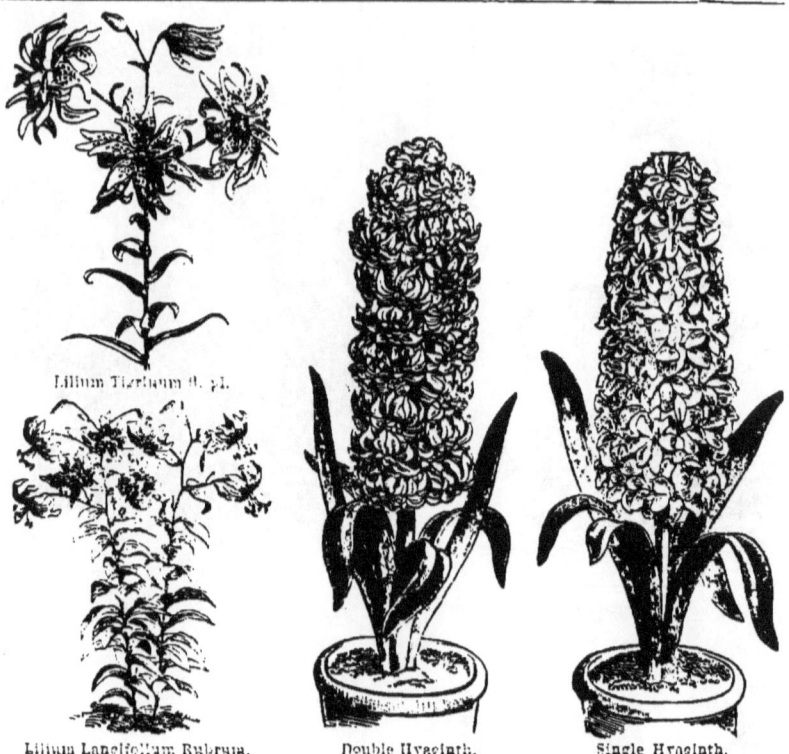

Lilium Tigrinum fl. pl.   Lilium Lancifolium Rubrum.   Double Hyacinth.   Single Hyacinth.

Hyacinths. (DUTCH.) Double and single. The Hyacinth is a beautiful flowering bulb, well suited for open ground or pot culture. They should be planted from October till February. If planted in pots it is well to keep in a cool, rather dark place, till they are well started, when they can be placed in the full light and sun. Double and single, 10 cents each; $1.00 per dozen.

Narcissus. Bulbs of the easiest culture, planted from November to January.

Double White, sweet scented. Yellow Mixed, Polyanthus Narcissus. White " " "
Price, 5c. each; 50c. per dozen.

Lilium tigrinum. Tiger Lily. A well known variety, very showy and of easy culture; 10 cents each.

Lilium tigrinum fl. pl. This is a new variety; it is perfectly double, and the petals are imbricated almost as regularly as a camellia flower. Novel and fine, 15 cents each.

JAPAN LILIES.

Lilium auratum. Golden Band Lily. This is a very handsome lily; the flowers are large and white, each petal having a yellow stripe. It is of easy culture. A loamy, dry soil suits it best, and planted one inch deep.

The past season I had occasion to see several of this noble lily in bloom, and it is really fine; half a dozen flowers opening at the same time and measuring from six to nine inches across. It is very fragrant. I expect some fine bulbs, same as I had last year, imported direct from their native country.

Flowering bulbs, 25c. each.

Lilium lancifolium album. Pure white, Japan Lily, 30 cents each.

Lilium lancifolium rubrum. White and red spotted, 15 cents each.

Lilium lancifolium roseum. Rose spotted, 15c. each.

These Japan Lilies are very beautiful and fragrant. Should be planted from October till January. Perfectly suited to this climate.

Pæonia sinensis. Chinese or herbaceous Pæonia. Herbaceous plants of different colors and great beauty; they should be planted during fall in a shady situation, as they flower early in spring. If planted too late they will not flower perfectly; 25c. each.

Ranunculus. Double Flowering. The roots can be planted during fall

Double Tulip.

Lilium auratum.

Single Tulip.

Tuberoses, double flowering.

Ranunculus.

Scilla peruviana.

and winter, either in the open ground or in pots. The French varieties are more robust than the Persian, and the flowers are larger. The ground should be rather dry, and if planted in the open ground, it will be well to have the spot a little higher than the bed or border.

French Ranunculus....25c. per dozen.

Scilla peruviana. These are green-house bulbs at the North, but here they are hardy, and do well in the open ground. There are two varieties —the blue and white. They throw up a shoot, on the end of which the flowers appear, forming a truss. Plant from October till January. 30 cents each.

Tulips. Double and single Tulips thrive better in a more Northern latitude than this, but some years they flower well here, and as they are cheap, a few flowering bulbs will pay the small amount they cost. They should not be planted later than December, and placed very shallow in the ground; not more than one-third of the bulb should be covered. When near flowering they require a good deal of moisture. Single and double, 50 cents per dozen.

Tuberoses. Double Flowering. They are ornamental for the garden, and very valuable for making bouquets, on account of their pure white color and great fragrance. Plant during the spring months. Strong bulbs, 10 cents each; 75 cents per dozen.

See what our customers say about F<small>ROTSCHER</small>'s S<small>EEDS FOR THE</small> S<small>OUTH</small>.

Moss Point, Miss., July 17, 1888.

The seeds were splendid, *Dahlias* and Tube Roses are beautiful. The madam believes in *Frotscher's* seeds every time.

L. M. Hand.

Cofield P. O., La., June 5, 1888.

Having dealt with you for the last five years, I must say that I have always been very well pleased with your seed, and have found you to be very prompt in filling my orders.

Mrs. F. M. Bertheaud.

Devall P. O., La., July 25, 1888.

I have given your seeds a fair trial, and have found them to be invaluable.

James R. Devall.

THE NEW YORK SEED DRILL.
MATTHEWS' PATENT.

I take pleasure in calling your attention to a perfect Seed Drill. This Drill was invented and perfected by the father of the seed-drill business—Mr. E. G. Matthews. It has been his aim for *years* to make a perfect drill and do *away* with the *objections found* in all others, and in the New York he has accomplished it. Its advantages over other drills are as follows:

1. Marker-bar under the frame, held by clamps, easy to adjust to any width by simply loosening thumb nuts.
2. Adjustable plow, which opens a wide furrow, and can be set to sow at any depth.
3. Open seed conductor to show seed dropping.
4. *Bars in seed conductor*, for scattering seed in wide furrows, prevents disturbing strong plants when thinning out—an important feature.
5. Ridged roller.
6. Dial plate in full sight of operator, and made of patent combination white metal which prevents rust.
7. Dial plate set on fulcrum, and hence holds close up, preventing seed from spilling.
8. It has a large seed-box with hinged cover.
9. Machine will stand up alone when not in use, not liable to tip over.

It is the SIMPLEST, MOST COMPACT and EASIEST DRILL TO HANDLE, being only 32 inches long.

It covers the seed better and runs very easy.

Packed in crates for shipping. Weigh about 45 pounds. Price, $10.00.

MATTHEWS' HAND CULTIVATOR.

The MATTHEWS' HAND CULTIVATOR is one of the best implements in use for weeding between row crops, and for flat cultivation generally, and is an indispensible companion to the seed drill.

It is thoroughly constructed throughout, very durable; easy to operate. *A boy can do as much with it as six men with hoes.* It spreads from 6 to 14 inches.

Price, $5.00, boxed.

and will cut all the ground covered, even when spread to its greatest extent. Its teeth are of a new and improved pattern and thoroughly pulverize and mellow the soil. The depth of cultivating may be accurately gauged by raising or lowering the wheels, which is quickly done by the use of a thumb screw.

THE CHAUTAUQUA CORN AND SEED PLANTER.

Patented April 4, 1882.

Unequalled in Simplicity, Durability and Efficiency.

THE BEST IS THE CHEAPEST. PERFECTLY SIMPLE. SIMPLY PERFECT.

DIRECTIONS.

To set the seed cup.—Loosen the set-screw and draw out the inside or narrow gauge far enough to drop the desired number of seeds. Then tighten the screw. For ordinary planting, only the narrow gauge should be moved. In putting in phosphate, or a large quantity of seed, both the narrow and wide gauges should be drawn out together. By taking out the screws, the gauges may be drawn entirely out.

In experienced or careful hands the machine will plant perfectly in any kind or condition of soil, mellow or soddy, dry or wet.

To operate the planter.—Place the blades in the ground to the desired depth, in advance of you, having the "step" to the front, as in the cut, without its touching the ground. Then pressing down forward on the handle, walk forward. The step will press on the ground and then the blades will be opened, the seed deposited in the ground and a charge taken for the next hill. After walking past the planter, still pressing on the handle, lift it from the ground to place for the next hill; as this is done the charge of seed will be HEARD rattling down upon the steel blades, and the operator will know the seed is ready for the next hill. Use the planter as you would a cane, or as much so as possible. *The blades must always enter the ground closed, and come out open.*

Its Efficiency. — We claim that the "Chautauqua" is not equalled as a dropper and planter. By actual trial in the field with a number of good planters, it has been shown that our machine will cover the seed in different soils and at different depths, shallow or deep, better than any other planter. *Our new improved seed slide*, having double gauges for adjusting the seed cup, enables the planter to *drop accurately small or large seed* in the quantity desired.

Price, $2 25.

GARDEN IMPLEMENTS.

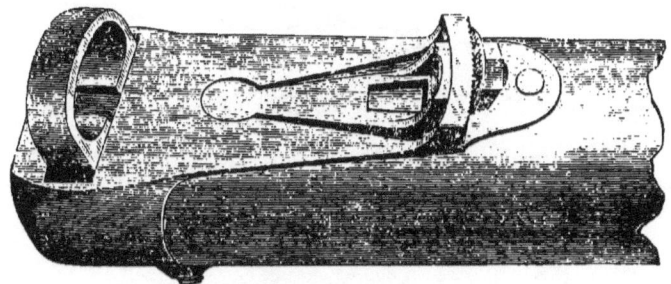

Loop Fastener, swing socket Scythe Snath.

Ladies' Set, Floral Tools. No. 5.

Boys' Favorite Set.

Weeding Hoe and Rake Combined.

O. G. Hand Pruning Shear.

Lang's Weeder.

Dutch, or Scuffle Hoe.

French Perfection Shear.

Saynor's Pruning Knife, No. 192.

Saynor's Pruning Knife, No. 194.

122 RICHARD FROTSCHER'S ALMANAC AND GARDEN MANUAL

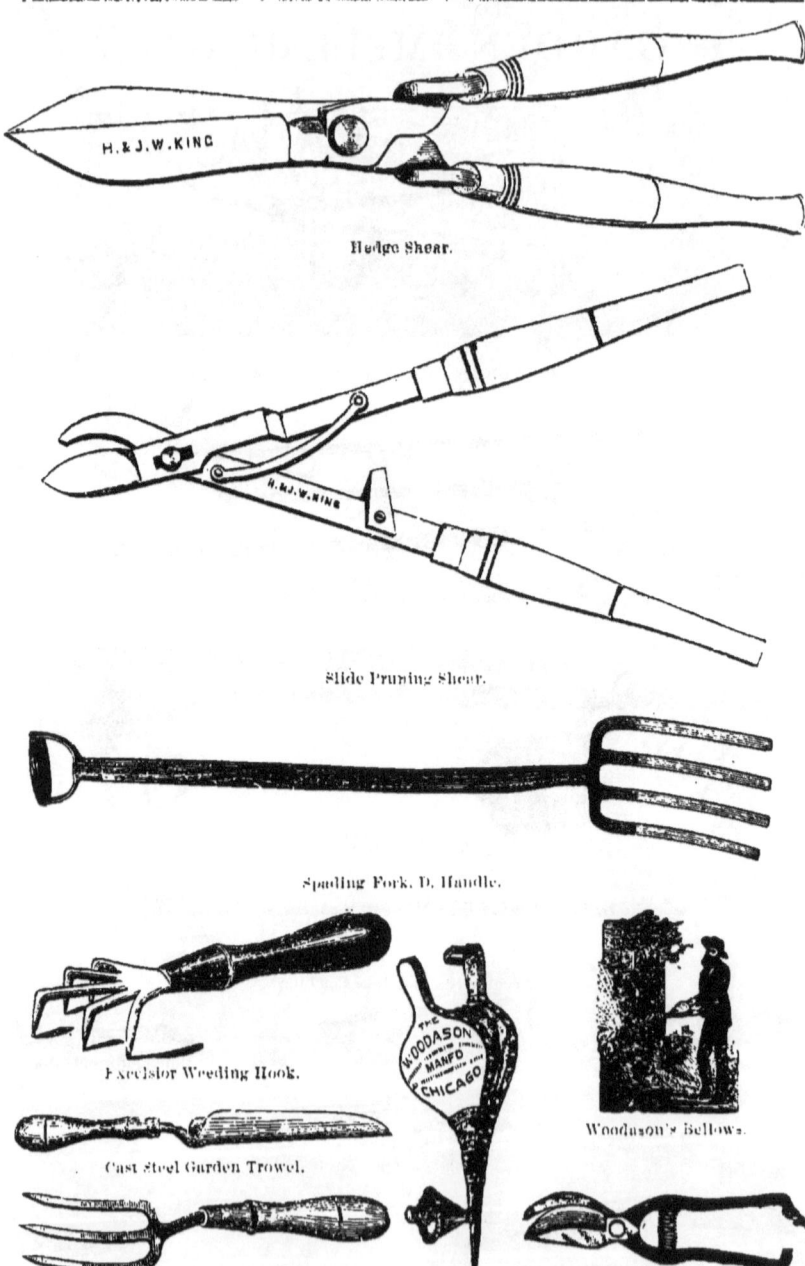

Hedge Shear.

Slide Pruning Shear.

Spading Fork, D. Handle.

Excelsior Weeding Hook.

Cast Steel Garden Trowel.

Strawberry or Transplanting Fork.

Woodason's Bellows.

Weiss' Hand Pruning Shear.

PRICE-LIST OF GARDEN IMPLEMENTS.

DEAKIN'S IMPROVED BRASS GARDEN SYRINGES.
(AMERICAN.)

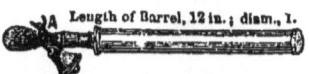

No. A.—Length of barrel, 12 inches; diameter, 1 inch, with one stream and spray rose. Price, $2.25.

No. 2. Ladies' Syringe; length of barrel, 14½ inches; diameter 1 3/8 inches; with one stream and two spray roses. The two roses, when not in use, are screwed on the sides of the barrel, as shown in cut. Price, $4 25.

No. 3.—Length of barrel, 18 inches; diameter, 1½ inches. Best Plate Valve Syringe, large size, with one stream, two spray roses and side pieces on barrel. Price, $6 50.

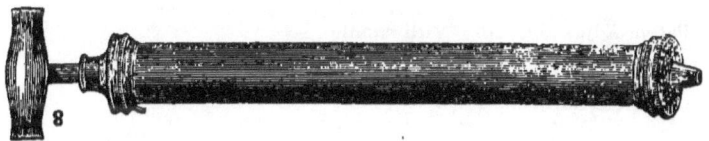

No. 8.—Length of barrel, 18 inches; diameter, 1¾ inches. Best Conical Valve Syringe, extra large diameter and length of barrel, with cross handle and one spray rose. Price, $8 00.

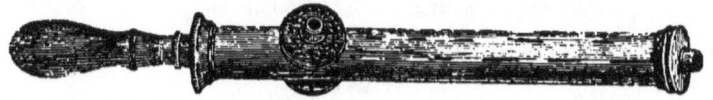

No. 11.—(Second Quality.) Length of barrel, 18 inches; diameter, 1½ inches. Open Rose Syringe, full size. Two spray roses and one stream. Slide attachments. Price, $4 25.

Lewis' Brass Syringe, spray only, 1¾ by 20 inches,... 1 75

The Deakin's Syringes are known to be the best manufactured in America, and are far superior to the imported.

HOES.

W. A. Lyndon's Louisiana, No. 00—Field	$0 80
" " No. 0— "	0 85
" " No. 1— "	0 90
" " No. 2— "	1 00
" " No. 3— "	1 10
W. A. Lyndon's Louisiana, No. 0—Toy	0 75
" " No. 1— "	0 75
" " No. 2— "	0 80
" Broad, Field No. 000	0 40
" " " No. 00	0 45
" " " No. 0	0 50
" " " No. 1	0 55
C. A. Maynard's No. 2	0 55
" No. 4	0 65
Briggs & Witte's Palmetto No. 2	0 40
" " No. 3	0 45
Sandusky Tool Co's Planter's No. 2	0 30
" " " No. 6	0 40
" " No. 3/0	0 25
" " No. 4	0 35
Two Pronged German Forged Steel	0 60
Iron City Grub No. 1	0 50
Champion with handle	0 75
Enterprise Socket with handle	0 40
Two Pronged Weeding, with handle ...40c. and	0 50
Four " " " "	0 50
Dutch or Scuffle, with handle	0 60
Solid Shank Cotton, with handle, No. 00	0 50
" " Planter's " No. 000	0 45
" " " " No. 2	0 60
Tillia Patent Adjustable, No. 1 with handle	0 55
" " " No. 2 "	0 65
" " " No. 4 "	0 75
German Pattern Garden, No. 7/0 "	0 35
" " " No. 5 0 "	0 40
" " No. 3/0 with handle	0 40
" " No. 1/0 " "	0 45
" " No. 2 " "	0 50
" " No. 4 " "	0 60
" " Grub or Sprouting, No. 7/0 with handle	0 45
" " " " No. 5 0 " "	0 50
" " Two Prong Grape with handle	0 75

RAKES.

Enterprise. Cast Steel, 6 teeth	$0 30
Geneva Tool Co's, Cast Steel, 10 teeth, (Braced)	0 45
" " " " " 12 " "	0 50
" " " " " 14 " "	0 60
" " " " " 16 " "	0 70
Challenge Rakes, Malleable Iron, 10 teeth	0 30
" " " " 12 "	0 40
" " " " 14 "	0 45
" " " " 16 "	0 50

Wooden Head, (12 Iron teeth)	$0 50
Wooden Hay Rakes.	25c and 0 30
English Wrought-Iron Rakes (10 teeth) without handle	0 50
" " " (12 " " "	0 60
" " " (14 " " "	0 70

SPADES.

Ames' Long Handled (extra heavy)	1 10
Ames' " " Bright	0 90
Ames' Bright, D. Handle	0 90
Rowlands' Long Handled,	0 75
Johnson's " " Bright	0 70
French Steel, Bright, without handles	$1 10 to 1 15

SHOVELS.

Rowland's Short Handled, (square)	0 75
Ames' Bright Long Handled, (round point)	0 90
Rowland's Long Handled, (round point)	0 75
Rowland's " " (square)	0 75

SCYTHE SNATHS.

Handles for French Scythe Blades (with Ring and Wedge)	0 90
No. 0, Plate Heel, American " " "	0 65
No. 00, Patent Loop Fastener	0 75

SICKLES.

English (welded), No. 2	0 40
" " No. 3	0 45
Scotch (riveted back,) No. 0	0 50
" " No. 1	0 60
English " No. 2	0 50
" " No. 3	0 60
" " No. 4	0 75
French Sickles, No. 1	0 40
" " No. 2	0 45

SHEARS.

Hedge Shears, 8 inches	1 75
" " 10 "	2 00
Pruning Shears No. 1, Wiss. A	1 75
" " No. 2, "	1 65
" " No. 3, "	1 50
" " No. 4, "	1 40
Pruning Shears No. 2, Wiss. B	1 65
" " No. 3, "	1 50
" " No. 109, " Steel Springs, 9 in.	2 00
" " No. 110, " " " 10 "	2 25
" " No. 111, " " " 11 "	2 50
" " No. 100, Lee's Cast Steel, 9 "	1 25
" " No. 100, " " " 10 "	1 50
" " American Sheeptoe	0 75
" " O. G. No. 2, Saynor, Cooke & Ridal	1 50
" " No. 655, " " " 7 in.	1 65
" " No. 655, " " " 8 "	1 80

Pruning Shears, French Perfection No. 1 .... $2 75
" " " " No. 2 .... 2 50
" " " " No. 3 .... 2 25
" " Extra Heavy French, (Pat. Brass Spring.)........ 3 00
Slide Pruning Shear, No. 1 .... 2 50
" " " No. 2 ..... 3 00
" " " No. 3 .... 3 50
" " " No. 4 .... 4 00

KNIVES.
H. & J. W. King's Pruning .... from 60c to 1 25
Saynor & Cook's .... from 75c to 1 60
Saynor & Cook's Budding .... $1 00 and 1 25
Aaron Burkinshaw's Pruning and Budding ...... from 40c to 0 80
Geo. Wostenholme's Pruning I. X. L 0 75

FORKS.
Geneva Spading, Long Handled 0 75
" " " " (strapped) 0 80
Spading Short Handled (strapped) .... 75c, 1.00 and 1 25
Manure Improved Ferrule Long Handled, 6 tine (strapped)...... 1 30
" Enterprise Long Handled, 4 tine (strapped) 0 70
" Premium " " 4 tine " 0 70
" Geneva " " 4 tine " 0 70
" " " " 5 tine " 0 90

POTATO HOOKS.
Long Handled, 6 tine....... 60c and 0 65
" " 4 tine (flat)...... 40c and 0 50
" " 4 tine (round) 0 50
" " 4 tine, Extra Heavy........ 0 70

SCYTHES.
French, First Quality (polished), 22 inches........ 0 75
" " " " 24 " 0 85
" " " " 26 " 1 00
" " " " 28 " 1 10
" Second Quality (blue) 22 " 0 65
" " " 24 " 0 75
" " " 26 " 0 85
" " " 28 " 1 00
American Grass 0 75
Blood's Champion Grass.... .... 0 75
" " Bramble, 20 to 26 inches 0 75

The French Scythe Blades are imported by me, and are of the best quality; none better can be had.

FLORAL TOOLS.
The Boy's Favorite—Hoe, Spade and Rake......... 2 00
No. 5.—4 pieces, Hoe, Rake, Spade and Fork (Ladies' Set) 1 00

PRUNING SAWS.
Diston's 12 inch No. 7 .... 0 90
" Compass 12 inch 0 50
" Crescent 12 " 0 75
" Duplex 16 " 1 00
Avery's Duplex 18 " 1 00
Brown's 18 inch 0 75

WOODASON'S BELLOWS.

Double Cone (for insect powder)		$4 00
Single " "		1 00
Atomizer (for liquid and powder)		2 00
Pure Pyrethrum Powder for above bellows	per box	0 50

MISCELLANEOUS.

Excelsior Weeding Hooks		0 25
American Transplanting Trowels	10c to	0 20
English " " 7 inch		0 50
Diston's Transplanting Trowels, (solid shank) 6 inch		0 45
Enterprise " "		0 20
Transplanting Forks, (Steel)		0 35
" " (Malleable Iron)	20c and	0 25
English Bill or Briar Hooks		1 25
Lang's Hand Weeder		0 25
Patent Adjustable Tool Handle, with 4 pieces		0 75
Toy Spades		0 40
Toy Shovels		0 50
Dutch or Scuffle Hoes	45c and	0 50
Western Files, 12 inch (flat)		0 35
Fork Handles		0 20
Hoe Handles	15c and	0 20
Rake Handles		0 15
Spade and Shovel Handles		0 25
Trowbridge's Grafting Wax	per lb. 40c; per ¼ lb.	0 15
Scotch Whetstones		0 20
American Indian Pond Whetstone		0 10
Darby Creek Whetstone		0 10
French Whetstone		0 15
Hammer and Anvil for beating French Scythes		1 50
Raffia, (for tying)	per lb.,	0 40

WATERING POTS.

6 Quarts, Japanned	0 40
8 " "	0 50
10 " "	0 65
12 " "	0 75
16 " "	0 90
Extra Heavy (hand made) No. 1, 20 Quarts	2 00
" " " No. 2, 16 "	1 75
" " " No. 3, 14 "	1 50
" " " No. 4, 10 "	1 25
" " " No. 5, 8 "	1 00

The latter are made of the best material, and have very fine rose heads; they are made by a mechanic who has been furnishing the vegetable gardeners for years with these pots, and has improved upon them until they are perfect for the purpose.

Having received many enquiries on the culture of Alfalfa, I reprint the following letter, written by E. M. Hudson. Esq., a close observer on the subject, to give information thereon:

VILLA FRIEDHEIM,
Mobile County, Ala., September 7th, 1878

Mr. R. FROTSCHER, New Orleans, La.

Dear Sir:—Your letter of the 3d inst. has just reached me, and I cheerfully comply with your request to give you the results of my experiments with *Lucerne or Alfalfa*, and my opinion of it as a forage plant for the South.

I preface my statement with the observation that my experiments have been conducted on a naturally poor, piney woods soil (which would be classed as a sandy soil), varying in depth from six inches to one foot. But I have good red clay sub-soil, which enables the soil to retain the fertilizers applied to it, thus rendering it susceptible of permanent enriching.

Three years since, when my attention was first directed to Alfalfa, I sought the advice of the editor of the *Journal of Progress*, Professor Stelle, who informed me that, after attempting for several years to cultivate it, he had desisted. He stated that the plant, at Citronelle, in this county, died out every summer, not being able to withstand the hot suns of our climate. Discouraged but not dismayed, I determined to test the matter on a small scale at first. Having procured some seeds in March, 1876, I planted them on a border in my garden, and gave neither manure nor work that season. The early summer here that year was very dry; there was no rain whatever from the first of June to the 23d of July, and from the 2d of August to the 15th of November not a drop of rain fell on my place. Yet, during all this time, my Alfalfa remained fresh, bloomed, and was cut two or three times. On the 1st of November I dug some of it to examine the habit of root-growth, and to my astonishment found it necessary to go 22 inches below the surface to reach anything like the end of the top roots. At once it was apparent that the plant was, by its very habit of growth, adapted to hot and dry climates. It is indeed a "child of the sun."

Encouraged by this experiment, in which I purposely refrained from giving the Alfalfa any care beyond cutting it occasionally, last year I proceeded on a larger scale, planting both spring and fall, as I have done again this year, to ascertain the best season for putting in the seed. My experience teaches that there is no preference to be given to spring sowings over those of autumn, *provided* only, there be enough moisture in the soil to make the seed germinate, which they do more quickly and more surely than the best turnips. Two winters have proved to me that the Alfalfa remains green throughout the winter in this latitude, 25 miles North of Mobile, and at an altitude of 400 feet above tide-water. Therefore I should prefer fall sowing which will give the first cutting from the first of March to the 1st of April following. This season my first cutting was made on the 1st of April; and I have cut it since regularly every four or six weeks, according to the weather, to cure for hay. Meanwhile a portion has been cut almost daily for feeding green, or soiling. Used in the latter way (*for under no circumstances* must it ever be pastured), I am able to give my stock fresh, green food, fully four weeks before the native wild grasses commence to put out. I deem it best to cut the day before, what is fed green, in order to let it become thoroughly wilted before using. After a large number of experiments with horses, mules, cattle and swine, I can aver that in no instance, from March to November, have I found a case when any of these animals would not give the preference to Alfalfa over every kind of grass (also soiled) known in this region. And, while Alfalfa makes a sweet and nutritious hay eagerly eaten by all kinds of stock, it is as a forage plant for soiling, which is available for at least nine months in the year, that I esteem it so highly. The hay is easily cured, if that which is cut in the forenoon is thrown into small cocks at noon, then spread out after the dew is off next morning, sunned for an hour, and at once hauled into the barn. By this method the leaves do not fall off, which is sure to be the case, if the Alfalfa is exposed to a day or two of hot sunshine.

It has been my habit to precede the Alfalfa with a clean crop - usually Rutabagas, after which I sow clay peas, to be turned in about the last of July. About the middle of September or later I have the land plowed, the turn-plow being followed by a deep sub-soil-plow or scooter. After this the land is fertilized and harrowed until it is thoroughly pulverized and all lumps broken up. The fertilizers employed by me are 500 lbs. fine bone-dust (phosphate of lime) and 1000 lbs. cotton seed hull ashes per acre. These ashes are very rich in potash and phosphates, containing nearly 45 per cent of the phosphate of lime — the two articles best adapted to the wants of this plant. I sow all my Alfalfa with the Matthews' Seed Drill, in rows 10 inches apart. Broad-cast would be preferable, if the land was perfectly free from grass and weeds; but it takes several years of clean culture to put the land in this condition, sowing in drill is practically the best. No seed sower known to me can be compared with the Matthews' Seed Drill. Its work is evenly and regularly done, and with a rapidity that is astonishing; for it opens the drill to any desired depth, drops the seed, covers and rolls them, and marks the line for the next drill at one operation. It is simple and durable in its structure, and is the greatest labor-saving machine of its kind ever devised for hand-work.

When my Alfalfa is about three inches high, I work it with the Matthews' Hand Cultivator. First, the front tooth of the cultivator is taken out, by which means the row is straddled and all the grass cut out close to the plant; then the front tooth being replaced, the cultivator is passed between the rows, completely cleaning the middles of all foul growth. As often as required to keep down grass, until the Alfalfa is large enough to cut, the Matthews' Hand Cultivator is passed between the rows.

Alfalfa requires three years to reach perfection, but even the first year the yield is larger than most forage plants, and after the second it is enormous. The land must, however, be made rich at first; a top-dressing every three years is all that will thereafter be required. The seed must be very lightly covered, and should be rolled, or brushed in, if not sowed with a Matthews' Seed Sower. Whenever the plant is in bloom it must be cut; for, if the seed be left to mature, the stems become hard and woody. Also whenever it turns yellow, no matter at what age, it must be cut or mowed; for the yellow color shows the presence of some disease, or the work of some small insect, both of which seems to be remedied by mowing promptly. My experience leads me to the conclusion that fully five tons of cured hay per acre may be counted on if proper attention be given to deep plowing, subsoiling, fertilizing and cleanliness of the soil. These things are indispensable, and without them no one need attempt to cultivate Alfalfa.

In conclusion, I will remark that I have tried the Lucerne seed imported by you from France, side by side with the Alfalfa seed sent me by Trumbull & Co., of San Francisco, and I cannot see the slightest difference in appearance, character, quantity or quality of yield, or hardiness. They are identical; both have germinated equally well, that is to say, perfectly.

In closing, I cannot do better than refer you to the little treatise of Mr. C. W. Howard, entitled: "A Manual of the Grasses and Forage Plants at the South." Mr. Howard, among the very first to cultivate Lucerne in the South, gives it the preference over all other forage plants whatever. My experience confirms all that Mr. Howard claims for it. Certainly, a plant that lasts a generation is worthy of the bestowal of some time, patience and money to realize what a treasure they can secure for themselves. I confidently believe that in years from this date the Alfalfa will be generally cultivated throughout the entire South.

I am, respectfully yours,
E. M. HUDSON,
Counsellor at Law,
20 Carondelet Street, New Orleans.

JERUSALEM ARTICHOKE.

This tuber is well known, and has been described by me in my former Almanacs. It is used for the table, also for stock feed. It does best in a rich loam; should be planted and cultivated like potatoes. They yield very heavy.

Price, per bushel, $2.50—per gall., 35 cents.

DESCRIPTIVE LIST
— OF —
SOME VARIETIES OF THE SORGHUM FAMILY.

As a forage plant for early cutting, to be fed to stock, I do not think that anything is equal to the Amber Sorghum, such as I have been selling for years, imported from Kansas. After several cuttings, the branching varieties of Sorghum, also called Millo Maize, may be preferable, but more so for seed than forage.—The Teosinte will give more fodder than any of the Sorghums. Some varieties not before described and rather new here are the following:

Yellow Millow Maize, or Yellow Branching Dhouro, grows same as the White Branching kind. The only difference exists in the size of the seed, which is twice the size of the white variety.—It is said to be somewhat earlier, seeds planted in April will ripen seed in July.—On account of its branching habit this grain should be planted in four or five foot rows, and two to three feet in the drill, according to the strength of the land, two plants in a hill. The cultivation is like corn.

Price, 15c. per lb; postage extra, 8c. per lb. by mail—10 lbs. $1.00 by Express or Steamer.

KAFFIR CORN.

This grain was distributed in small quantities from the Georgia State Department of Agriculture in 1878, and in the hands of Dr. J. H. Watkins, of Palmetto, Campbell County, Ga., it has been preserved and fully developed, and was first brought to public notice through him in 1885. The seed offered for sale is from his own growing, the genuine and pure stock; crop of 1888.

It is a variety of Sorghum, non Saccharine, and distinctly differing in habit of growth and other characteristics from all others of that class. The plant is low, stocks perfectly erect, the foliage is wide, alternating closely on either side of the stalks.

It does not stool from the root, but branches from the top joints, producing from two to four heads of grain from each stalk. The heads are long, narrow and perfectly erect, well filled with white grain, which at maturity is slightly flecked with red or reddish brown spots. Weight, 60 lbs. per bushel.

The average height of growth on good strong land, 5½ to 6 feet; on thin land, 4½ to 5 feet. The stalk is stout, never blown about by winds, never tangles, and is always manageable, easily handled. A boy can gather the grain heads or the fodder. The seed heads grow from 10 to 12 inches in length, and product of grain on good land easily reaches 50 to 60 bushels per acre.

It has the quality common to many Sorghums of resisting drought. If the growth is checked by want of moisture, the plant waits for rain, and then at once resumes its processes, and in the most disastrous seasons has not failed so far to make its crop. On very thin and worn lands, it yields paying crops of grain and forage, even in dry seasons in which corn has utterly failed, on the same lands.

The whole stalk, as well as the blades, cures into excellent fodder, and in all stages of its growth is available for green feed, cattle, mules and horses being equally fond of it, and its quality not surpassed by any other known variety. If cut down to the ground, two or more shoots spring from the root, and the growth is thus maintained until checked by frost.

The Kaffir Corn may be planted in the latter part of March, or early in April. It bears earlier planting than other Millets or Sorghums. It should be put in rows not over three feet apart, even on best land, and it bears thicker planting than any other variety of Sorghum; should be massed in the drill on good land, for either grain or forage purposes, and also on thin land, if forage mainly is desired. No plant can equal it for quality and quantity of grain and forage on thin lands. Use 3 to 5 lbs. of seed per acre. Price of seed, 15c. per lb., postage extra, 8c. per lb. by mail; lots of 10 lbs. for $1.00.

TEOSINTE.

(Reana luxurians.)

This is a forage plant from Central America. It resembles Indian Corn in aspect and vegetation, but produces a great number of shoots 3 to 4 yards high; it is perennial, but only in such situations where the thermometer does not fall below freezing point. Cultivated as an annual, it will yield a most abundant crop of excellent green fodder.

Considering the Teosinte a superior forage plant, the following extract of a letter from Mr. Chas. Debremond of Thibodeaux, La., will give additional light on the cultivation of same.—In describing his experience with Teosinte, he advises planting the seed in February, so as to have the plants up early in March, as it takes some 14 or 20 days for the seed to germinate. He prefers planting in rows, as giving a heavier crop than when in hills; and as its growth during the first month is very slow, he gives it a good hoeing for its first cultivation, using only the plough thereafter.

He also advises cutting the stalks for green food when about 4 feet high, and specially recommends cutting them close to the ground, as tending to make a much heavier second growth than when cut higher. His horses, mules and cattle eat the stalks with great avidity, leaving no part unconsumed, and prefer it much to green Indian Corn or Sorghum.

Price, $1.75 per lb.; 50c. per ¼ lb.; 20c. per oz. Postage prepaid.

LIST OF A FEW VARIETIES OF FRUIT TREES,
SUITABLE FOR THE SOUTHERN STATES.

LE CONTE PEAR.

This new Southern pear is as vigorous in growth as the China Sand, and is an enormous bearer. The fruit is large, pale yellow, juicy melting, and of good quality, doing better in the South than elsewhere. It bears transportation well, and commands the highest prices at the North. Time of ripening begins about the middle of July. So far, this pear has never been known to blight. It promises to be the pear for the South.

Rooted one year old trees, 3 to 6 feet 20 cts. each; $2.00 per dozen. 4—8 feet, 25 cts. each; $2.50 per dozen.

KIEFFER'S HYBRID PEAR.

A variety from Philadelphia; a hybrid between the China Sand and Bartlett, both of which it resembles in wood and foliage. It has the vigor and productiveness of its Chinese parents. Fruit large and handsome; bright yellow and red cheek; flesh tender, juicy and well flavored. It comes into bearing at an early age. Ripens end of September, or beginning of October.

Two year old trees, well branched, 30c. each; $3.00 per doz.; one year, 20c. each; $2.00 per dozen.

BARTLETT PEAR.

This well-known variety, one of the finest pears in cultivation, has been successfully cultivated here; but occasionally it has blighted. Since the introduction of the LeConte, trials have been made with success, that is by grafting this, and other fine varieties, upon the LeConte;—by so doing, the trees are imparted with the vigor of the latter, growing stronger, and making finer and healthier trees. I have a limited number of trees, grafted on the LeConte Stock, for sale.

One year old trees, 3 -4 feet, 25 cts. each; $2.50 per dozen.

Two years old, well branched, 5—6 feet high, 35c. each; $3.50 per dozen.

DUCHESS D'ANGOULEME PEAR.

Another popular variety which does well in this section.—On LeConte Stock. Two years old, well branched, 30c. each; $3.00 per dozen.

HOWELL PEAR.

One of the best for here. Tree is an upright free grower; it is an early and profuse bearer.

Two years old, on LeConte Stock, 30c. each; $3.00 per dozen.

CLAPP'S FAVORITE PEAR.

A large new pear, resembling the Bartlett; but does not possess its musky flavor. Fine texture; juicy, with a rich, delicate, vinous flavor. It is very productive. On LeConte Stock.

Two years old, 30c. each; $3.00 per dozen.

JEFFERSON PEAR.

Another blight proof pear, very distinct in habit and growth from other varieties under cultivation. Cannot be stated yet under what particular type or species it should be classed.

It ripens in Central Mississippi from the 1st—10th of June, is in the market with the earliest peaches, and brings the highest prices. It is above medium size, color bright yellow, with a bright, deep crimson cheek. It is ripe and marketed before LeConte is ready to ship. It is poor in flavor.

Price, one year old trees, 5–6 feet, 30c. each; $3.00 per dozen.

WILD GOOSE PLUM.

A native variety from Tennessee, where it is highly esteemed for market. It is a strong grower; the fruit is large and of good quality.

Price, 25c. each; $2.50 per dozen.

MARIANNA PLUM.

A new plum from Texas, supposed accidental seeding of the Wild Goose. It is a rapid grower. Grows from cuttings; it never throws up any suckers or sprouts. Fruit as large, good and handsome as the Wild Goose; one to two weeks earlier, hangs on better, ships well; ripens and colors beautifully, if picked a few days previously. It is the best of the Chickasaw type.

Price, 5–6 feet high, 30c. each; $3.00 per dozen.

KELSEY'S JAPAN PLUM.

The *Prunus Domestica*, or European varieties, have proven worthless in the South generally. The above will take their place promising good results, being of Asiatic origin. The Kelsey Plum is from two to two and a half inches in diameter, heart-shaped, rich yellow, with purple cheek. Parties who have been fruiting it here in the South, pronounce it the most magnificent plum they have seen; it weighs from four to six ounces. It excels all other plums for canning and drying, and will carry for a long distance better than any other kind. Matures middle of August to September. Do not fail to try it.

Price, 30c. each; $3.00 per dozen.

OGAN AND BOTAN PLUMS.

Two other Japan varieties. They are vigorous, handsome growers; branches smooth with rich light green foliage.

The Ogan is a large yellow variety, ripens early, and is very sweet. The **Botan** is very large, reddish blue; a good keeping and shipping fruit. Japan fruit does well here generally; everybody should try a few of these plums.

Price, 30c. each; $3.00 per dozen.

APRICOT PLUM.
(PRUNUS SIMONI.)

A new plum from North China. It was fruited for the first time in 1885, by T. W. Munson, of Denison, Texas—the well-known nurseryman. The fruits, when ripening, shine like apples of gold, and become of a rich vermilion when ripe. It is very firm and mealy, and equal to any Plum; has never been attacked by the Curculio. It will carry any desired distance.

Tree very thrifty, upright; early and abundant bearer.

Price, one year old trees, 50c. each; $5.00 per dozen.

PEACH TREES.

I have a fine assortment of Southern grown Trees, selected from the well-known Nurseries of Gaines, Coles & Co. They consist of the following varieties, viz:

FREE STONES.	FREE STONES.	CLING STONES.
Jessie Kerr.	**Stump the World.**	**General Lee.**
Amsden.	**Thurber.**	**Stonewall Jackson.**
Alexander.	**Old Mixon.**	**Old Mixon.**
Early Louise.	**Crawford's Late.**	**Lemon.**
Fleitas St. John.	**Smock.**	**Heath.**
Mountain Rose.	**Picquet's Late.**	**Nix White Late.**
Foster.	**Lady Parham.**	**Stinson's October.**
Crawford's Early.		**Butler.**
Amelia.		**Chinese.**

As they follow in the list they ripen in succession. Price, 25c. each; $2.50 per dozen.

JAPAN PERSIMMON.

This new valuable fruit has been fruited for the last few years. Most varieties are of excellent quality; twice and three times as large as the native kind; very attractive when the fruit is ripe.

Assorted varieties. Price, 50c. each; $5.00 per dozen.

GRAPE VINES.

Have some selected varieties for the table, and for making wine. The following is a list of them, viz.:

Champion. Large black, poor quality but sells readily, being the earliest in the market.

2 years old, 10c. each; $1.00 per dozen.

Moore's Early. Large size and very early, good for table use. Price, 25c. each.

Delaware. Well known. Regarded as best American Grape; it does well in the South, with good soil and high culture. Price, 20c. each; $2.00 per dozen.

Goethe. Light pink; very fine for table use. It is the best of the Roger's hybrids. Price, 20c. each; $2.00 per dozen.

Triumph. This is a late variety; bunches very large, golden when fully ripe, fine as best foreign, and sells equally well; melting pulp, small seeds, vigorous as Concord, of which it is a hybrid seedling. Rarely it rots; stands pre-eminently at the head as a late table grape. Price, 25c. each.

Norton's Virginia. An unfailing, never rotting, red wine grape of fine quality. Price, 20c. each; $2.00 per dozen.

Cynthiana. Very much like the latter; same price.

Concord. Early; very popular; good for market. Some years it rots. 10c. each; $1.00 per dozen.

Ives. Ripens with the Concord. Good for wine; vigorous and productive. 15c. each; $1.50 per dozen.

Herbemont (McKee). A most popular and successful red or purple grape in the south; excellent for table or wine. McKee is identical with it.

Price, 20c. each; $2.00 per dozen.

Prices for other Nursery Stock will be given on application.

CELESTE OR CELESTIAL FIG.

I have only a limited supply of one year old trees of this variety. They have been raised from cuttings in a sandy loam; are well rooted, and raised to a single stem; not in sprouts, as is often the case, when raised from suckers taken off from old trees.

The cultivation of this fruit has rather been neglected, which should not be so, as the fig is always a sure crop, with very little attention. It has commenced to be an article of commerce, when preserved; shipped from here it sells quite readily North, put up in that way. The Celeste is the best for that purpose, not liable to sour like the yellow skinned varieties, and sweeter than other dark skinned kinds.

Price, 20c. each; $2.00 per doz.; packed and delivered on steamboat, or R. R. depot.

White Marseilles and **Lemon**, both early. Price, 25c. each.

SUCKER STATE STRAWBERRY.

We have various sorts of soil in Louisiana, and the Strawberry suitable to and succeeding equally well in poor or rich land, can only be determined by practical experiment.

There are but few varieties which adapt themselves to all soils and latitudes, hence the importance of planting those which experienced fruit growers have tested and found profitable. A Strawberry having all the good qualities, has not, and perhaps never will be discovered; still in choosing, it is well to purchase plants having as many good points as possible. This I claim for the Sucker State.

It is bisexual; having both, stamens and pistils perfect. The foliage is very heavy, protecting the fruit from beating rains and hot sun. It is very prolific, large size, good quality, and cone shaped. Color bright red, very attractive, and in addition will ship well. I offer this variety at the following prices.

60c. per 100, $5.00 per 1000.

Have other varieties, *Wilson's Albany*, *Finch's Seedling*, etc., at same price.

LOUISIANA SOFT SHELL PECANS.

This is a variety of nuts which only grows South, and is a sure crop here. Those who planted Orange trees twenty years ago, lost most of their labor in January, 1886, when seven-eighths of trees were killed by the severity of the weather. If Pecan trees had been planted instead, they would have brought a handsome income, and continued to increase every year in their production, furnishing a never failing crop for a whole century.

What I offer are of the choicest quality, 75c. per pound; large roundish paper shell; another good quality of long shape, 60c. and 50c. per pound. I also have good sized pecans at 40c. per pound; if sent by mail 8c. per pound postage must be added.

EXTRA CLEANED BIRD SEED.

I make a specialty to put up choice re-cleaned bird seed in cartoons holding one pound. These cartoons contain a mixture of

SICILY CANARY, HEMP, GERMAN RAPE, AND GERMAN MILLET,

all re-cleaned and of best quality.

Have also plain Canary put up in same way, one pound cartoons; this is of the very best quality and also re-cleaned.

Price, 10c. per cartoon; 3 cartoons, 25c.

Have also in bulk, the above as well as Hemp and Rape.

Cuttle Fish Bone, 5c. a piece; 50c. a pound.

NOVELTIES FOR 1889,
AND SOME VARIETIES OF SEED OF SPECIAL MERIT.

Osage Musk Melon.

New Water Melon, "Seminole." The above Melon has been originated by W. M. Girardeau, of Monticello, Fla. He describes the same as being oblong in shape, smooth, and beautifully proportioned. It is of two colors, gray and light green; the latter seems to be just a darker coloring of the former, the gray color greatly predominates. Melons of both colors are exactly the same in shape, size, color of seed, and flavor.

It is *extra early, extra large, enormously productive, and of most delicious flavor*. It is in all respects a perfect melon.

Price, 10c. per package; 20c. per oz.; per ¼ lb., 60c.; per lb., $2.00.

The Osage Musk Melon. This new Melon has been only two years in the Chicago Market, but has become the favorite sort in nearly all the leading hotels and restaurants. It is small and slightly netted, but of exquisite fine flavor. The seed I offer is of the genuine stock; recommend same highly for family use. Perhaps when grown here, it will get larger.

Price, per package, 10c.; ¼ oz., 35c.; 1 oz., 60c.; ¼ lb., $2.00; 1 lb., $7.50.

New Golden Andalusia Wax Pole Bean. This Bean originated at Andalusia, Bucks Co., Pa., with a celebrated bean grower. The illustration, made from nature, gives some idea of their wonderful productiveness. The pods are broad, thick, very fleshy and entirely stringless, and retaining their important qualities until almost ripe. The pods when fully grown are five to six inches long, rich, buttery, and fine flavored when cooked. The vines cling well to the Poles. They commence to bear when quite young, and continue to bear profusely for a long time. The beans when dry are round as a bullet, pure white in color, and also make a fine shell or winter bean.

The stock of seed this season is so small that I can offer it only in packages.

Price, per package, 15c.; 4 packages for 50c.

Thorburn's Extra Early Flat Beans.—**"Pride of Newton."** The originator of this new bush bean says: It is of robust growth, with very long, flat pods, which are light green. This is undoubtedly the earliest and most productive bush bean in cultivation. The plants on account of their bushy growth,

must have plenty of space in the rows; sown thinly they will produce from forty to fifty pods on a plant.

Price, 15 cts. per packet, containing about 100 beans.

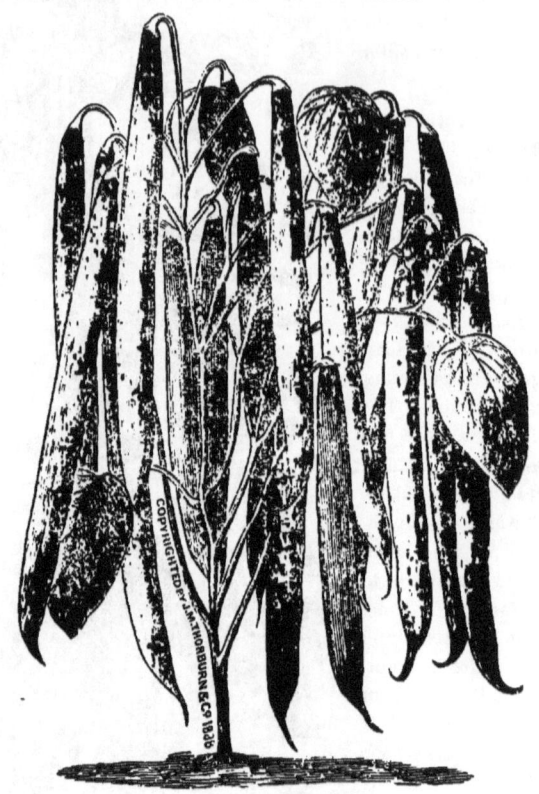

Pride of Newton Bean.

Phlox Drummondii Alba, fl. pl.
This is really the first double flowering Phlox introduced. Fully two-thirds of the plants raised from this seed will give pure double white flowers. They can be used for bouquets, at the same time they are ornamental in the garden.

Price, per packet, 20c.

Phlox Drumondii, alba fl. pl.

PLANTER'S & GARDENER'S PRICE-LIST.

COST OF MAILING SEED.

Orders for ounces and ten cent papers are mailed free of postage, except *Beans, Peas* and *Corn.* See page 4 in regard to seeds by mail. On orders by the pound and quart an advance of eight cents per pound and *fifteen cents per quart must be added to quotations for postage.*

SPECIAL DISCOUNT.

On all orders, amounting to $ 5.00 and over, 10 % discount.
"   "   "   10.00   "   12   "
"   "   "   20.00   "   15   "

For larger quantities, special prices will be given on application.

The above discount is on all seeds except *Potatoes, Onion Sets, Shallots* and *Grass Seeds,* which are net cash.

VARIETIES.		PRICES.		
		Per ounce.	Per ¼ lb.	Per lb.
ARTICHOKE.				
Large Green Globe (Loan)		$0 50	$1 75	$6 00
Early Campania		40	1 50	5 00
ASPARAGUS.				
Conover's Colossal		10	20	20
		100	1000	
" " Roots 3 years old		$0 75	$6 00	
		Per quart.	Per peck.	Per bushel
BEANS—Dwarf, Snap or Bush.				
Extra Early Six Weeks or Newington Wonder.		$0 20	$1 25	$4 50
Early Mohawk Six Weeks		20	1 25	4 50
Early Yellow Six Weeks		20	1 25	4 50
Dwarf German Wax, (stringless)		25	1 25	5 50
Dwarf Golden Wax		25	1 50	6 00
Wardwell's Dwarf Kidney Wax		40	1 50	6 00
White Kidney		20	1 25	4 50
Red Speckled French		20	1 25	4 50
Early China Red Eye		20	1 25	4 50
Red Kidney		20	1 00	4 00
Best of All		25	1 50	6 00
Improved Valentine		20	1 25	5 00
BEANS—Pole or Running.	By mail, add 15c. per quart for postage.			
Large Lima		50	2 50	10 00
Carolina or Sewee		50	2 50	10 00
Southern Willow-Leaved Sewee or Butter		50	2 50	10 00
Horticultural or Wren's Egg		30	2 00	7 00
Dutch Case Knife		30	2 00	7 00
German Wax (stringless)		40	2 25	9 00
Southern Prolific		40	2 25	9 00
Crease Back		40	2 25	9 00
Lazy Wife's		40	2 50	8 00
Golden Wax Flageolet		40	3 00	10 00

Prices for larger quantities given on application.

VARIETIES.	PRICES.		
BEANS—English.	Per quart.	Per peck.	Per bushel
Broad Windsor	$0 25	$1 50	$5 00
BEET.	Per ounce.	Per ¼ lb.	Per lb.
Extra Early or Bassano	$0 10	$0 20	$0 50
Simon's Early Red Turnip	10	20	50
Early Blood Turnip	10	20	50
Long Blood	10	15	40
Half Long Blood	10	20	50
Egyptian Red Turnip	10	20	50
Eclipse	10	25	75
Long Red Mangel Wurzel	10	15	40
White French or Sugar	10	15	40
Silver or Swiss Chard	10	25	75
BORECOLE or CURLED KALE.			
Dwarf German Greens	15	40	1 00
BROCCOLI. Purple Cape	30	1 00	4 00
BRUSSELS SPROUTS	25	75	3 00
CABBAGE.			
Early York	25	60	2 00
Early Large York	25	60	2 00
Early Sugar Loaf	25	75	2 50
Early Large Oxheart	25	75	2 50
Early Winningstadt	25	75	2 50
Jersey Wakefield	30	1 00	4 00
Early Flat Dutch	25	75	2 50
Early Drumhead	25	75	2 50
Large Flat Brunswick	25	1 00	3 00
Improved Large Late Drumhead	25	1 00	3 00
Superior Large Late Flat Dutch	25	1 00	3 00
Improved Early Summer	25	1 00	3 00
Red Dutch (for pickling)	25	1 00	3 00
Green Globe Savoy	25	60	2 00
Early Dwarf Savoy	25	60	2 00
Drumhead Savoy	25	75	2 50
St. Denis or Chou Bonneuil	25	75	2 50
Excelsior	25	1 00	3·00
CAULIFLOWER.			
Extra Early Paris	75	2 50	10 00
Half Early Paris	75	2 50	10 00
Early Erfurt	75	2 50	10 00
LeNormand's Short Stemmed	1 00	3 00	10 00
Early Italian Giant	1 00	3 00	12 00
Late Italian Giant	1 00	3 00	12 00
Imperial	1 00	3 00	12 00
Algiers (fine)	1 00	3 00	12 00
CARROTS.			
Early Scarlet Horn	10	35	1 00
Half Long Scarlet French	10	25	80
Half Long Luc	10	30	1 00
Improved Long Orange	10	25	80
Long Red, without core	10	30	1 00
St. Valerie	10	30	1 00
Danver's Intermediate	10	25	80
CELERY.			
Large White Solid (finest American)	25	75	2 50
Heartwell's Perfection (very fine) short crop	40	1 25	5 00
Large Ribbed Dwarf	25	75	2 50
Turnip-Rooted	30	1 00	4 00
Cutting	15	50	1 50

VARIETIES.	PRICES.		
CHERVIL.	Per ounce.	Per ¼ lb.	Per lb.
Plain leaved	$0 15	$0 50	$1 50
COLLARDS	20	65	2 00
CORN SALAD	15	50	1 50
CORN.	Per quart	Per peck	Per bushel
Extra Early Dwarf Sugar	$0 25	$1 25	$4 00
Adam's Extra Early	20	1 00	3 00
Early Sugar or Sweet	20	1 25	4 00
Stowell's Evergreen Sugar	20	1 25	4 00
Golden Beauty	15	1 00	3 00
Champion White Pearl	15	1 00	3 00
Golden Dent Gourd Seed	15	1 00	3 00
Early Yellow Canada	15	75	2 50
Large White Flint	15	75	2 50
Blunt's Prolific, Field	15	1 00	3 00
Improved Leaming	15	1 00	3 00
Mosby's Prolific	15	75	2 50
Hickory King, (White)	20	1 00	3 00

(By mail, add 15c. per quart for postage.)

N. B.—Prices for larger quantities given on application.

CRESS.	Per ounce.	Per ¼ lb.	Per lb.
Curled or Pepper Grass	$0 10	$0 35	$1 00
Broad-leaved (grey seeded)	15	60	2 00
CUCUMBER.			
Improved Early White Spine	10	25	80
Long Green White Spine or New Orleans Market	15	50	1 25
Early Frame	10	25	80
Long Green Turkey	10	30	1 00
Early Cluster	10	25	80
Gherkin, or Burr (for pickling)	20	75	2 50
EGGPLANT.			
Large Purple, or New Orleans Market	50	2 00	6 00
Early Dwarf Oval	30	1 25	4 00
ENDIVE.			
Green Curled	20	75	2 50
Extra Fine Curled	20	75	2 50
Broad-leaved, or Escarolle	20	75	2 50
KOHLRABI.			
Early White Vienna	25	75	2 50
LEEK.			
Large London Flag, American grown	20	65	2 00
Large Carentan	30	1 00	3 00
LETTUCE.			
Early Cabbage or White Butter	20	60	2 00
Improved Royal Cabbage	20	75	2 50
Brown Dutch	20	75	2 50
Drumhead Cabbage	15	50	1 50
White Paris Coss	20	75	2 50
Perpignan	20	75	2 50
Improved Large Passion	20	75	2 50
MELON, MUSK or CANTELOUPE.			
Netted Nutmeg	10	35	1 00
Netted Citron	10	35	1 00
Pine Apple	10	35	1 00
Early White Japan	15	40	1 25
Persian or Cassaba	15	40	1 25
New Orleans Market (true)	15	50	1 50

VARIETIES.		PRICES.	
MELON, WATER.	Per ounce.	Per ¼ lb.	Per lb.
Mountain Sweet	$0 10	$0 25	$0 80
Mountain Sprout	10	25	80
Ice Cream (White Seeded)	10	35	1 00
Orange	15	50	1 50
Dark Icing	15	35	1 00
Rattlesnake (true)	10	35	1 00
Cuban Queen	10	35	1 00
Pride of Georgia	15	35	1 00
Mammoth Iron-Clad	10	35	1 00
Kolb Gem	15	40	1 25
Florida's Favorite	15	50	1 50
Oemler's Triumph	40	1 50	5 00
MUSTARD.			
Large Curled	10	25	75
Chinese Large Leaved	10	25	75
White or Yellow Seeded	05	15	40
NASTURTIUM.			
Tall	20	50	2 00
Dwarf	25	75	3 00
OKRA.			
Green Tall Growing	10	20	50
Dwarf White	10	20	60
White Velvet	10	25	75
ONION.			
Large Red Wethersfield	20	75	2 50
White or Silver Skin	30	1 00	3 50
Creole (sold out, new crop ready in July)			
ITALIAN ONION.			
New Queen	25	75	2 50
Bermuda (true)	20	60	2 00
ONION SETS.	Per quart.	Per peck.	Per bushel
White		Market Price.	
Red or Yellow		"	
SHALLOTS			
PARSLEY.	Per ounce.	Per ¼ lb.	Per lb.
Plain Leaved	10	25	75
Double Curled	10	25	80
Improved Garnishing	15	35	1 25
PARSNIP.			
Hollow Crown, or Sugar	10	25	75
PEAS.	Per quart.	Per peck.	Per bushel
Extra Early, (First and Best)	$0 25	$1 25	$5 00
Cleveland's Alaska	30	1 50	6 00
Tom Thumb	25	1 25	5 00
Early Washington	20	1 00	4 00
Laxton's Alpha	25	1 50	6 00
Bishop's Dwarf Long Pod	20	1 50	5 00
Champion of England	25	1 50	5 00
Carter's Stratagem	50	2 50	8 00
Carter's Telephone	50	2 25	8 00
McLean's Advancer	25	1 75	6 00
McLean's Little Gem	25	1 50	5 00
Laxton's Prolific Long Pod	25	1 50	5 00
Eugenie	25	1 50	6 00
Dwarf Blue Imperial	20	1 50	5 00
Royal Dwarf Marrow	20	1 00	3 50
Black-Eyed Marrowfat	15	1 00	3 50
Large White Marrowfat	20	1 00	3 50
Dwarf Sugar	30	2 00	8 00
Tall Sugar	30	2 00	8 00
American Wonder	30	2 25	7 00
Field or Cow Peas	Market Price.		

VARIETIES.	PRICES.		
PEPPER.	Per ounce.	Per ¼ lb.	Per lb.
Bell or Bull Nose	$0 30	$1 00	$3 00
Sweet Spanish Monstrous	40	1 25	4 00
Long Red Cayenne	30	1 00	3 00
Red Cherry	40	1 25	4 00
Golden Dawn Mango	30	1 00	3 00
Bird Eye	50	1 50	
Tabasco	50	1 50	
Chili	50	1 50	
Ruby King	50	1 25	4 00
POTATOES.	Per bushel	Per barrel.	
Russets	$1 00	$2 50	
Burbank Seedling	1 25	3 00	
Peerless	1 50	3 25	
Early Rose	1 50	3 25	
Extra Early Vermont	1 50	3 50	
Early Snowflake	1 50	3 50	
Early Beauty of Hebron	1 50	3 50	
White Elephant	1 50	3 50	
Rural Blush	1 50	3 50	

(Prices subject to fluctuation.)

POTATOES, SWEET.
Spanish Yam
Shanghai, or California Yam
Prices vary according to market. Quotations given on application.

	Per quart.	Per peck.	Per bushel
PUMPKIN.			
Kentucky Field	$0 25	$1 50	$5 00
	Per ounce.	Per ¼ lb.	Per lb.
Large Cheese	$0 10	$0 20	$0 60
Cashaw Crook-Neck (green striped) southern grown	10	25	75
Golden Yellow Mammoth	20	65	2 00
RADISH.			
Early Long Scarlet	10	20	50
Early Scarlet Turnip	10	20	60
Yellow Summer Turnip	10	25	80
Early Scarlet Olive-Shaped	10	20	60
White Summer Turnip	10	20	60
Scarlet Half Long French	10	20	60
Scarlet Olive-Shaped, or French Breakfast	10	20	60
Black Spanish (WINTER)	10	25	80
Chinese Rose (WINTER)	15	35	1 00
Chartier	15	35	1 00
White Strassburg	10	30	1 00
ROQUETTE	15	75	2 00
SALSIFY, American	20	60	2 00
Sandwich Island (Mammoth)	30	1 00	4 00
SORREL, (Broad-leaved)	15	50	1 50
SPINACH.			
Extra Large-leaved Savoy	10	20	50
Broad-leaved Flanders	10	20	60
SQUASH.			
Early Bush, or Patty Pan	10	25	75
Long Green, or Summer Crook-Neck	10	25	1 00
London Vegetable Marrow	15	50	1 50
The Hubbard	15	50	1 25
Boston Marrow	15	50	1 50
TOMATO.			
King of the Earlies	40	1 25	4 00
Extra Early Dwarf Red	25	75	3 00
Early Large Smooth Red	20	65	2 00

VARIETIES.	PRICES.		
	Per ounce.	Per ¼ lb.	Per lb.
TOMATO.—Continued.			
Tilden	$0 25	$0 75	2 50
Trophy, (selected)	40	1 25	4 00
Large Yellow	30	1 00	3 00
Acme	25	75	2 50
Paragon	25	1 00	3 00
Livingston's Perfection	25	1 00	3 00
Livingston's Favorite	25	1 00	3 00
Livingston's Beauty	30	1 25	4 00
TURNIP.			
Early Red or Purple Top (strapleaved)	10	20	50
Early White Flat Dutch (strapleaved)	10	20	50
Large White Globe	10	20	50
White Spring	10	20	50
Yellow Aberdeen	10	20	50
Golden Ball	10	20	60
Improved Purple Top Ruta Baga	10	20	50
Munich Early Purple Top	10	20	60
Milan Extra Early Purple Top	10	20	60
Purple Top Globe	10	20	50
White Egg	10	20	50
SWEET AND MEDICINAL HERBS.	Per pack.		
Anise	$0 10		
Balm	10		
Basil	10		
Bene	10		
Borage	10		
Caraway	10		
Dill	10		
Fennel	10		
Lavender	10		
Marjoram	10		
Pot Marigold	10		
Rosemary	10		
Rue	10		
Sage	10		
Summer Savory	10		
Thyme	10		
Wormwood	10		
GRASS AND FIELD SEEDS.	Per lb.	Per ½ bu.	Per bushel
Red Clover	$0 15		$7 50
White Dutch Clover	25		12 00
Alsike Clover	20		10 00
Alfalfa or French Lucerne	20		10 00
Lespedeza or Japan Clover	30	2 50	5 00
Kentucky Blue Grass. (Extra Cleaned)	15		1 25
Red Top Grass	10		1 25
English Rye Grass	10		1 50
Rescue Grass	25		3 00
Johnson Grass. (Extra Cleaned)	15		2 50
Tall Meadow Oat Grass	20		2 50
Meadow Fescue Grass	20		3 00
Orchard Grass	20		2 00
Hungarian Grass			
German Millet			
Rye		Market Price.	
Barley			
Red or Rust Proof Oats			
Sorghum	10		3 00
Broom Corn	10		3 00
Buckwheat	10		2 50
Russian Sunflower	10		
Burr or California Clover	(measured) per quart, 15c.; per bushel, $3.00.		

N. B.— Prices for larger quantities given on application.

TESTIMONIALS.

The following extracts are taken from a few of the many complimentary letters received during the ensuing year. This is to convince the public, who have had no dealings with my house yet, that

FROTSCHER'S SEEDS ARE THE BEST FOR THE SOUTH,

and have always given the utmost satisfaction.

It is a gratification for me to receive letters from my patrons, expressing their satisfaction, as it is my constant endeavor to please them.

AMITE CITY, LA., June 7, 1888.

I have just finished digging my potato crop. I planted on January 5th two barrels of potatoes purchased from you; one of Snowflake and one of Peerless. I have dug 60 bbls. of them, all large, smooth and white; they average from ½ to 1¼ lbs.   S. E. AKERS.

BAYOU SARA, LA., July 5, 1888.

I am very well satisfied with your seeds, as they came up well and were true to description. The *Early Summer Cabbages* were particularly fine, some heads weighing as much as 14 lbs., and were very uniform in heading. I like the *Velvet Okra* very much. I also have the finest Beets, Turnips, Carrots and Beans in this neighborhood grown from your seed.   THOMAS. W. BUTLER.

MADISON STATION, MISS., May 22, 1888.

It affords me much pleasure to assure you that your seeds have given perfect satisfaction at this place, and think the shippers will in future buy their seeds from you.   P. B. BRIDGES.

BERMUDA FIELD, near BATON ROUGE, LA., July 11, 1888.

Will say that the seeds bought of you for my spring and summer garden, gave the greatest satisfaction. Coming up beautifully and in a short time.
Dr. PETER RANDOLPH.

GRAND CHENIERE, LA., June 27, 1888.

I have been using your seeds for the past eight years, and consider them superior to any planted before.
WM. LAURENTS.

ST. ANDREW'S BAY, FLA., Sept. 11, 1888.

I cannot but speak in the highest terms of the seeds that I received from you last winter.   E. P. KINNEY.

SUNNY SIDE FARM, near PENSACOLA, FLA., June 12, 1888.

Since three years we have been using your seeds, and have always met with success. We must say they have given the greatest satisfaction every time. Your Garden Manual is one of the best, published for the South, and should be in the house of every Southern farmer and gardener.   CLOPTON BROS.,
Market Gardeners.

GRAND CHENIERE, LA., January 23, 1888.

I always want your seeds to plant. That is for *Southern climate;* as I have never failed with them yet. With me it is *Southern* seed vs. Northern seed, judgment in favor of *Southern* seed always.
J. A. DOXEY.

LAKE PROVIDENCE, LA., April 23, 1888.

From the 10 bbls. *Potatoes* purchased of you I will probably realize 200 bbls; all very fine.   J. J. ROBINSON.

BARTOW, FLA., February 13, 1888.

My garden shows your seed up in fine shape, and is admired by every one. I have the finest *Potato patch* in Polk Co. this season.   W. W. MOORE.

BAYOU SARA, LA., May 29, 1888.

The *"Red Rust Proof Oats"* you sent me last fall are fine. I cut a splendid crop of them two weeks ago.
A. T. GASTRELL.

CAMDEN, WILCOX Co., ALA., July 23, 1888.

I have usually sent to a northern seed house for my turnip seed, but I am so well pleased with the garden seed, which I have bought of you for the last two years, that I will give your turnip seed a trial also. A. G. ERVIN.

ST. ANDREWS BAY, FLA., Oct. 9, 1888.
Your seeds give better satisfaction than any other sold here; I will send you a large order shortly.
L. M. WARE.

JACKSON, MISS., Aug. 2, 1888.
Your seeds have given entire satisfaction; have found them all *true to name.*
F. A. WOLFE.

BEAUMONT, TEX., January 12, 1888.
Frotscher's Superior Flat Dutch Cabbage cannot be praised too highly; notwithstanding the bad weather we have had, each plant made a head as hard as a rock, and weighing from ten to fifteen pounds. It is the best cabbage that was ever grown here. H. W. Joachimi.

BALDWIN P. O., LA., February 27, 1888.
My husband has been using your seeds for many years, and has always been well pleased with them.
Mrs. M. A. DE LA GREVE.

UNION SETTLEMENT, LA., February 16, 1888.
I was very much pleased with the fruit trees that I got from you.
Mrs. JENNIE BURTON.

PATTERSON, TEXAS, February 6, 1888.
I was pleased with the German Millet seed that I got from you last Spring; it did splendidly. The *Extra Early Vermont Potato* is the best of all for this section; the yield is large, from 80 to 90 bushels per barrel; the *Beauty of Hebron,* also, gives full satisfaction.
GEORGE BENNER.

COTTONVILLE, LA., January 29, 1888.
RICHARD FROTSCHER,
New Orleans, La.
DEAR SIR:—
Your postal card, quoting prices of potatoes, received. Have received a shipment of 40 bbls. potatoes marked *"New York State Early Rose,"* purchased by Messrs. ——— of your city; but they certainly did not buy of you, as was asked

by me; because they did not have your brand on them, and are so badly mixed, of all shapes, colors and kinds, that I have concluded to send 20 bbls. back, I will keep the other 20 bbls. because the most of them were already cut before I was aware that they were so *good for nothing.* I telegraphed to Messrs. ——— to-night, and wrote them a letter which will go with the same mail as this, ordering 20 bbls. *Eastern Early Rose* from *R. Frotscher sure,"* of no one else; as I cannot afford to plant such mixtures as they sent before. Please fill the order with your best *Early Rose,* and notify me at once. I have had great trouble for several years in getting good sound seed, true to name, and knowing by six years experience, that your garden seeds are the best I can buy, I hope to receive as good an article of seed potatoes.
Respectfully,
R. G. BAXTER.

GULLETT'S STATION, LA., February 26, 1888.
The seeds that I got from you, and planted, are growing splendidly. I will soon have Beets ready for market; my Carrots are large and fine; my Lettuce is beautiful, as is also the Celery, and I must say, that I have never seen such fine Radishes as I have, grown from your seed. Mrs. A. H. STARK.

LAKE CHARLES, LA., January 28, 1888.
I have been using your seeds for the past three years, and have found them to be better than any other that I have used before. H. D. SUMRALL.

VILLAGE MILLS, TEX., February 4, 1888.
The *"Red Rust Proof Oats"* that I got from you, are doing O. K. in spite of the blizzard which we have had a short time ago. C. E. SMITH.

HERMITAGE P. O., LA., January 31, 1888.
Those seeds which I planted, that came from you, are "coming up" splendidly, and I am very well satisfied with same. Dr. W. W. MATHEWS.

TROYVILLE P. O., LA., January 29, 1888.
The Turnip seeds of your selection last fall, did spendidly, as did also your other seeds. Mrs. S. J. METCALFE.

WALKER SPRINGS, ALA., March 1, 1888.
I am very well pleased with your seed, are all up and looking fine.
JNO. F. MURPHY.

INDEX.

	PAGE.		PAGE.
Almanac	7 to 18	Le Conte Pear	132
Apricot Plum	133	Leek	49
Artichoke	123	Letter on "Alfalfa"	128 to 130
Asparagus	23	Lettuce	50 and 51
Bartlett Pear	132	Marianna Plum	133
Beans, (Bush)	24	Matthews' Hand Cultivator	119 and 120
Beans, (Pole)	24	Melon, Musk	51 and 52
Beans, (Dwarf, Snap or Bush)	24 to 26	Melon, Water	52 to 55
Beans, (Pole or Running)	27 and 28	Mustard	56
Beans, English	28	Nasturtium	56
Beets	29 to 31	New York Seed Drill	119
Bird Seed	135	Novelties	136 to 138
Borecole or Kale	31	Ogan and Botan Plum	133
Broccoli	31	Okra	56 and 57
Brussels Sprouts	31	Onion	57 and 58
Bulbous Roots	114 to 116	Parsley	59
Cabbage	32 to 37	Parsnip	59
Cauliflower	35 to 37	Peach Trees	133 and 134
Carrot	36 to 39	Peas	59 to 63
Celery	39 and 40	Pecans, Louisiana Soft Shell	135
Celeste, or Celestial Fig	134	Pepper	63 and 64
Chervil	40	Potatoes	64 to 68
Clapp's Favorite Pear	132	Pumpkin	68
Collards	40	Price-List, Planters and Gardeners'	139 to 144
Corn Salad	40		
Corn, Indian	41 to 44	Price-List Garden Implements	123 to 127
Corn and Seed Planter	120	Radish	69 and 70
Cress	44	Remarks on Raising Vegetables for Shipping	5 and 6
Cucumber	44 to 48		
Climbing Plants	112 to 114	Roquette	70
Directions for Planting	90 to 95	Salsify	70 and 71
Duchess D'Angouleme Pear	132	Seeds by Mail	4
Eggplant	48	Shallots	59
Endive	48 and 49	Sorghum	130 and 131
Flower Seeds	96 to 111	Sorrel	71
Garden Implements	121 to 122	Sowing Seeds	21
Grape Vines	134	Spinach	71
Grass and Field Seeds	80 to 89	Squash	71 and 72
Herb Seeds	80	Sucker State Strawberry	135
Hot Bed	20	Teosinte	131
Howell Pear	132	Testimonials	118, 138, 145 to 146
Japan Lilies	116 to 118	Tobacco Seed	80
Japan Persimmon	134	Tomato	72 to 76
Jefferson Pear	132	Turnip	76 to 79
Jerusalem Artichoke	130	Table showing Quantity of Seed required to the Acre	22
Kelsey's Japan Plum	133		
Kieffer's Hybrid Pear	132	Vegetable Garden	19
Kohlrabi	49	Wild Goose Plum	133

www.ingramcontent.com/pod-product-compliance
Lightning Source LLC
Chambersburg PA
CBHW030333170426
43202CB00010B/1113